TO BE JUST IS TO LOVE
Homilies for a Church Renewing

Homily Books by Walter J. Burghardt, S.J.

Tell the Next Generation (1980) (out of print)
Sir, We Would Like to See Jesus (1982) (out of print)
Still Proclaiming Your Wonders (1984)
Preaching: The Art and the Craft (1987)
Lovely in Eyes Not His (1988) (out of print)
To Christ I Look (1989) (out of print)
Dare to Be Christ (1991) (out of print)
When Christ Meets Christ (1993) (out of print)
Speak the Word with Boldness (1994)
Love Is a Flame of the Lord (1995)
Let Justice Roll Down Like Waters (1998)
Christ in Ten Thousand Places (1999)

TO BE JUST IS TO LOVE

Homilies for a Church Renewing

WALTER J. BURGHARDT, S.J.
Woodstock Theological Center

Paulist Press
New York/Mahwah, N.J.

Book design by Theresa M. Sparacio

Cover design by Cheryl Finbow

Illustrations by Rita Corbin

Library of Congress Cataloging-in-Publication Data

Burghardt, Walter J.
   To be just is to love : homilies for a church renewing / Walter J. Burghardt.
     p.   cm.
   Includes bibliographical references and index.
   ISBN 0-8091-4041-1 (alk. paper)
   1. Catholic Church—Sermons. 2. Sermons, American. 3. Christianity and justice—
Catholic Church—Sermons. I. Title.

BX1756.B828 T597 2001
252′.02—dc21

                                    2001038746

Published by Paulist Press
997 Macarthur Boulevard
Mahwah, New Jersey 07430

www.paulistpress.com

Printed and bound in the
United States of America

TABLE OF CONTENTS

ORDINARY TIME

MEMORIALS OF SAINTS

WEDDING HOMILIES

MEDLEY

PREFACE

This collection, the 13th volume of my homilies published by Paulist Press, has much in common with the more recent sets. Each homily has for its springboard one or more of the liturgical texts designated for the occasion, whether a Sunday, a weekday, a memorial or feast of saints, a wedding, or a special event such as Reformation Sunday. In consequence, the Prior Testament and the New enter intimately into the construction of each homily. Understandably so, for our congregations gather not for a lecture in philosophy (much as human reason, enlightened by grace, must play its part) but for insight into revelation—what God has said and might be saying now.

Specifically, as before, the Bible is part and parcel of my homilies because an overarching theme is biblical justice. Not that Scripture ignores the legal and the ethical (witness the Pentateuch). Rather that the justice most prominent in the Bible, from the call of Abraham in Haran to the exile of John on Patmos, is fidelity to the demands of relationships arising from a covenant—relationships to God, to humans, to the earth. Love God above all earthly idols. Love every human person as an image of God, a child of God, like another self, especially the poor and the downtrodden. Touch each "thing," each reality that is not God or the human person, with respect, with reverence, even with awe, as a gift of God not to be clutched possessively but shared generously.

It is this vision of biblical justice that links my homilies to live issues, to real people, to injustices that pervade parishes and disfigure dioceses—injustices that keep our country from being genuinely a "land of the free," and that create killing fields from the North of

1

Ireland through the Middle East to South Africa. As a result, my readers may complain of frequent repetition: biblical justice, biblical justice, biblical justice. My justification and consolation is the "parable" in Luke 18:1–8: the widow who keeps pestering the unjust judge, keeps clamoring "I want justice, I want justice, I want justice"— until he gives in, if only to get this mad woman out of his hair.

Remember, too, that all genuine living, even God's life, is a matter of relationships. To preach relationships is to preach biblical justice. The need? Courage to touch the gospel to relationships that divide the human family: poverty, racism, physical and sexual abuse, homelessness, unemployment, thievery in high places, immigration; the list is legion. These issues that divide our congregations remind me of the parishioner in the film *Mass Appeal,* storming out of church after a homily on social injustice, shouting at the pastor, "I don't come to church to be preached at!"

Courage, yes, the courage of Jeremiah and Jesus, but prudence, too, in the Thomistic sense: putting reason into virtue. We do not *solve* complex issues in a homily; we raise consciousness, raise awareness. Challenge, yes, but encouragement as well. It demands that we preachers never stop learning what God's revealed Word means, that we constantly learn what the justice issues are where we live and proclaim, and that we put the two together with a care for the sacredness of words and a love for the people we are privileged to serve.

Walter J. Burghardt, S.J.
October 3, 2000

FROM ADVENT TO LENT

1
A NEW MILLENNIUM:
TO BE JUST IS TO LOVE
Second Sunday of Advent (A)

- Isaiah 11:1–10
- Romans 15:4–9
- Matthew 3:1–12

Good friends in Christ: This afternoon can be critical for us.[1] Your program tells us this homily will focus on love. It makes sense, for this is Advent, and once again the Son of God in baby flesh is begging us to love as he loves. But it is also "the brink of the third Christian millennium," your effort to bring fresh life to your Catholic love. And so your chairman has asked me to integrate in this single homily three sets of realities. (1) Stress this central theme: staying close to God by loving the Lord your God and your neighbor as yourself. (2) Reflect on the readings for this second Sunday of Advent: Isaiah, Paul, and Matthew. (3) Weave into the homily insights on how justice enters in: how it affects your personal, professional, and civic lives; how you might grow in understanding justice as a constitutive element in the preaching of the gospel; and how you can be involved locally and nationally in promoting justice.

My original reaction? I don't have time for so thick a book. On second thought, Jim Daniel is on to something: not only the intimate relationship between love and justice, but an awareness that what he described has been my life as a priest and preacher for almost a decade.

So then, with gratitude to your chairman, three points, three questions. (1) How, concretely, do love and justice come together for the Christian? (2) How does this relationship stem from Scripture—from prophets like Isaiah and Jesus? (3) How ought this relationship penetrate the way you and I live and love, work and play, dance and dream, especially as this third Christian millennium stretches before us? Not, I hope, a lecture; rather an effort to link God's Word to our life.

5

I

First, how do love and justice come together for the Christian? To grasp that, you have to think beyond our ordinary understanding of justice. You see, when I say "justice," the philosopher, the ethicist, says: Justice means giving every man, woman, and child what each deserves, what each can claim as a right. Not because they are Jews or Christians, not because they are brilliant or beautiful, not because they are prosperous or productive. Only because they are human beings—can they for that reason lay claim to food, a job, a living wage, decent housing, to being treated with respect.

When I say "justice," the lawyer, the jurist, the judge thinks of Lady Justice, the woman with scales and a sword, blindfolded in token of impartiality, swayed neither by love nor by prejudice, moved only by what is laid down in law.

The Hebrews of old knew all that, lived by it. They knew that unless we give people what they deserve and what has been written into law, life becomes a jungle, the survival of the fittest, the rule of the swift, the shrewd, the savage. Such justice, they knew, is indispensable for civilized living. But they lived by something even more important, something that came directly from God. It was what the prophet Micah trumpeted to his people:

> With what shall I come before the LORD,
>   and bow myself before God on high?
> Shall I come before Him with burnt offerings,
>   with calves a year old?
> Will the LORD be pleased with thousands of rams,
>   with ten thousands of rivers of oil?
> Shall I give my first-born for my transgression,
>   the fruit of my body for the sin of my soul?
> He has told you, O mortal, what is good;
>   and what does the LORD require of you
> but to do justice, and to love kindness,
>   and to walk humbly before your God?
>   (Mic 6:6-8)

Do justice. For Micah, not what people deserve. Biblical justice is fidelity.[2] Fidelity to what? To the demands of relationships that stem from a covenant with God. What relationships? To God, to people, to the earth. To God: Love God above all else, above everything created: "You shall love the Lord your God with all your heart, all your soul, all your mind. This [Jesus declared] is the greatest and first commandment" (Mt 22:37-38). To people: "You shall love your neighbor as yourself." This, the second commandment of the law and the gospel, this, Jesus declared, "is like" loving God (v. 39). To the earth: I mean, treat all of God's creation, whatever is neither human nor divine, with reverence, with respect, as a gift of God, as a trace of divinity.

This is how justice is more than being fair, living according to the rules, never giving anyone less than he or she deserves. This is how justice is more than what President Clinton declared after the Oklahoma City bombings: "We shall see to it that the criminals receive justice." Where does the difference lie? One word: *love*. I can do all that human reason or human law demands without loving anybody. I can do all that God asks out of sheer fear, afraid of going to hell. I can keep every contract, meet every obligation, treat every man or woman who crosses my life with respect, simply because I am naturally decent, without love ever entering the picture, without actually caring about anyone.

Divine justice demands that I love. Demands that nothing I cherish on earth—man or woman, wealth or wisdom, reputation or pleasure—take priority over God. "You shall have no other gods before [or: besides] me" (Exod 20:3). "You shall not make for yourself an idol" (Deut 5:8). Demands that I see in every man, woman, and child an image of God, no matter how flawed; cherish each like another self, another "I," especially the poverty-stricken and the persecuted, the despised and the downtrodden, the bedeviled and the bewildered. Demands that I touch God's good earth, the "things" of God, with the reverence that is distinctive of love.

II

How does this stem from Scripture? You must know that the command "Love God above all else" did not originate with Jesus. It was God's command to Israel, "Hear, O Israel: The Lord is our God, the Lord alone. You shall love the Lord your God with all your heart, all your soul, all your might. Keep these words in your heart. Recite them to your children and talk about them when you are at home and when you are away, when you lie down and when you rise" (Deut 6:4–7). Jesus simply repeated his Father's command, said it was "the greatest and first commandment" (Mt 22:38).

You must know that the command "You shall love your neighbor as yourself" occurs first not in Matthew but in Leviticus (19:18). And the neighbor was not just the Jew next door. The Lord had commanded: "You shall not oppress a resident alien; you know the heart of an alien [you know how an alien feels], for you were aliens in the land of Egypt" (Exod 23:9; see 22:21). More than not oppressing, "you shall also love the stranger, for you were strangers in the land of Egypt" (Deut 10:19; see 24:17–18). Why? Because "the Lord your God...loves the strangers" (Deut 10:18).

You heard Isaiah prophesy that an ideal king would administer justice in favor of the weak and lowly, that justice would be "the belt around his waist, and fidelity the belt around his loins" (Isa 11:4–5). Listen to Isaiah in another place:

> Is not this the fast that I choose:
>> to loose the bonds of injustice,
>> to undo the thongs of the yoke,
> to let the oppressed go free,
>> and to break every yoke?
> Is it not to share your bread with the hungry,
>> and bring the homeless poor into your house;
> when you see the naked, to cover them,
>> and not to hide yourself from your own kin?
>> (Isa 58:6–7)

You heard St. Paul tell the Christians of Rome, "Welcome one another, just as Christ has welcomed you" (Rom 15:7). It is a conclusion that follows from Jesus' own commandment, his insistence in a sentence that for a Christian says it all: "Love one another as I have loved you" (Jn 15:12). This was the Jesus who summed up the program for his own ministry in the synagogue of his hometown Nazareth: "The Spirit of the Lord is upon me, for [the Lord] has anointed me; He has sent me to preach good news to the poor, to proclaim release for prisoners and sight for the blind, to send the downtrodden away relieved" (Lk 4:18).

III

So then, a truth to scotch-tape to your refrigerator: Biblical justice, the justice Jesus inherited from his ancestors, not only *includes* love; it *is* love. Which raises an extraordinarily practical issue. You see, what I have said about biblical justice is not intended for our heads alone, new knowledge to be tucked away for some disenchanted evening. How does this touch the way we live? What John the Baptist thundered in today's Gospel, "Repent, for the kingdom of heaven has come near" (Mt 3:2). What Jesus proclaimed after John, "Repent, and believe in the good news" (Mk 1:15). To repent is not simply beating my breast in sorrow. Repent means changing the way I think and act. It is a conversion—not necessarily from sin to sanctity, but turning each day closer to the Christ whose image I am. Believing in the good news is not simply repeating the Creed each weekend at Mass; it means a faith that is alive, that lives what it utters. And here biblical justice can make the difference, for living is relationships, and biblical justice is fidelity to relationships. Take each facet.

1. "Love God with your whole heart." Not a prescription for prayer alone, for a mystical embrace of God in the shelter of my room. When the Lord God issued that first commandment, God had immediately in mind idols like the golden calf the Israelites worshiped when Moses delayed coming down from Mount Sinai. Today's idols? Too many for one homily. How decide whether you and I have an idol? Take to heart how a remarkable third-century theologian named Origen saw it. "God...knows that what a man loves with all his heart and soul and might, this for him is God." And he added pungently for us: "Let each one of us now examine himself and silently in his own heart decide which is the flame of love that chiefly and above all else is afire within him, which is the passion that he finds he cherishes more keenly than all others.... [T]hat for you is God."[3]

A splendid examination of conscience for a new millennium: What is it I actually love with all my heart, all my soul, all my might? Is it God? Or is it the things I own, possessions that are legitimately mine: my home, my company, my money? Is it power, in politics or business? Is it fame, a good name, applause? Is it a Toyota, a Harley-Davidson, a private jet? Or, perhaps even more sadly, nothing? Is there nothing I love with all my heart and soul and might? Not even God? Two thousand years of Christ in our flesh, on our altars, in our bodies, in our hearts—is he actually number one in my life?

Which is the passion I cherish more keenly than all others?

2. "Love your neighbor as yourself." Not an easy command to interpret. I cannot believe God meant: As much or as little as you love yourself, so much or so little love shall you lavish or trickle on others. A solid Scripture scholar says Jesus is speaking of "a right form of self-love."[4] Perhaps. I have suggested, from other biblical experts: I must love every human person like another self, another "I," treat every person as an image of God.

Here is a primary facet of your spirituality and mine. Oh yes, our spirituality has to be centered in the Eucharist, for, as Vatican II declared, "The liturgy [especially the Eucharist] is the summit to

which the Church's activity is directed; at the same time it is the
source from which all her power proceeds."[5] But the Eucharist is not
a private party, where we can snuggle up to Jesus and forget all our
troubles. The Eucharist sends us out to be eucharists to our world. I
mean that, like the eucharistic Christ, we too become present to
people, really present. A presence of the whole person—not only my
mind and money but flesh and spirit, emotions and passions. A presence that, like Jesus' real presence, springs from love and leads to
love. "Love one another as I have loved you."

Is this realistic? We have our problems with the world outside.
Can we always love the illegal immigrant, ever love the Libyan ter-
rorist, the Oklahoma City bomber, the rapists in Rwanda, the violent
in the Nation of Islam? All good questions. Pressed by time, I suggest
that for 2000 we begin with love within. I mean, within our own
Catholic communities. Let me explain.

The eve before his death Jesus prayed for us, "As you, Father, are
in me and I am in you, may they also be [one] in us, so that the world
may believe that you have sent me" (Jn 17:21). St. Paul told us, in rap-
turous syllables, that "in the one Spirit we were all baptized into one
body...and we were all made to drink of one Spirit" (1 Cor 12:13); that
no one of us can say to any other, "I have no need of you"; that "the
members of the body that seem to be weaker are indispensable" (vv.
21–22); that "If one member suffers, all suffer together with it; if one
member is honored, all rejoice together with it" (v. 26).

One body? What does the world outside see in us? A body
fractured. We cannot disagree without disliking; we use of one
another the harsh language of enemies; all too many Catholics see
in John Paul II not a graced guide given us by Christ, but a dodder-
ing old man who is simply not "with it." The Eucharist that we call
our sacrament of unity divides us from the gathering song to the
final dismissal. Shall we worship in Latin or English, sing with St.
Louis Jesuits or bask silently in Bach, kneel or stand during the
eucharistic prayer, receive Christ in hand or on tongue, shake
hands for "Peace" or embrace or stare straight ahead? Not academic questions. Never have I seen the Body of Christ so torn by
lack of love. Is this how we prove to the world that the Father has
sent Christ to it?

3.   Treat the earth, the "things" of God, with reverence, as gifts
of God. One powerful idol today, what many 20th-century men and
women worship, was identified clearly by John Paul II. He called it
"the civilization of 'consumption' or 'consumerism'." It is

the excessive availability of every kind of material goods for the benefit of certain social groups, [which] easily makes people slaves of "possession" and of immediate gratification, with no other horizon than the multiplication or continual replacement of the things already owned with others still better.... [It] involves so much "throwing-away" and "waste."[6]

You know, the food Washingtonians waste each day could feed all the homeless and hungry in the District of Columbia. We see no pro basketball because millionaire owners are battling millionaire players for more millions. Smog covers L.A., chemicals kill the Chesapeake, refrigerators and air conditioners are depleting the world's ozone layers—a critical factor for cancer. Do you know that in 1992 the Union of Concerned Scientists issued a declaration over 1,575 signatures that said in part: "Human beings and the natural world are on a collision course. Many of our current practices put at serious risk the future that we wish for human society and the plant and animal kingdoms, and may so alter the living world that it will be unable to sustain life in the manner that we know."[7]

In the third millennium will we believe with John Paul II that "[our] responsibility within creation and [our] duty toward nature and the Creator are an essential part of [our] faith"?[8]

Let me sum up with a picture. When you kneel before the Christmas crib, let your imagination run loose. Gaze there on a single, all-embracing community: God, people, nature. God: the Child Jesus, the God-man. People: Joseph and Mary, the lowly shepherds, and the awesome kings. Nature: the wood of the manger and the hay, the oxen and the donkey, a single star above. God, people, nature. Our salvation depends on three relationships. Do I love God above all else? Do I love each sister and brother as Jesus loves me? Do I touch each "thing," each creature of God, with reverence? Only thus will the next millennium bring us closer to the Father, to the kingdom of God, to God's reign over all creation.

Our Lady Star of the Sea Catholic Church
Solomons, Maryland
December 5, 1998

2
MOTHER OF GOD
FOR A NEW MILLENNIUM
Solemnity of the Blessed Virgin Mary,
Mother of God, and Giving of the Name Jesus

- Numbers 6:22–27
- Galatians 4:4–7
- Luke 2:16–21

Within an hour's time, all manner of madness will occur from Times Square through D.C. to Bethesda. Cheering and kissing, champagne and sherry, fireworks and brass bands—whatever it takes to ring in a new millennium. Even checking your computer to see if it knows how to deal with 2000. Nothing strange about that. Not even strange that we Catholics usher in Christianity's third millennium with a Eucharist. After all, Eucharist means thanksgiving, and what more profound thanks for two millennia than recapturing at an altar the Last Supper and Calvary of the God-man who is himself the new age?

Still, tonight's liturgy[1] might strike you as somewhat strange. Tonight's Eucharist highlights the mother of God's Son. Why begin the new millennium with Our Lady, with the mother of Jesus? First let me tell you why it makes Christian sense, why it should delight you; then let me suggest how Our Lady might inspire our lives, renew Catholics the world over, as the clock strikes millennial midnight; let me end with a difficulty that challenges our renewal, and a Catholic truth that should encourage us mightily despite all difficulties.

I

First, why begin the third millennium with Our Lady? Because with Our Lady the first Christian millennium began. Let your imagination loose; roam back 2000 years. Picture not thriving Jerusalem, center of Jewish worship, picture rather an obscure Jewish village, Nazareth, a small backwater, perhaps 150 people in all. The village of which apostle-to-be Nathanael asked, "Can anything good come out of Nazareth?" (Jn 1:46). Picture a Jewish girl, perhaps 14 years old, engaged to a carpenter or mason named Joseph. Possibly busy about the house, cleaning, cooking. Out of nowhere an angel appears, addresses her, "Greetings, favored one. The Lord is with you." Favored by God. How? Because "you will conceive in your womb and bear a son, and you will name him Jesus. He...will be called the Son of the Most High" (Lk 1:29–32).

Mary is puzzled, understandably: She is a virgin, has not come together with Joseph. Ah, says the angel, not to worry. "The Holy Spirit will come upon you, the power of the Most High will over-shadow you." No more questions from Mary; immediately, "Here I am, the Lord's servant [the Lord's bondmaid, the Lord's slave]. Let it happen to me as you say" (Lk 1:38).

At that moment the first Christian millennium broke through. At the simple yes of a Jewish girl. A yes to God that changed all of history. A yes to God that Mary would continue to murmur all her life: a yes when her Son left her, a yes even when her neighbors rejected him, a yes to his three years of ministry, a yes to his crucifix-ion, a yes when he left this earth to return to his Father.

That is why the mother of Jesus has come down through Catholic tradition as the model believer, the model woman of faith. Little wonder that her kinswoman Elizabeth exclaimed of her: "Blessed is she who believed that what was spoken to her by the Lord would be fulfilled" (Lk 1:45). Mary is Jesus' first disciple, the perfect example of what it means to believe, to follow Jesus, to say yes to our Lord. Never forget those startling words of Jesus, "My mother and my brothers are those who hear the word of God and do it" (Lk 8:21). Not a rejection of Mary; quite the contrary. She above all others heard the word of God and did it, listened to her Lord speak-ing and acted on it.

This is not to separate Mary from her Son, put her on a pedestal above him. All her life on earth and into eternity, Mary points to her Son. That is why today's Gospel ends with the simple but significant sentence on Jesus' circumcision: His parents named him Jesus, the name an angel had told Mary she would give to the Son of the Most High. Mary in separation from Jesus, in iso-lation from her Son, makes no Christian sense. Even now she says silently to us what she said so eloquently to the servants when the marriage feast at Cana ran out of wine, "Do whatever [my Son] tells you" (Jn 2:5).

II

"Do whatever my Son tells you." This leads directly into my second point: how Mary's yes to God might inspire our lives, renew Catholics the world over, as we begin the third Christian millennium.

You see, all by itself 2000 means nothing more than 1999. An hour from now, Russia will continue to destroy the Republic of Chechnya, AIDS will still assail Africa, 13.3 million American children will still be asleep hungry. Each day 2,200 of our youngsters will drop out of school, 80 teenagers will be raped, 500 adolescents will begin using illegal drugs, a thousand begin drinking alcohol. An uneasy neutrality will still segregate all too many whites and blacks, locals and immigrants, the haves and the have-nots. And so on into the night. Very simply, 2000 is likely to be more of the same, unless.... Unless we who profess to follow Christ listen to God's word as Mary did, listen and do it.

Where might you and I hear God, hear Christ, speaking to us? Not in a vision; not usually through an angel in your kitchen, in my living room. Where then?

A living example is the liturgy, every Eucharist, this Eucharist. Recall what the Second Vatican Council declared: Christ "is present in his word, because it is he himself who speaks when the holy Scriptures are read in the church."[2] Not words wafted away on the wind. Spoken to you, spoken to me. Expecting a response. And we do respond. When the lector declares, "The Word of the Lord," we exclaim, "Thanks be to God!" We mean, "Yes, yes. So it is. This is indeed God speaking. Speaking to me."

That yes can be dangerous—if I am listening as Mary listened. Am I actually listening when Jesus declares that on Judgment Day he will say to some, "Come, inherit the kingdom. For I was hungry and you gave me food. I was thirsty and you gave me something to drink, I was a stranger and you welcomed me, I was naked and you gave me clothing, I was sick and you took care of me, I was in prison and you visited me" (Mt 25:34–36)? Does it get through to me that my relationship to Christ depends on my relationship to the less fortunate: to the poor, to the hungry on my street, to the immigrant's children denied healthcare, to the sick and lonely in my parish, to the several thousand on death row across the country?

I cannot, I dare not, tell you exactly what God is asking of any one of you when you hear God speaking. I do know that, like Mary after the shepherds left the stable, you too have to "treasure" what you hear, "ponder" it in your heart (Lk 2:19). You too may be puzzled, have to ask questions, have to think hard thoughts. But most importantly for this new millennium, resolve to listen to God's Word, Old Testament and New, as Mary listened, aware that it is God who is talking to you. And when you discover what it means for you, what God is asking of you, have the graced strength to answer, "Here I am, Lord, your servant. Let it happen to me as you say."

Remember, too, that God never asks more than we can bear; and we can bear more than we suspect, because it is God's strength that becomes our strength. As St. Paul put it to the Christians of Rome: "He who did not withhold His own Son, but gave him up for all of us, will He not with him also give us everything else?" (Rom 8:32).

A new millennium indeed. You see, we Christians can change our world—if we listen to our Lord as Mary listened—if we act on what we hear as Mary acted. If midnight strikes on that resolve, this parish will enjoy a rebirth. And I do mean "enjoy." A joy the world cannot give; the joy Mary experienced as she felt God's own Son within her.

III

Finally, two swift words: a difficulty that challenges our renewal, and a Catholic truth that should encourage us.

An enormous problem leaps out from your very presence here. You are here, I suspect, because you sense in your hearts what the Second Vatican Council declared in technical language: "The liturgy is the summit to which the Church's activity is directed; at the same time it is the source from which all her power proceeds.... From the liturgy, and especially from the Eucharist, grace is channeled into us, and the sanctification of men and women...[is] most effectively achieved."[3]

Here, right here where you sit, is the Church at its best, God's grace at its most powerful, Catholic worship at its peak, Communion in the very body and blood of God's Son. But do you know how many Catholics in our country share our Eucharist at least twice a month? Thirty percent; three Catholics out of ten. We speak optimistically of evangelizing the world, of carrying out Jesus' command to "make disciples of all nations" (Mt 28:19). We might well begin within our homes, within our schools, within our parishes.

How? First by a profound renewal within ourselves, by becoming increasingly men and women of prayer. Not just an Our Father here, a Hail Mary there, an occasional act of contrition. I mean men and women whose ears are open to God speaking to us. Men and women who listen to God and say yes. Men and women who by our

Catholic example channel God's grace to our spouses, to our children, to our relatives, to our friends, even to those who do not share our faith. Men and women who are not ashamed to proclaim that we love God above all else, that we love all God's children as reflections of God—especially those who hunger and thirst, the naked and the homeless, the ill and the imprisoned. Yes, good friends in Christ, 2000 can be more than a new millennium. It can mean, it should mean, a new person: each of us renewed by listening to God's Word as attentively as Mary did; renewed by welcoming our Lord's body and blood eagerly into our own bodies; renewed by saying yes to whatever God wants: "Let it happen to me as you say." Mary's yes changed our world for ever; your yes can change the acre of God's world you walk. You are more powerful than you know. Not because you are brilliant or beautiful, not because you are wealthy or wise. Simply because each of you can declare with St. Paul, "I can do all things through Him who strengthens me" (Phil 4:13). Graced as you are by God, with Christ himself within you, all things are possible. Believe it! Live it!

Our Lady of Lourdes Church
Bethesda, Maryland
December 31, 1999

3
FORGIVENESS, FREEDOM, FESTIVITY
First Sunday of Lent (B)

- Genesis 9:8–15
- 1 Peter 3:18–22
- Mark 1:12–15

At this moment we Christians are somewhat overwhelmed. We are into a new millennium, this is a jubilee year, and now Lent has struck. Is there a way to bring all three together, without turning each of you into a three-headed creature, meandering around mumbling "millennium, jubilee, Lent; millennium, jubilee, Lent"? I think so. But how?

Start with millennium. For us it's not just an unusual number, 2000. It's a reminder; it projects a person; it tells us that Jesus Christ has been around for two thousand years, is alive and well, is demanding that we do something to make his presence real. Lent suggests what we might do: 40 days in which we ought to be increasingly initiated into the paschal mystery, sharing the dying and rising of Jesus. And jubilee makes that initiation concrete, for it recalls a year in Hebrew history when debts were to be relaxed, slaves were to be liberated, the land was to lie fallow—no sowing, no reaping. It speaks of forgiveness, of freedom, of festivity. A swift program for Lent that is practical, links you to Jesus, and keeps you from turning Lent into ashes on your forehead, ill humor on your lips, and a sour taste in your mouth.

I

First, Lent is for forgiveness. Because this is what the dying/rising of Jesus is all about. His life, from Bethlehem to Calvary and beyond, is summed up in three words: "Father, forgive them" (Lk 23:34). Forgive not only the soldiers who crucified him;

17

forgive every human being born into this world. How might we share, how ought we share, in this redemptive work of Jesus? One suggestion, highly personal, not at all easy.

Begin with the words of Jesus: "Pray this way: Father, forgive us our sins, as we have forgiven those who have sinned against us. For if you forgive others their transgressions, your heavenly Father will also forgive you; but if you do not forgive others, neither will your Father forgive your transgressions" (Mt 6:9, 12, 14–15). Jesus is talking about something terribly important, frighteningly human. He is talking about love and hate, about likes and dislikes, about friends and enemies, about cold silences and shrugged shoulders. Two millennia after he was born and died to forgive us, he is asking us to make the first move when we have hurt another, to make the first move if we are the ones hurt. He is asking us to love others as his Father loves us.

What does this mean? It means that, like God the Father, we are to take the initiative in loving, take the first step in forgiving. God doesn't wait, aloof and aloft in solitary splendor, stroking a gray beard like a shrewd psychiatrist, till we come to our senses. Like the father of the prodigal, God runs to meet us. Before we can actually say "I have sinned against you," God who knows our hearts kisses us in forgiveness, dresses us in new garments of innocence, throws a party for us among the angels. In fact, unless God took the initiative, took the first step, we could never come to God at all.

How does this touch your Lent and mine? Recall the parable of the Prodigal Son. Where forgiveness is concerned, I have a choice. Like the elder brother of the prodigal, I can stay outside, aloof from the party, enjoying my anger, reveling in my wretchedness, refusing to forgive or be forgiven. Or I can let go of yesterday, join the party, celebrate God, celebrate myself, celebrate my brothers and sisters, celebrate...life.

Good friends, let your imaginations loose. Imagine every man, woman, and child in this parish who has hurt another asking that person's forgiveness. Imagine each one who has been hurt taking the first step, seeking the other out: "Can we talk together? Can we try to be friends?" A jubilee indeed, cause for jubilation. You want a renewal? In your parish, in your marriage, in your family, in your inner self? Learn the lesson the apostle Peter learned: "Lord, how often should I forgive? Seven times?" "No, Peter, seventy times seven" (Mt 18:21–22). A vivid way of saying there is no end to forgiving, no limit.

I am not saying forgiving is easy, a simple matter. I have no magic words for the Jew whose grandparents were gassed by Nazis, no persuasive speech for Palestinians and Israelis locked in historic hate, no heart balm for parents enraged at their daughter's rapist, no facile solution for the enormous debts poorer countries owe the richest. I do say, you and I have to start where we are, look into our own experience of hurt, of anger, our own refusal to be reconciled. It can be done, if we stare long enough at a cross on which our God hung...the cost of forgiveness...the cost of forgiving you and me.

II

Second, Lent is for freedom. I mean freedom from the captivities that hold so many of our sisters and brothers in bondage. Let me focus on one bondage: the poverty that imprisons our children. How many? In the richest country on earth, 13.3 million children grow up below the poverty line. Every five seconds a child is born into poverty. Every minute a child is born without health insurance. Every two minutes a baby is born weighing less than five pounds, eight ounces. Every 18 minutes a baby dies.

These are not cold statistics. Each of these is flesh and blood; all are precious to the God who shaped them. This is not the simple lifestyle of the child Jesus in Nazareth. This is the poverty that stunts minds and mangles bodies. This is the poverty that leads to crack and cocaine, to violence for a pair of Reeboks, to guns that prove you a man. This is the poverty that imprisons: I mean the poverty that keeps millions of children in chains, unable to break out of these shackles, haunted by our easy axioms: "They're born lazy." "They don't want to learn." "They don't care to work." And, unlike guns and cigarettes, our children have no powerful lobby.

As so often, so now in Lent I have a dream. I dream that in every parish of our "land of the free," each family with a fair amount of this world's goods will seek out, will discover, one child in need. One child, one need. The needs are legion: a wheel chair or a warm jacket, a tutor or a storyteller, a shoulder to rest on or an ear to listen, tuition or a tutor, a pair of shoes or a pair of skates, insurance or lunch money, toys or schoolbooks, reading glasses or an X ray, perhaps even a dinner for a family at your home. Is this an impossible dream? Or is it not one way to live out our Lord's exhortation that we let the children come to him, "for it is to such as these that the kingdom of heaven belongs" (Mt 19:14)?

One child...one need. With a little imagination we can share the freedom we take for granted; with a little imagination we can touch to a child the words of Jesus on Judgment Day, "I was in prison and you visited me" (Mt 25:36).

III

Third, Lent is for festivity. Festivity is another word for celebration. Sound strange to you, celebrating during Lent? It shouldn't. It won't, if you spend some hours of your Lent in contemplation. Not some mystical, spaced-out ecstasy. Everyday contemplation as Carmelite William McNamara defined it: "a long loving look at the real." The real? Anything and everything that is: a setting sun, a ruddy glass of Burgundy, a child licking a chocolate ice cream cone, a striding woman with wind-blown hair, Christ Jesus. But contemplation is not study. I don't analyze or argue, describe or define. I'm one with it. My favorite example: lounging by a stream, one hand in the water, I can react in either of two ways. I can exclaim, "Ah, yes, H_2O!" Or I can let the water trickle gently through my fingers, experience it, feel it. In his Spiritual Exercises, St. Ignatius Loyola is constantly doing just that. In the meditation on sin he is not satisfied with a definition of sin: "Sin is an offense against God." Even more importantly, smell the stench of sin!

So too with Lent. It's a good thing to think about the redemptive meaning of Calvary, what we strange creatures called theologians spend much of our time explaining. Even better, far better, simply look long and lovingly at a crucifix: Look at the crucified Jesus, link a pierced hand to yours, hear him say, "I'm here because I love you," No need for words; he knows what lies in your heart. For a change of pace, simply let yourself *feel* what comes of it. Perhaps sadness for the sins, yours and mine, that brought him there. Perhaps gratitude for a God-man who of his own free will chose a cross to reveal how important you are to him. Best of all, joy—yes, delight—because, as the evangelist John puts it from the lips of Jesus, "God so loved the world that He gave His only Son, so that everyone who believes in him may have eternal life" (Jn 3:16). This is how amazingly God loved you; this is how God made it possible for you to share God's own life now and for ever. Don't try to prove it, don't analyze it; feel it, sense it, touch it! Feel the profound joy that Jesus promised no human being can take from you.

This is what I mean by festivity: *Celebrate* the cross. Each September 14th the Church celebrates what it calls "the *triumph* of the cross." The cross is not defeat, disaster; not failure, frustration, to be rectified, remedied, by a resurrection—40 days of unrelenting sadness. Jesus' resurrection is God's declaration that the cross itself is victory, that love has triumphed.

So, these 40 days keep a crucified Christ in front of you—the Christ you see here or the cross in your imagination. Experience him for what he may say to you. Let him speak to you. Of a dying that gives life, of a love that destroys hate, of a forgiveness that is changing you, transforming you, while you look lovingly at his tortured flesh. Make Lent a long, loving look at Jesus crucified. Give your mind a rest. Let the senses, your emotions, have a field day.

In fact, try it during this Eucharist. It's not a distraction to be confessed. The Eucharist is a replay of the Supper and the cross: "This is my body, given for you" (Lk 22:19). Remember what you will exclaim as you "proclaim the mystery of faith": "When we eat this bread and drink this cup," what? "We proclaim the death of the Lord until he comes." Touching him, tasting him, you will be proclaiming a death that is God's victory over death. Is it any wonder that untold numbers of Catholics share Eucharist each day of Lent? Not something "nice" added on to Lent. Simply proclaiming the death of the Lord each day—proclaiming it the way Jesus himself invented it: his body given for you...each day.

Let's pull it all together. These three points may strike you as a strange way to live your Lent. I am not downplaying traditional practices; I am not claiming it's a bad idea to "give up" something for Lent. Surrendering sin is always a good choice. Even some of the hand-me-down "sacrifices" we graying Catholics imbibed before Vatican II: R-rated movies, the cherry-topped sundae, the cigarette, the sugar in our wake-up coffee. You can even make a decent case for Slim Fast and Jane Fonda's body-building routine. I'm only afraid that none of these is likely to put you or me in touch with Jesus' journey to the Jerusalem of his destiny, with the dying/rising of Jesus, is likely to change us at some deep level, or trigger a resurrection to new life on Easter Sunday.

This, after all, is what Lent is all about: an increasing, day-by-day sharing in Jesus' journey to Jerusalem. You see, his journey has to be our journey. Yes, we journey as risen Christians; we are redeemed; we have been made new by his sacrifice, his cross. But we are still on pilgrimage, we do not "have it made." (1) We are still in need of God's forgiveness, still need to forgive others as Jesus continues to forgive us. (2) We still need to live Jesus' own program on earth, as we find it in Luke's Gospel (Lk 4:18). The Spirit of the Lord is upon you and me The Lord has anointed you and me to proclaim God's good news to the poor, release our sisters and brothers from the chains that oppress them, send the downtrodden away relieved. (3) We need to recapture a Christian festivity. I mean a sense of celebration as we look long and lovingly at the cross. Not joy in blood, joy in the love that transformed sheer suffering into sacrifice. We still must take seriously the German philosopher Nietzsche's criticism more than a century ago: "You Christians do not look redeemed."

So then, dear Christians, look redeemed! Three steps: (1) Forgive and let yourself be forgiven. (2) Break the chains that keep one image of God enslaved. (3) Celebrate the cross that made it possible for all of us to believe, to hope, to love. It can change your Lent. More importantly, in changing your Lent it can change your life. As the saying goes, "Have a happy one!"

Holy Trinity Church
Washington, D.C.
March 12, 2000

4
THIRSTY? BLIND? DEAD?
Fifth Sunday of Lent (A)

- Ezekiel 37:12–14
- Romans 8:8–11
- John 11:1–45

This evening let me link three Gospels. Gospels that are uniquely appropriate for Lent, for continuing conversion to Christ. The Gospels for the third, fourth, and fifth Sundays of Lent: the woman at the well, the man born blind, Lazarus raised from the dead. Why these three? Because, early in the Church's life, these three Gospels played a large part in the development of Lent, in the process of conversion that led to Christian initiation. How? They compelled the catechumen to ask three questions: Where do I thirst? In what ways am I blind? And what part of me is dead?

I

First, the Samaritan woman at the well (Jn 4:5–42). Jesus asks her for a drink of water. She responds, "You are a Jew—how can you ask me, a Samaritan, for a drink?" To which Jesus replies, "If only you recognized the gift of God and who it is that is asking you for a drink, you would have asked him instead, and he would have given you living water." When she asks in wonder how he proposes to get water from a deep well when he hasn't even a bucket, Jesus tells her:

> Everyone who drinks this water [from the well]
> will be thirsty again.
> But whoever drinks the water I shall give him
> shall never be thirsty.
> Rather, the water I shall give him
> will become within him a fountain of water
> leaping up unto eternal life.

23

"Living water." What did Jesus mean? Very simply and very profoundly, a twin gift: the word Jesus speaks to us, and the Holy Spirit Jesus gives to us. I mean God's unique revelation through God's own Son in our flesh, and the Third Person of the Blessed Trinity within us. These are the twin gifts symbolized by living water that leads to eternal life. On the one hand, the wisdom that comes from the lips of Jesus and transforms our thinking; on the other hand, the divine Person Jesus left with us to transform our living.[1]

Now the Samaritan woman was thirsty. For well water indeed. But from the story in John she thirsted for much more. She had been married five times. Call it a thirst for happiness, call it a sex drive, call it a yearning to be alive. Jesus promises her a "water" that will exceed anything she could possibly imagine, a way of living that will keep her from ever being thirsty again: God's own word in her mind, God's own Spirit in her heart.

Now for today's question: Where is your thirst and mine? Some of it is quite clear, because it is so universally human. We yearn to be happy, healthy, loving and loved; we want a close family that cherishes one another; we want to be someone, do something, feel good about ourselves, sense that our lives have some meaning. And many are like the freshmen who entered Harvard on her 350th anniversary in 1986: Their choice of Harvard and their hopes for living focused on (1) money, (2) power, (3) fame.

Where am I profoundly thirsty—perhaps, like the Samaritan woman, without knowing it? Christians that we are, do we recognize God's gift? Do I long to hear God's word proclaimed in the liturgy, or do I hope it will be short? I suspect you would agree with the Second Vatican Council when it proclaims, "Christ is present in his word, since it is he himself who speaks when the holy Scriptures are read in the church."[2] This is not like listening to *Shakespeare in Love*[3] or Mozart's *The Magic Flute*. This is Jesus speaking—speaking to you and me. This is God's living water, water that gives you and me a breath of God's own life. When we hear Jesus speaking, we should react the way the two disciples reacted to a risen Jesus they did not recognize on the way to Emmaus: "Were not our hearts burning within us while he was talking to us on the road, while he was opening the Scriptures to us?" (Lk 24:32). Minds opened, hearts on fire.

Similarly for the second gift. You know, I never cease to be amazed that, with the Holy Spirit within me, I can eat and sleep, work and play, pretty much the same as the unnumbered unbelievers who people my city. No wonder the charismatics leap and shout for joy: They *feel* God's Holy Spirit inside them and all around them. In theory at least, you and I should look like the early apostles when they "were filled with the Holy Spirit" (Acts 2:4), looked so different at nine o'clock in the morning that the Jews around them said, "They are filled with new wine" (v. 13); they are drunk.

The ironic thing is, you and I don't have to thirst for God's word and God's Spirit; Jesus is actually speaking to us and the Holy Spirit is really living within us. What we must thirst for is the grace to recognize, to realize, to feel in our bones what is actually happening to each one of us—and then to live to the full the kind of life God's word and God's Spirit demand of us.

Pray, if you can, for the thirst Jesus felt on the cross when he murmured, "I am thirsty" (Jn 19:28). Physically thirsty indeed, as thirsty as the wealthy man in hell asking Abraham to send Lazarus "to dip the tip of his finger in water and cool my tongue, for I am in agony in these flames" (Lk 16:24). But more importantly, athirst out of love, thirsting to drink the cup of suffering and dying. Jesus longed, agonizingly, to complete what he had been born to do: to die out of sheer love—love for us. Dare I ask for so profound a love?

II

Turn now to the man born blind (Jn 9:1–41). A fascinating drama. In our project Preaching the Just Word, we hold a "scrutiny" liturgy in which five of the participants dramatize this Gospel. Very powerful. (Powerful even when on one occasion the man cured of his blindness forgot where he had put his eyeglasses, and at the end of the Gospel was seen groping his way perilously through the room.) Understandably, most of us who listen to this Gospel tend to focus on the man born blind and healed by Jesus. Not so Jesus. Important indeed is this single physical miracle. But Jesus has something broader and deeper in view.

Notice how the man born blind is brought to an ever-deepening knowledge of Jesus. Follow his progress. Questioned by his neighbor, all he knows is, "that man they call Jesus" smeared mud on his eyes, sent him to Siloam to wash. Questioned more searchingly by the Pharisees, "What have you to say about him?" he is able to assert, "He is a prophet." Interrogated still more insistently by the Pharisees because "we don't know where he comes from," he defends Jesus with passion and some irony: "Now that's strange! Here you don't even know where he comes from, yet he opened my eyes.... If this man were not from God, he could have done nothing." They throw him

out of the synagogue; Jesus finds him. In response to Jesus' own inter-
rogation, he comes to see Jesus as "the Son of Man." Not only are his
eyes opened, gradually his mind and heart as well. Indeed he sees—
more than with his eyes.

Now notice the Pharisees. They become more and more stub-
born, hardened, inflexible in refusing to see the truth. They begin to
doubt that the poor fellow was born blind; they question his parents;
they even try to trap him by making him repeat the details of his healing; they vilify him, malign him, abuse him. Imagine someone "born
steeped in sin" daring to "lecture" devout Pharisees! When Pharisees
protest, "Surely you're not saying we too are blind?" Jesus answers
tellingly, devastatingly: "If only you were blind, then you would not be
guilty of sin. But now that you claim to see, your sin remains."

A masterful portrait of increasing insight on the one hand, hard-
ening blindness on the other.[4] But Jesus is not speaking to one man
born blind and to a small number of Pharisees becoming blind. He
came to our earth as the light not simply of Israel but of the world.
Each of us, you and I, we were born blind. Our minds were darkened—
darkened by the sin St. Paul says "came into the world through one
man" (Rom 5:12). Jesus was born; Jesus lived; Jesus died to take away
that darkness: "I am the light of the world. Whoever follows me will
never walk in darkness but will have the light of life" (Jn 8:12).

The light shone first for you and me when water flowed down
our foreheads, the baptism early Christians called "illumination,
enlightenment." We actually experienced the light as we grew up, as
God's word slowly, gradually penetrated our minds. For the light of
Christ is what we call "revelation." It is Jesus in our flesh, on our
earth, telling us about God's secret life, telling us what it means to be
alive, what it means to love, what it means to die.

At this very moment the light that is Christ is alive within you,
within me. The Gospel of the man born blind is not just a lovely
story with a happy ending. As always, the Gospel is meant to challenge us. It raises a question: How alive is the light within *me?* The
truths Jesus was born to teach us, are they part and parcel of my
mind, or is God's revealing word mainly between the covers of a
book? Is the light blazing, shining brightly, or flickering like a dying
fire? Where am *I* blind? What is it *I* don't see? Am I a cafeteria
Christian, selecting this part of God's message, rejecting that? If I
don't see it, that's the end of it? Is one of the books in my home *the*
Book? Harsh questions, yes, but terribly important when God's Son
died to dispel our darkness, to keep us who believe in him from
groping in the dark.

III

Turn now to Lazarus raised from the dead (Jn 11:1–45). Again a gripping story. Let me focus on Lazarus' sister Martha. She is disturbed: "Lord, if you had been here, my brother would never have died." Jesus assures her, "Your brother will rise again." Martha is not consoled: "I know he will rise again in the resurrection on the last day." Sounds splendid, doesn't it? Not to Jesus, not adequate at all. For Martha has misunderstood. She thinks Jesus is uttering the usual words of comfort Jews expressed when someone died. You see, in Jesus' time the ordinary Jew believed in the resurrection of the body on the last day. An official Jewish prayer in the first century includes this sentence: "You, O Lord, are mighty for ever, for you give life to the dead."[5] Then why was Jesus unhappy with Martha? Listen to him:

> I am the resurrection and the life;
> he who believes in me,
> even if he dies, will come to life.
> And everyone who is alive and believes in me
> shall never die at all.

"Never die at all?" Are you puzzled? Don't be. You will indeed die a physical death. I mean, your body will be severed from the spiritual part of you, what *we* call your soul—spiritual not only because you cannot see it, more importantly because therein lives the Holy Spirit. Physical death is real. But physical death is not the whole story. The spiritual part of you, your soul, will never die in you who believe, precisely because it is the dwelling place of the Holy Spirit. This is the life Jesus calls "eternal" life. Eternal because that life of the Spirit is in you now and will not cease when the body is severed from it. Now, and when you die, and after death until God restores your body to you, you are and will be alive. Alive with God's own life. Never, never will you die completely, never die totally.

Don't let anyone downplay "spiritual" life. It's not a question of ghosts. It's not something wispy, filmy, gauzelike, gossamer. Spiritual life is the life you have right now because you are a temple of the Holy Spirit; and that Holy Spirit will not leave you when the body crumbles into dust. That is why we Christians can speak of the "communion of saints." It is the community of all those who are alive in Christ, whether in heaven, in the anteroom of heaven we call purgatory, or still down here on earth. Whatever you do, don't sell your dear departed short. They live; they are alive, more alive than they have ever been.

But once again Lent confronts us with a question: How alive am I? Where am I dead? You know what it feels like to be fully alive physically, when you feel so full of life you can scarcely bear it. Do you remember the film *Chariots of Fire,* on the 1924 Paris Olympics? Remember one of the British runners confessing "When I run, I feel God's pleasure"? Filled with the Holy Spirit, we should feel God's pleasure, God's presence, God's love. Not only grasp it in an idea. Philosopher Jacques Maritain insisted that the height, the acme, the summit, the highest point of human knowing is not a concept, an idea; no, "man/woman feels God."

At this very moment you possess an incredible gift: God—Father, Son, and Holy Spirit—alive within you. The problem: How alive are you? "This is eternal life," Jesus said the eve of his crucifixion, "that [those whom the Father has given me] know you, the only true God, and Jesus Christ whom you have sent" (Jn 17:3). Not sheer intellect; rather, the knowledge that implies "immediate experience and intimacy."[6] Ultimately, the knowledge that is love.

We Christians see so clearly when certain features of human life are at issue: family, education, money, jobs. But we can be distressingly blind where eternal life is at stake: the life that is God within us now, the life we hope to live in God's presence for ever.

Lent is traditionally a period of self–denial, giving up. But not the cream in my coffee, not the Godiva chocolates, not the Jerry Springer show. Deny rather what is far more important—the temptation to take yourself for granted: "This is the way I am"; the inclination to continue living just as you always have. No, Lent is for searching. I, this Christian man or woman, what am I actually thirsting for? Has it anything to do with Jesus speaking to me and the Holy Spirit living in me? What is it I do not see? Is there something that blinds me to the light that is Christ, keeps me from grasping, accepting, living the truths for which he died? Where am I not fully alive, not trembling with the joy Jesus promised no human being can take from me?

These three questions do not aim at making me feel bad. Quite the contrary: They have for purpose to make me better than I already am. In three ways: (1) to satisfy my thirst for God's word and God's Spirit; (2) in the light of Christ, to look at myself, at my world, at my God with stunning clarity; (3) to come gloriously alive in Christ, more alive than I've ever been. Then it is that Easter will dawn for *me,* and my eyes too will be opened, and like the disciples at Emmaus I will really and truly recognize Jesus in the breaking of the bread.

So then, these two final weeks of Lent, pray passionately for a threefold grace: to be thirsty, to see, to be alive. "Dear Jesus crucified for me: Help me, first, to yearn, to long for, to thirst ever more agonizingly for every word that falls from your lips, never to feel satisfied until the Holy Spirit within me is a living, fiery presence I cannot ignore. Second, lift the scales from my eyes, the cataracts from my vision, so that I can see with your eyes, understand with your mind, judge with your clear insight. Third, bring to life whatever good may have died in me: the joy I had in simply being alive, the love that was once aflame in me, the compassion that has been smothered in self-pity. Grace me to "feel God's pleasure" each moment I live.

"If you grace me this threefold way, dear Jesus, then when I finish my journey to Jerusalem, I will be able to murmur with your own hope, 'Father, into your hands I entrust my spirit.' "

St. Thomas' Church, Whitemarsh
Fort Washington, Pennsylvania
March 21, 1999

5

FOR THE REST OF LENT, LOOK REDEEMED
Fifth Sunday of Lent (B)

- Jeremiah 31:31–34
- Hebrews 5:7–9
- John 12:20–33

Good friends in Christ: Just about every Sunday, Jesus says some-thing to us that delights us or inspires us or encourages us: "You are the salt of the earth, the light of the world" (Mt 5:13–14); "This is my commandment: Love one another as I have loved you" (Jn 15:12); "My peace I give to you" (Jn 14:27). Today Jesus says something that may trouble us: "I solemnly assure you, unless the grain of wheat falls into the earth and dies, it remains alone [just a grain of wheat]. But if it dies, it bears much fruit" (Jn 12:24). This grain of wheat that must die to bear fruit: What does it say about Jesus? What does it say about us? And how might it touch these final weeks of our Lent?

I

First, Jesus. Here is a brief parable on the lips of God-in-flesh, the parable of the Seed that Dies. What does the parable mean? Very simply, what will give life to all women and men is Jesus' death. The hour has come for Jesus to be lifted up in crucifixion: "When I am lifted up from the earth, I shall draw all men and women to myself" (Jn 12:32). When he is "lifted up." The way God chose to bring all of humanity to life, to God's life, was through death. The death of God's Son. Death not on a soft mattress; death on a criminal's cross.

I have often wondered, wonder even now, is it possible to make sense out of this? It's not the way I would have gone about bringing God's life to people. Oh yes, I resonate to one part of

God's plan: I love the idea of God's Son taking my flesh, becoming what I am, walking my earth, eating my bagels. But the rest of it? If he had to be born, it would not have been in a stable. If he was to grow up, it would not have been in a backwater town like Nazareth. If he had relatives, they would not have thought he was mad, not have allowed townspeople to try tossing him over a cliff. He would have ridden into Jerusalem not on the back of a donkey but triumphantly on a chariot. When he spoke with authority, no Pharisee would have challenged him. No Judas would have dared sell him with a kiss, no soldier crown his head with thorns, strip him of his garments, lash his back with whips, nail him to a tree, laugh at him while he died. No, he would have come with power, the power proper to God's Son.

I know, God's thoughts are not my thoughts. But why this, why the way of the cross? Why did the seed have to die, die so cruelly? Was there no other way? Of course there was! A single breath of Bethlehem's baby could have brought us God's life, because it was the breath of God. A single "Father, forgive them" from the home in Nazareth, because it was the word of God. A single day's fast in the wilderness, because it was the hunger of God.

Then why this? Why a cross? Five simple monosyllables in the Gospel of John: "God so loved the world" (Jn 3:16). No, I cannot plumb, cannot fathom, the depths of a crucified love, cannot understand how God could possibly express love in ways so dread-full. All I know is that behind the cross is the finest four-letter word in our vocabulary: love. We might all too easily forget a Jesus who came striding into our world, into Jerusalem, with irresistible power, sweeping all before him like a Christian Caesar. We could all too easily pass over a Jesus behind our altar with a crown of gold on his head, a royal cloak on his shoulders, a scepter in his hand. What the world cannot forget, believer and unbeliever alike, what you and I dare not disregard, is the Jesus you see before you, stripped of everything...everything except his love.

So did God love you and me. Such is the love that bears fruit, the love that gives life. Such is the love we memorialize when we sing, "Dying, you destroyed our death." You and I are alive with God's life at this moment because the Son of God died for us. Such is the love that makes it all but impossible not to love him in return.

II

Love in return. It suggests my second point: What does the seed that dies say about us? Jesus told us flatly, plainly, what it says: "Whoever does not carry his [or her] cross and follow me cannot be my disciple" (Lk 14:27). What cross? It is only rarely that this cross is shaped of wood and nails. It may have happened to the apostle Peter in the persecution of Nero, to the apostle Andrew some years later; it is hardly likely to be your lot or mine.

You know what we call a cross. A cross is any kind of trial or trouble. Like what? Headache or heartburn, anxiety or fear, discouragement or depression, discrimination or oppression, hunger or thirst, grief at a dear one's death, discrimination, loneliness, a sense of being victimized. A cross is whatever clashes with our sense of well-being. The list is all but endless.

Bur for a Christian the word "cross" has a special meaning. Cross links our trial or trouble to Christ. In the Christian vision, no cross need be an isolated experience, simply something to be endured, resented, cursed. I may not be able to explain why this cross has been laid on my shoulders: why a cancer is eating my flesh away, why I have lost my job to downsizing, why my nearest and dearest have been torn from me by death. But there it is, a fact. I may not be able to cry with St. Paul, "I rejoice in my sufferings," but I have the graced strength to add with him, "In my flesh I am completing what is lacking in Christ's afflictions for the sake of his body, the Church" (Col 1:24). I can say with conviction the old, ever-new Morning Offering: "Dear Jesus, I offer all my joys and sufferings of this day for all the intentions of your Sacred Heart, in union with the Holy Sacrifice of the Mass throughout the world, in reparation for my sins, and in particular for the special intentions recommended by our Holy Father for this month."

What we dare not forget is that "in the one [Holy] Spirit we were all baptized into one body" (1 Cor 12:13). This body St. Paul compares to our physical body. So compact is it that no member can say to any other, "I have no need of you" (v. 21)—not pope to peasant, not rich to poor, not powerful to powerless...not I to you. So unified by baptism that "If one member suffers, all suffer together with it" (v. 26). With Christ as our head, so compact are we that what I suffer can bring healing to a child in war-torn Croatia, strength to an AIDS victim in Africa, comfort to a wasted heart next door. But only if we recognize with St. Paul that "[we] can do all things in him who strengthens [us]" (Phil 4:13).

FOR THE REST OF LENT, LOOK REDEEMED   33

Fifty-nine years ago, one year a priest, I was privileged to bless
a paralyzed lady in a New York City hospital. For 25 years she had
not moved from shoulders to feet. And yet, because she was so wondrously aware of this Body of Christ, its oneness in him, this lady's
smile and tears, her faith and courage were more powerful for
unnumbered people she never saw than anything I did in my robust
health, save for the Sacrifice of the Mass. It was the Christ in her, the
Christ of Calvary, who made her cross an instrument of healing for a
whole little world that knew her not.

Good friends: In the Body of Christ that is the Church we have
an "internet" more powerful than the technological network we
justly call a modern miracle. It is the grace of Christ flowing through
humanity like another blood stream—flowing through humanity by
your faith and mine, your hope and mine, your love and mine.

III

Which leads me to my third point: How might all this touch these
final weeks of Lent? Touch you? I suggest this: Remember your dignity,
the privilege that is yours as Christians. St. Paul phrased it powerfully:
"We are always carrying in the body the death of Jesus, so that the life
of Jesus may also be made visible in our bodies" (2 Cor 4:10).

My point is: Dying with Jesus is not limited to our final cross,
our last breath on earth. For a Christian, for you and me, dying with
Jesus is a lifelong process. Why? Because dying with Jesus is a dying
to sin and a dying to self.

A dying to sin. For you and me, I suspect, sin is not usually
some earth-shaking assault on the Ten Commandments: breaking
and entering, murder, adultery. For Lent, I focus on what is surely
more frequent, what we call "sins of omission": what I don't do. For
"sins of omission" are not always trivial, of little importance. Not to
forgive is not trivial. Never to visit the sick, the housebound, the
lonely, even the imprisoned, is not trivial. Not to encourage the
despondent, never to praise someone you don't like, these are not
trivial. Not to thank God for the air I breathe and the food I eat is
not trivial. Not to admit in words that I am wrong is not trivial. And,
of course, not to compliment a preacher for a superb three-point
homily! Not always sins in the strict sense, not often serious, at times
simply imperfections, but added up they can paint an unpretty picture of a thoughtless Christian.

A dying to self. From experience, I realize that I am least Christian when I make the world revolve around me: my likes and dislikes, my hiatal hernia and my ingrown toenail, my needs and my wants, the honors of yesterday and the fears for tomorrow, my books and my honorary degrees. A splendid Lent is to "let go." Let go of yesterday; not forget it, simply not live in it, not imagine that in some bygone past was the heyday of my existence, nostalgia for a past that will never be repeated or surpassed. Rather, as a centuries-old *Salutation of the Dawn* put it:

> Listen to the exhortation of the dawn!
>   Look to this day!
> For it is life, the very life of life.
> In its brief course lie all the verities and realities of your existence:
>   The bliss of growth,
>   The glory of action,
>   The splendor of beauty.
> For yesterday is but a dream,
> And tomorrow is only a vision;
> But today well-lived makes every yesterday a dream of happiness,
> And every tomorrow a vision of hope.
> Look well therefore to this day!
> Such is the salutation of the dawn.[1]

It is the importance of the "now" in Christian living. It is the urging of the Psalmist, "O that today you would listen to [God's] voice!" (Ps 95:7). Today. Salvation is now; God's grace is now; the cross is now. Above all, remember this: Dying to sin, dying to self is not something negative. If I die to sin, I am rising to Christ, rising with Christ. If I die to the selfish self in me, I am allowing the selfless Christ within me to come alive, help me share my gifts with the less fortunate, send graces of courage and consolation through other members of his Body. Therein lies the deep joy Jesus promised no human can take from us.

I have long been amused by comedian W. C. Fields' remark, "Every morning start the day with a smile...and get it over with." Amused, but not impressed. I am much more impressed by an unusual sculpture in an abbey on an island off the southeast coast of France. It has for its title "The Smiling Christ." Jesus is imprisoned on the cross; his head is leaning somewhat to the right; his eyes are closed—in death, I think; but on his lips is a soft, serene smile.

This is not to deny the tragic in human living, the cross in our lives. I am simply insisting that even during Lent we are risen Christians. Even as we make our own journey to Jerusalem through the bittersweet of human living, we have not been left orphans. The Trinity is tented within us: a Father who, John Paul I told us, is also our Mother; a Christ who will shortly fill our flesh with his body and blood, soul and divinity; a Holy Spirit who is light for our minds, strength for our wills. Such is the gift from a cross outside Jerusalem. Greater love than this no one has ever had.

Finally, for a few short moments, fix your eyes on the crucified Christ behind this altar. Focus not on the thorns, not on the nails; focus on the love that led him there. To recapture that love, put on his lips a soft, serene smile. And then, for the rest of Lent, look redeemed. Smile—the way you smile when you're in love.

Holy Trinity Church
Washington, D.C.
April 9, 2000

6
UNTIL HE HAS ESTABLISHED JUSTICE
Holy Week, Monday (A)

- Isaiah 42:1–7
- John 12:1–11

These past five weeks, something quite remarkable has stayed with me. It has to do with the liturgies of Lent. I am instructed, delighted, saddened—all sorts of ideas and emotions that stem from the way the readings present Jesus to us. There is the hungry Jesus in the wilderness, refusing to let Satan move him from his mission, deter him from his destiny. There is the Jesus transfigured before Peter, James, and John, where the law and the prophets bear witness to him. There is the Jesus who is living water for the thirsty, light for the blind, life for the dead. And all this time, in every situation, there is the Jesus moving inflexibly on his journey to Jerusalem.

And this evening? "Here is my servant" (Isa 42:1). Jesus the Servant: the first of the four Isaian Servant Songs that the Church applies to Jesus. But a very specific facet of this servant: "He will bring forth justice to the nations" (v. 1); "He will faithfully bring forth justice. He will not grow faint or be crushed until he has established justice in the earth" (vv. 3–4).

Made to order for a three-point homilist: (1) justice, (2) Jesus, (3) you and I.

I

First, justice. I ask a philosopher what justice is, and he replies: Justice means giving to every man, woman, and child what they deserve, can claim as a genuine right. Not because they are rich or powerful. No, only because they are human, shaped of the same

36

flesh and spirit as you and I. I ask a lawyer what justice is, and she replies: Our goddess is the Roman *Justitia,* the lady with scales and a sword, blindfolded in token of impartiality. The legal ideal? Equality before the law.

All well and good. Highly important, for without ethical and legal justice, human living becomes inhuman, society is a jungle, the preserve of the strong, the shrewd, the savage. For human living, indispensable; for Christian living, inadequate. Why? Because our gracious God has revealed a broader justice, itself a comprehensive spirituality, a total way of living unto God.

We call it biblical justice. Not that the ethical and legal are absent from God's Book; rather that a justice even richer pervades the law and the prophets, finds a high point in Jesus.

You see, the way in which ancient Israel played out its life is in sharp contrast with the rugged individualism scholars like Robert Bellah see scarring our society. To live was to be united with others, related. Not only family with tribe and kinfolk, but "king with people, judge with complainants, the community with the resident alien and [with the] suffering in their midst—and all with the covenant God."[1] In this context, justice is fidelity to the demands of a relationship. How is God just? Because God is always faithful to God's promises. When are men and women just? When they are in right relationship to God, to God's people, to God's earth. Love God above all else, all idols; love every man, woman, and child like another self; touch God's good earth with reverence.

That is why, in the Hebrew vision, Eden was the first Camelot, a creation God found "very good" (Gen 1:31). Why? Because for one brief stretch of time simply everything was in proper relation: humanity *(adam)* to God, humans among themselves, human and nonhuman reality toward one another.

As we know, sin shattered these relationships—the first sin and the accumulated sins of the centuries: man and woman severed from God, severed from one another, severed from the earth that sustained them. Our traditional understanding of sin, "an offense against God," is good as far as it goes. But in Scripture, sin involves also the sundering of community. Israelite life was a ceaseless story of struggle for community, of lapses into disintegration, division, enmity. If biblical justice is fidelity to the demands of a relationship, then sin is a refusal of responsibility; sin creates division, alienation, dissension, rejection; sin dis-members the body. Sin wounds the single, all-embracing, triadic community God had in mind: God, God's people, God's "things." All sin is social, just as all grace is social.

What is new in biblical justice? Ethical justice and legal justice, for all their significance, for all their strong demands, do not demand...love. Israel's God did.

II

Such is the justice Jesus inherited, the justice that sparked his ministry. What was "new" in his justice? To the love commanded in Leviticus, "You shall love your neighbor as yourself" (Lev 19:18), Jesus gave an utterly new quality: "This is my commandment: Love one another as I have loved you" (Jn 15:12). Here is the Servant of justice past compare.

How did Jesus serve God's justice? How did he love us? His whole life, his very death, was a ceaseless struggle to make all relationships right. Run through the Gospels with that in mind. Take Jesus' miracles. The miracles do not primarily prove Jesus' power. The leper is not only cured; a human being ostracized from society, banished to the edge of his city, is restored to his community (Mk 1:40–45). Jesus heals a withered hand on the Sabbath, to stress a right relationship to God: "The Sabbath was made for men and women, not men and women for the Sabbath" (Mk 2:27). A paralyzed man is not simply loosed of his paralysis; he is restored to God's friendship: "Son, your sins are forgiven" (Mk 2:5). That dear word "son." Take the man possessed, a wild man, "among the tombs and on the mountains, howling and bruising himself with stones," wrenching his chains apart. Jesus not only drives out an unclean spirit; Jesus sits with the man, talks to him, listens to him. When he wants with all his heart to stay with Jesus, Jesus refuses, sends him home to his dear ones, asks him to proclaim to them how much the Lord has done for him (Mk 5:1–20). An apostle to his own!

Take Jesus' lesson in Christian leadership. When his disciples argue, centuries before Mohammed Ali, "Who's the greatest?" Jesus takes a little child in his arms, an example then of a social nobody— no status, no social importance, a symbol of humility, of dependence. "Whoever wants to be first must be last of all and servant of all" (Mk 9:35). The model? Jesus himself, who "came not to be served but to serve" (Mk 10:45).

Take the widow's mite (Mk 12:41–44). This widow I shall never forget. Not only because in dropping into the temple treasury all she

had to live on, "by the totality of her self-giving" she was foreshadow-
ing "the complete self-giving of Jesus on the cross."[2] Instructed by
insightful scholars, I now see Jesus lamenting a "tragedy of the day."[3]
This widow had been encouraged by religious leaders to give as she
did. Jesus condemned the value system that motivated her action—a
poor widow persuaded by the hierarchy of her religion to plunk into
the treasury her last penny. It was Jesus' quiet but passionate rebuke
to a structure of sin; Jesus was condemning a social injustice.

The Servant of justice indeed. On some disenchanted evening,
thumb through Mark, see how in large measure it is the "little
people" who lay uncommon claim to Jesus' attention, his effort to
restore right relationships. Mull over them: fishermen and a fevered
lady, the possessed and the paralyzed, those hungering for food or
the Word, the deaf and blind and leprous, sinners and a tax collector, a woman hemorrhaging for 12 years and a young man all too
rich, a poor widow and two crucified bandits.

III

The Servant of justice indeed—the suffering Servant. But it
hardly ends with Jesus. "This is my commandment: Love one
another as I have loved you." As disciples of Jesus, as ministers
ordained or to be ordained, we too are summoned to be servants of
justice. In the way we live and the way we preach. Not growing faint,
not crushed, until, as far as in us lies, we have established justice in
our acre of God's good earth. Not only a justice that gives to others
what they can claim as a right. Not only equality and impartiality
under the law. With all that, proclaiming with passion God's justice:
fidelity to relationships that stem from our covenant with God cut in
the blood of Christ. Love God above all else; love every child of God
like another self; touch all of God's creation with reverence.

This is not to forsake the liturgy for social action. The liturgy is
the very presence of the Servant of justice in the people assembled,
in the Word proclaimed, in the body and blood shared. Like Jesus'
parables, the liturgy—homily and symbols—does not force decisions
on people. It generates insight, gives fresh perspective, invites them
to discover what God's kingdom is all about—and leaves the rest to
their graced freedom.

How? The liturgy reveals and celebrates our relationship with
God. Each Preface begins, "It is right to give God thanks and praise."
It is right—a weak translation of the Latin, *Vere dignum et iustum est.*

Iustum: To praise and thank God always and everywhere "is a matter of justice."

The liturgy reveals and celebrates our relationship to sisters and brothers. Not that it tells the faithful exactly what to do. They do not gather with a single mind. They gather, across our social, political, and economic differences, to say "Our Father," to speak of themselves as "we." But in fact, "the liturgical assembly reflects, not the justice of the Kingdom, but the divisions of social groupings." It is "a tension rather than an achievement."[4] Still, the tension cannot be relaxed. If it is, "the Christian community falls from the justice of God and relapses into the thoughtless acceptance of an unjust world."[5]

The liturgy reveals and celebrates our fidelity to creation. God's "things" can be used to build up relationships or destroy them—from a jug of wine to nuclear energy, from bread shared generously to luxuries clutched feverishly. The breaking of bread, our sharing in the one Christ, cries out against the way we turn the creation committed to our care into slaves of our greed—yes, into weapons of power and destruction.[6]

Servants of justice indeed. But only if we do not sever social action from the most powerful source of grace at our command. Only if we and our people recognize that our self-giving to God's justice draws its power from this hour—from the Servant who still proclaims to the world in and through us, "This is my body given for you" (Lk 22:19). Only if, as suffering servants, we are prepared to walk the way of the cross that is inseparable from proclaiming God's justice, prepared to follow the Servant who "was despised and rejected by others, a man of sorrows, one from whom others hide their faces" (Isa 53:3).

Suffering servants of God's justice—a pertinent meditation this Holy Week. It was Jesus' priestly vocation. It is yours.

Theological College
Washington, D.C.
March 29, 1999

7
MY SERVANT WILL BRING FORTH JUSTICE
Holy Week, Monday (B)

- Isaiah 42:1–7
- John 12:1–11

Last year, on this same Monday of Holy Week, I preached here to many of you.[1] I focused on the first reading, on the first of the four Isaian Servant Songs that the Church applies to Jesus. A specific facet of this Servant: "He will bring forth justice to the nations. He will faithfully bring forth justice. He will not grow faint or be crushed until he has established justice in the earth" (Isa 42:1, 3–4). I asserted that the justice this Servant of justice inherited was not simply ethical justice: giving every man, woman, and child what they deserve. Rising above the ethical was biblical justice: fidelity to relationships that stem from a covenant. Three relationships. To God: Love God above all else. To people: Love every human being as an image of God, however flawed; love every sister and brother like another self. To the earth: Touch all of God's material creation with reverence.

I insisted that this is the justice we inherit from the Old Testament and the New: from the Psalms and the prophets, from the Suffering Servant Jesus. I said that our liturgy is the very presence of the Servant of justice in the people assembled, in the Word proclaimed, in the body and blood shared. For the liturgy reveals and celebrates our relationship to God, to our sisters and brothers, to all of God's creation.

What for lack of time I did not do was put flesh and blood on these relationships, bring the principles down to earth. This evening allow me to suggest three specific areas where, as disciples of the pre-eminent Servant of justice, in the way we live and the way we preach, you and I may "not grow faint or be crushed" until we have

41

established justice in our acre of God's world. Three groups: the impoverished, the imprisoned, the immigrant.

I

First, the impoverished, the poor. Focus on the most vulnerable: our children. In the richest country on earth, one out of five grows up below the poverty line—16.5 million. Some vital statistics, deadly statistics:

1 in 2 will never complete a single year of college.
1 in 3 is born to unmarried parents.
1 in 3 is behind a year or more in school.
1 in 4 lives with only one parent.
1 in 5 lives in a family receiving food stamps.
1 in 7 has no health insurance.
1 in 8 never graduates from high school.
1 in 11 lives at less than half the poverty level.
1 in 12 has a disability.
1 in 13 was born with low birthweight.
1 in 24 lives with neither parent.
1 in 60 sees parents divorce in any year.
1 in 137 will die before first birthday.
1 in 620 will be killed by guns before age 20.[2]

Deadly statistics indeed. Discouraging statistics, when we remember that two thousand years have passed since the new era of justice began, when the Suffering Servant Jesus would not "grow faint or be crushed until he has established justice in the earth." On Good Friday we Catholics across our country will do well to kiss the feet of the crucified Christ. We will do even better if in some practical fashion each Catholic were to wash the feet of a crucified image of Christ. I mean, reach out to one of our little sisters and brothers, heal one hurt. One child, one hurt.

II

Second, the imprisoned—the justice in our penal system. Why this in a Holy Week homily? Because imprisonment is one of the captivities God's Son took our flesh to do something about. Because it is intimate to the Jubilee Year we are celebrating. Because it raises a nerve-tingling moral issue: Is our justice to be retributive or restorative, sheer punishment or renewal as well? In our country about two million men and women are in prison—half a million more than the next incarcerating country, mother Russia. This "land of the free" has one-quarter of all the people incarcerated in the world. Of these two million, 48 percent are black, 18 Hispanic. The remaining one-third are white. "What they have in common with their black and brown brothers is that they're poor, addicted, under-educated, and jobless."[3] Recidivism rate? 70 percent for juveniles, 63 percent for adults.

The problem, you know, is not far from you and me. Listen to the full-time Catholic chaplain at the D.C. jail, with 20 years of stories, of listening:

> Most of [the inmates] grew up in poverty, in dilapidated public housing. Most of them dropped out of high school when they were in their first or second year. Their literacy level is at the fifth-grade level. Eighty percent are addicted to drugs or alcohol, or a combination of both. Sixty percent of that 80 percent are non-violent offenders.[4]

When he began his ministry two decades ago, this chaplain confesses, he "was under the general belief...that our justice system...is fair, impartial, and balanced. But...my early naivete has long since gone away. I now recognize that our system of criminal justice is not fair, is not impartial, and is not balanced."[5]

Many judges, many in correction and policing, would admit that our system is broken. The retributive model of justice—punishment, retaliation—is inadequate; we must look for another model. And another model has begun to show promise, in New Zealand especially, in about 600 U.S. jurisdictions in small ways. It is based on biblical justice, a justice that focuses on healing. It is called restorative justice, a justice that restores peace, security, trust. It gets the people involved. "The one who has offended and the victim sit down together with mediators and begin to put the thing back together."[6]

Which model works? With the punishment model, two-thirds of former prisoners commit another crime and return to prison. The restorative or treatment model "is associated with an average reduction in crime by 25 percent."

Take a swift look at capital punishment. Most Americans, most Catholics, still support it. But a sea change is taking place. New York's District Attorney has told us that the death penalty actually hinders the struggle against crime, fuels the flames of violence, exacts a terrible price in dollars, lives, and human decency.[7] The

conservative Republican governor of Illinois has halted all execu-
tions in his state because the system is "fraught with error," because
13 convicts scheduled for death have been exonerated, because of
12 executed one is now believed to have been innocent.[8] Pope John
Paul II insists that in our humanity we have developed to a point
where execution is no longer necessary to preserve the moral order.
And when was the last time you heard a priest preach that all human
life is sacred, even the life of a rapist, a serial killer?

III

A third group of the downtrodden: immigrants. Since 1903 we
have cherished a poem by Emma Lazarus inscribed on a tablet in the
pedestal of the Statue of Liberty. It ends with five resplendent lines:

> Give me your tired, your poor,
> Your huddled masses yearning to breathe free,
> The wretched refuse of your teeming shore.
> Send these, the homeless, tempest-tost to me,
> I lift my lamp beside the golden door!

Almost a century has passed and our welcome to immigrants is
wearing thin. There are problems our American ancestors did not
have to face. Numbers: As I speak, Hispanics compose 28 percent of
Texas, about 31 percent of California. Soon after 2050, non-Hispanic
whites may form a minority of our population. And so, as I crisscross
our country in my project Preaching the Just Word, I find controversy
raging. Is the new migration doing harm to our economy? Is unskilled
labor taking jobs from natives? Can we possibly merge Hispanics,
Koreans, Vietnamese, and Anglo-Americans into a parish that is a single, well-knit, loving community? One example, at once serious and
humorous: In building the new cathedral in Los Angeles, how can we
fit 52 cultural Madonnas into one church structure? Yes, fifty-two.

A fresh problem, unknown a century ago: For lack of custom-
ary detention space, thousands of our immigrants are housed in jails,
side by side with convicted criminals; contact with lawyers can be
extremely difficult; at times families are broken up. In Elizabeth,
New Jersey, a religion program was halted because the subject under
discussion was Matthew 25:36: "I was in prison and you visited me."
The problems are many and mind-boggling, due not to ill will, but to
unprecedented numbers and the awesome task of examining hundreds of thousands of histories.

In so chaotic a situation, how can you and I, how can our people, be servants of justice? I suggest a small beginning. Recall the Hebrew ideal, legislated for a people that had experienced enslavement, exile, domination: "You shall not oppress a resident alien; you know how an alien feels, for you were aliens in the land of Egypt" (Exod 23:9; see 22:21). More than not oppressing, "You shall also love the stranger, for you were strangers in the land of Egypt" (Deut 10:19; see 24:17).

You may still ask: Why all these secular statistics in a homily—in Holy Week? After all, a homily is not a lecture. One basic reason. This evening take up your breviary; turn to Week 3, Friday; take the Daytime Prayer; find the psalm-prayer. It comes immediately after you have prayed Psalm 23: "My God, my God, why have you forsaken me?...And my soul shall live for Him." Read the psalm-prayer aloud, slowly: "Father, when your Son was handed over to torture and seemed abandoned by you, he cried out to you from the cross and death was destroyed, life was restored. By his death and resurrection, may we see the day when the poor man is saved, the downtrodden is lifted up, and the chains that bind people are broken."

Priests and priests-to-be: Holy Week is about dying/rising. But not simply the dying/rising of Jesus. And not simply the dying/rising of the well and the wealthy, the fortunate and the free. It is about the dying/rising of the poor, the downtrodden, the enchained. It is about the impoverished, the imprisoned, the immigrant. The prayer the Church prays for them does not stop with prayer, is not ended on your knees. The prayer is for biblical justice, the justice God's Son took our flesh to preach and live. A justice of which he was the Suffering Servant.

But it is not only he; it is we who are not to "grow faint or be crushed" until we have "established justice in the earth." And we as priests will help establish justice by hearing the just word, living the just word, and preaching the just word.

Hearing the just word. I mean listening not only to Jesus but to the cries of the poor, the disadvantaged, the oppressed. You can hear it from the 16.5 million little ones with so little hope. You can hear it from the silver screen, voices from *Dead Man Walking* and *The Green Mile*. You can hear it from thousands of immigrants in detention centers across the country. Hearing it somewhat as Mother Teresa heard it when she cradled a baby with AIDS or carried a dying Indian into her home in Calcutta.

Living the just word. You and I are uncommonly blessed. As priests, we are assured three square meals a day, a roof over our heads, clothes on our backs, insurance for our health, compassion in our dying. Not a guilt trip. Simply a reminder against the consumerism John Paul condemns, slavery to possessions, continually replacing what we have with something better. A reminder that we, like Jesus, have come not to be served but to serve.

Preaching the just word. Not an easy task. A task of persuasion and grace. To make cold statistics on poor children excite families that already have problems enough. To change the hearts of 70 percent of Catholics who support capital punishment. To persuade our people of Jesuit sociologist Joseph Fitzpatrick's assertion, "Whenever migrations are in progress, you can be sure that the finger of God is writing, often in strange ways."[9]

It can be done. Precisely because the task of persuasion is a task of grace. It is not our own initiative that creates God's justice. This is what Calvary was all about. From this Holy Week stems the grace you and I need to be effective servants of justice. But here a warning. If grace stems from the preeminent Suffering Servant, grace calls for suffering servants. To listen with head and heart to the cries of the poor, to live a life of compassion for the downtrodden, to preach fidelity to all relationships with passion as well as intelligence and discretion—it will hurt. You are not likely to be shot down like Archbishop Romero, cruelly butchered like the six Jesuits at the University of Central America, massacred like the four women missionaries in El Salvador. But if you're not hurting at all, it's a pretty good sign you're not really working at it.

Yesterday the Suffering Servant rode into Jerusalem on a donkey. May I submit that in God's plan you and I rode with him, rode into the city of *our* destiny as well? How precisely share that donkey, that destiny? There, my brothers, is the rest of your Holy Week and mine. Take a moment now to pray that, as priests in the likeness of Jesus, you may not grow faint, may not be crushed, until you have established justice, God's justice, in your little acre of God's kingdom.

Theological College
Washington, D.C.
April 17, 2000

8
CROSS OF CHRIST,
CROSS OF THE CHRISTIAN
Good Friday (ABC)

- Isaiah 52:13–53:12
- Hebrews 4:14–16; 5:7–9
- John 18:1–19:42

Good friends in Christ: Today's solemn celebration, our Good Friday, allows only two short homilies. Actually, one homily in two acts. My first act focuses on the cross of Christ; my second act, on the cross of the Christian.

I

First, the cross of Christ. There is a sadness to Good Friday. How could there not be? Perhaps the saddest day of the year. God's own Son died. The Son of God in our flesh died. Not peacefully at home in Nazareth; not on a soft bed. The most shameful of deaths: on a cross. Between two bandits. His mother standing pale and shaken a few yards away. Nails pinning his hands and his feet. Roman soldiers gambling for his garments. Crowds of his fellow Jews mocking him. The chief priests, the scribes, and the elders taunting him; "If you are really God's Son, come down from the cross—come down and we will believe" (Mt 27:41–42).

If that were all, it would be sheer tragedy, room for grief and nothing more. But there is another side to it. Three swift statements—simple on their face, profound in their meaning. The cross is life, the cross is love, and so the cross is joy.

The cross is life. The greatest paradox in history: life through death. "Dying, you destroyed our death." Jesus told the Jews, "And I, when I am lifted up, will draw all men and women to myself" (Jn 12:32). When he is "lifted up." He had already told Nicodemus

47

what it meant to be lifted up. Remember the Israelites in the wilderness, many bitten by poisonous serpents? Remember how Moses "made a serpent of bronze and put it upon a pole; and whenever a serpent bit someone, that person would look at the bronze serpent and live" (Num 21:9)? Listen to Jesus: "Just as Moses lifted up the serpent in the wilderness, so must the Son of Man be lifted up, that everyone who believes may have eternal life in him" (Jn 3:14-15). Eternal life: life now and now for ever.

What Calvary did was to take a human race that was dead in sin and make it possible for all of us to come alive in Christ. What does that mean? It means that, because Jesus died, you and I can now have God living in us: Father, Son, and Holy Spirit dwelling in each of us as in a temple. In St. Paul's breathtaking expression, "God's love has been poured into our hearts through the Holy Spirit that has been given to us" (Rom 5:5). We are temples of God, as truly as is the tabernacle in this cathedral.

That is why St. Paul could cry, "We proclaim Christ crucified, a stumbling block to Jews and foolishness to Gentiles, but to those who are the called, both Jews and Greeks, the power of God and the wisdom of God" (1 Cor 1:23-24). We *proclaim* Christ crucified; we *glory* in the cross. With the sign of the cross we bless ourselves and one another; with the cross we bless our food; with the cross we bring a child into the Church; with the cross we consign the dead to God; with the cross we even drive out devils. For the cross of Christ is life, gives life, makes us come alive like other Christs. How? It enables us to believe what is unbelievable, to hope for life for ever in the face of death, to love God and one another as Jesus has loved us.

This it is to be alive; and it stems from a cross outside Jerusalem. This was the divine exchange: God's Son lived our life so that we could live his life.

And the cross is love. We are not alive simply because Jesus died. We are alive because he died out of love. "Greater love than this no one has: to lay down life itself" for those we love (Jn 15:13). "In this is love," the First Letter of John declares, "not that we loved God but that He loved us and sent His Son to be the atoning sacrifice for our sins" (1 Jn 4:10). It is love that transmutes sheer suffering into sacrifice. Christ "loved me," Paul declares in wonder, "and gave himself for me" (Gal 2:20).

Without love, Calvary would have been worthless, useless, the most tragic example of capital punishment in history. It was not so. "God so loved the world that He gave His only Son" (Jn 3:16). God's Son so loved the world that he took our flesh. Not a head trip; not to simply know what we go through. He loved us so intensely that he wanted to experience what we experience as we experience it: our successes and our failures, our delight and our grief, our joy and our tears. Yes, our dying. He wanted to love as we love. Only love, God's love, makes sense out of this. And when Jesus left us, he left us with the most incredible proof of his love: himself, body and blood, soul and divinity—the very sacrament of love. "This is my body given for you" (Lk 22:19).

Therefore what? Therefore joy! Not pleasure in a bleeding, dying Jesus. Joy in the gift, joy in his love, joy in his presence within us, all around us. Joy in Jesus alive and active in everything he has created, from the amoeba to the farthest star. Joy because death itself has been defeated. Little wonder poet Gerard Manley Hopkins could sing, "The world is charged with the grandeur of God."[1] Despite sin and war, despite disease and death, Christ our Lord is here.

Joy because we die not into dust, into nothingness; we die into life, life more complete, more intense, more satisfying than anything we now experience, life face to face with God, with our Lady, with our dear ones. Life without end. Joy because we die into love. For, in the encouraging words of God's own Book, "'What no eye has seen, nor ear heard, nor the human heart conceived, what God has prepared for those who love Him,' these things God has revealed to us through the Spirit" (1 Cor 2:9; see Isa 64:4). What the God who *is* Love has prepared for us.

Christ our life, Christ our love, Christ our joy! A sad day indeed, but not the sadness of a disaster. We need not wait for Easter to rejoice. At this moment we are risen Christians—men and women who know we have been redeemed, redeemed by a cross, men and women who say over and over, "*By your cross* you have set us free. You are the Savior of the world." As you kiss Jesus' crucified feet, let your tears be seasoned with joy.

II

So far, the cross of Christ. Now, the cross of the Christian. We begin with a fact of life: suffering. Here, three questions. (1) Why is suffering a problem? (2) Is there a Christian solution? (3) How bring the cross of Christ into our daily lives?

First, why is suffering, the Christian's cross, a problem? One reason goes back to our God. For those of us who have grown up with a God whose very name is Love, much human suffering makes little or no sense: infants with Down's syndrome, a young woman comatose for seven years, families wiped out in auto accidents, thousands of Guatemalans exterminated by an earthquake, six million Jews destroyed in the Holocaust—the mysteries are endless. Remember Job? "That man was blameless and upright, feared God and turned away from evil" (Job 1:1). And yet God let Satan destroy his animals, kill his sons and daughters, inflict loathsome sores on him head to foot, till he cursed the day he was born. He found human wisdom bankrupt, could not understand why this was happening to *him*, came face to face with a God who refused to explain, who simply appealed to his love and trust.

A second reason. Many years ago, in a synagogue in White Plains, New York, I tried to take a step toward Catholic-Jewish reconciliation. I recalled that for the last eight centuries most Jewish interpreters had seen in Isaiah's Suffering Servant the Jewish people, had seen in his sufferings not only the agony of the Captivity but the whole Jewish people. I suggested the redemptive power of Jewish suffering—for them and for me. At best, a magnificent failure. From their history the Jewish people see no spiritual value in suffering. "Its value is that, as we use our free will to eliminate it, there will be less."[2]

A third reason. There are intelligent Christians who see no good, no purpose, in suffering. Some feminist theologians reject theologies of the cross because they "glorify suffering even when...identification with the suffering Jesus provides comfort in the harsh reality of women's lives."[3]

Is there a Christian solution? Yes indeed, but it too is shrouded in mystery. It goes back to St. Paul addressing a Christian community: "I am now rejoicing in my sufferings for your sake, and in my flesh I am completing what is lacking in Christ's afflictions for the sake of his body, the Church" (Col 1:24). It does not mean that somehow Jesus did not suffer enough. It means that his cross does not have its full effect unless it becomes the cross of the Christian.[4] It means what Jesus declared: "If anyone wants to come after me [wants to become my disciple], let him deny himself [stop being self-centered], take up his cross each day, and follow me" (Lk 9:23).

The mystery in all this is the mystery of God's grace. As the Body of Christ, we Christians are so intimately linked with him and with one another that what we do, for good or ill, affects the Body or some part of it. A Presbyterian novelist/preacher compared humanity to an enormous spider web:

If you touch it anywhere, you set the whole thing trembling.... As we move around this world and as we act with kindness, perhaps, or with indifference, or with hostility, toward the people we meet, we too are setting the great spider web a-tremble. The life that I touch for good or ill will touch another life, and that in turn another, until who knows where the trembling stops or in what far place and time my touch will be felt. Our lives are linked. No man [no woman] is an island....[5]

Within the Body of Christ that insight is even more telling. Listen to Jesus: "Unless the grain of wheat falls to the earth and dies, it remains alone [just a single grain of wheat]. But if it dies, it bears much fruit" (Jn 12:24).

In a word, the cross of the Christian is the cross of Christ—or can be if...if we bring the cross of Christ into our daily lives. If we can murmur each morning, "Dear Jesus, I offer you my prayers, works, joys, *and sufferings* of this day, for all the intentions of your sacred heart, in union with the holy Sacrifice of the Mass throughout the world, in reparation for my sins, for the intentions of all our associates...."

Not only words in the morning; the life of the whole day. From womb to tomb we have to let go. Let go of where we've been, let go of the level of life where we are now, so as to live more fully. Let go of childhood and adolescence, of good looks and youthful energy, of health and hair, of a high-paying job or the joys of mothering, of activity and applause, of anger and revenge, of dear ones who die and friends who move away. Let go of so much that helps us to say with Italian actor Roberto Benigni, "Life is beautiful."[6]

Not simply because we must, because we have no choice. Rather because we want to, because the way of the cross is the way of Christ. Oh yes, to let go is to die a little. It's painful; it can be bloody; and so we hang on, clutching our yesterdays like Linus's blanket, refusing to grow. And yet, it is only by letting go of yesterday that we can grow more fully into Christ today. We do not forget our yesterdays; we simply dare not live in them.

Not if we want to follow the Christ who let go of his "glory with the Father" to share our humanity; let go of comfortable Nazareth to preach his gospel to a wider world; let go of his divine dignity to endure the disdain of his countrymen; let go of those closest of friends like Peter, who loved him but could not watch one hour with him in his agony; let go of an apostle who betrayed him with a kiss; let go of his awesome power to hang all but naked on a criminal's cross; let go of life itself, trusting in his Father's goodness to raise him from the dead.

To follow the suffering Christ. Not because we must; because we love. Because by love we turn sheer suffering into sacrifice. Because by our sacrifice we touch Christ to others; for in this close-knit Body of Christ, only God knows "in what far place and time my touch will be felt." Pain need not be wasted. Not if every distress, every "installment in dying,"[7] is my gift to another through Christ. Not if my very last gift of love, to my Lord and my sisters and brothers, is a faith-filled "Father, into your hands I entrust my spirit" (Lk 23:46).

St. Matthew's Cathedral
Washington, D.C.
April 2, 1999

FROM EASTER TO PENTECOST

9
ONE HEART, ONE MIND
Second Sunday of Easter (B)

- Acts 4:32–35
- 1 John 5:1–6
- John 20:19–31

About ten minutes ago you heard a startling sentence. I wonder if it actually did startle you. It was the very first sentence in the very first reading, a sentence from the second book St. Luke wrote, the Acts of the Apostles, a companion volume to his Gospel. Luke is speaking of the earliest days of our church. And how does he describe that church? "The whole multitude of those who believed was of one heart and mind" (Acts 4:32). I preach on that single sentence today for three good reasons: (1) It gives us a glimpse into what the infant church was like—the ideal and the real. (2) It brings the ideal into America 2000. (3) It compels us to confront the ideal in our church with our experience of the real.

I

First, St. Luke declares that in the infant church there was a single heart, a single mind. For that to be true, there had to be a basic unity. And earlier in his story Luke tells us what that unity meant in the concrete, in day-to-day living. "They continued to devote themselves to the teaching of the apostles, to a communal form of life, to the breaking of the bread, and to the prayers" (2:42). Four qualities characterized Jerusalem's Christians. (1) They believed what the Church at that time was teaching. (2) They lived their lives not as independent individuals but as a single community, dependent each on every other, brothers and sisters in Christ. (3) Their worship had for its focus the Eucharist: the bread

55

broken, the cup shared. (4) They prayed together—perhaps in the temple, perhaps elsewhere as well.

Luke adds a fascinating feature of church life in Jerusalem. "There was never a needy person among them, for those who owned property or houses would sell them, bring the proceeds of what was sold, and lay them at the feet of the apostles; and it was distributed to each according to one's need" (4:34–35).

Is this an accurate picture of life in the primitive Jerusalem community? Unwavering faith, complete harmony, utter unity, undeviating devotion to prayer and worship, common ownership of property and possessions? Probably not. It is more likely a foil, a contrast to the scandal and the squabble Luke will soon describe. One example: "There was a complaint of the Hellenists [Jewish Christians who prayed and read their Scriptures in Greek] against the Hebrews [Jewish Christians who prayed and read in Aramaic or Hebrew] that their widows were being neglected in the daily distribution of food" (6:1). And you may remember Ananias and his wife Sapphira. Ananias "sold a piece of property" and with Sapphira's knowledge "put aside for himself some of the proceeds," gave the apostles only part of the proceeds (5:1–2). When they were found out, when they were accused harshly by Peter, both of them dropped dead.

Luke's picture of unity is an ideal; the reality was never realized to perfection. Still, the ideal is important, for it reveals what the Lord expects his disciples to aim at. And what was that? Jesus told us in his Last Discourse, in his prayer for his disciples: "I pray...that they all may be one, just as you, Father, are in me and I in you, that they also may be [one] in us...I in them and you in me, that they may be brought to completion as one. Thus the world may come to know that you sent me and that you loved them even as you loved me" (Jn 17:20–23).[1]

II

This moves me to my second point: How does the early Jerusalem situation touch our Catholic life in the United States today? As with Jerusalem, so with us, let me suggest two aspects of our Catholic existence: the ideal and the reality. Begin with the ideal. Here is where the four qualities Luke attributes to Jerusalem's Christians deserve our consideration. "They continued to devote themselves to the teaching of the apostles, to a communal form of life, to the breaking of the bread, and to the prayers."

First, you and I are gifted beyond our deserving. What is that gift? A precious monosyllable: faith. We believe what the earliest Christians believed, "the teaching of the apostles," what God has told us through Christ and his Holy Spirit. What that is has been summarized beautifully by the Second Vatican Council:

> What was handed on by the apostles includes everything which contributes to the holiness of life and the increase in faith of the People of God; and so the Church, in her teaching, life, and worship, perpetuates and hands on to all generations all that she herself is, all that she believes.
>
> [But] there is a growth in the understanding of the realities and the words that have been handed down. This happens through the contemplation and study made by believers..., through the intimate understanding of spiritual things they experience, and through the preaching of those who have received through episcopal succession the sure gift of truth.[2]

Second, like the early Christians, with the early Christians, you and I are part of a unique community. Vatican II calls it the People of God. For St. Paul, we are the Body of Christ. A body into which we were inserted when saving waters bathed our bodies in baptism. A body that has the risen Christ as its head. A body whose members are so intimately linked that no one of us can say to any other, "I have no need of you" (1 Cor 12:21). Not pope to peasant, not the rich to the poor, not the learned to the simple, not I to you or you to me. A body wherein "if one member suffers, all suffer together with it; if one member is honored, all rejoice together with it" (v. 26).

Third, like the early Christians, you and I are privileged to share in "the breaking of the bread." Breaking the bread Sunday after Sunday, even day after day, may dull the miracle that is Eucharist: the risen Christ present in our gathering together, present in the Word proclaimed, present in unbelievable intimacy when his body enters our bodies in a "communion" no mere human could ever have imagined. As Pope Pius XII declared, with the risen Christ within us we are what we have received.

And there is more. Listen to a lover of liturgy who back in 1981 expressed in striking syllables the equalizing, leveling power of the Eucharist:

> Where else [other than at Eucharist] in our society are all of us—
> not just a gnostic elite, but everyone—called to be social critics,
> called to extricate ourselves from the powers and principalities
> that claim to rule our daily lives in order to submit ourselves to
> the sole domination of the God before whom all of us are
> equal? Where else in our society are we all addressed and sprin-
> kled and bowed to and incensed and touched and kissed and
> treated like *somebody*—all in the very same way? Where else do
> economic czars and beggars get the same treatment? Where else
> are food and drink blessed in a common prayer of thanksgiving,
> broken and poured out, so that everybody, *everybody* shares and
> shares alike?[3]

Fourth, like the primitive Christians, you and I are graced to share "the prayers," to pray together. It sounds so simple, doesn't it? It is, but when you think of it, striking in its simplicity. Take the Our Father we shall shortly chant together. It is *our* Father to whom we pray as Jesus taught us to pray. And we pray not only *with* one another; we pray *for* one another: that God's will may rule all of our hearts, God's food nourish all of us, God forgive all of us as we all forgive all who have offended us, God deliver all of us from the power of the Evil One. The Our Father is not the prayer of hundreds of isolated egos; it is the prayer of this community precisely as a community, each of us wondrously aware of all of us.

III

Such is the ideal, whether for early Jerusalem or America 2000. And as we struggle to realize the ideal, we cannot avoid the reality— the real that clashes with the ideal. Let me touch briefly on each of our four areas.

First, "the teaching of the apostles" as it has developed through almost 20 centuries. Much as we Catholics respect what we are taught, we are divided on a number of issues: from contraception to Communion in the hand, from papal authority to the ordination of women, from prochoice on abortion to justice and injustice within the Church itself.

Second, such differences inevitably affect our life in commu-nity. We are wonderfully and fearfully human, all of us. When we feel fiercely about something, tempers flare up, friendships are fractured, words become violent weapons—even among Catholics. St. Paul might well say to us what he said to the Christians of Corinth: "It has been reported to me...that there is quarreling among you" (1 Cor 1:11). Not civilized disagreement—angry wrangling, the antagonism of enemies.

Third, the Eucharist, which has traditionally been our supreme symbol of oneness, now divides us, at times mortally. Shall we stand or kneel, play Palestrina or sing the St. Louis Jesuits, greet one another with a hug or a handshake or not at all, work quietly for women priests or create a Eucharist of our own? And what shakes me and shivers me, only about 30 percent of American Catholics share the Eucharist at least two Sundays a month, the most powerful source of grace within the Church.

Fourth, we have in large measure forgotten how to pray together. Group rosary seems limited to wakes, families rarely say "grace before meals" or thank God together before retiring to bed, and our legal judges are debating whether a public school football team may say a prayer together for victory.

Good friends in Christ: A homily is hardly the place to solve profound problems. But it is the place for an encouraging challenge. Each one of us—your homilist included—would do well some disenchanted evening to go back to the sentence in Acts that shaped this sermon: The followers of Jesus "continued to devote themselves to the teaching of the apostles, to a communal form of life, to the breaking of the bread, and to the prayers." Not primarily an examination of conscience, desirable as this might be. Rather, focus on that sentence as the risen Christ's Easter gifts to you. I mean: (1) You have been gifted by God to believe truths about God and yourself you could not possibly discover for yourself. (2) You form a unique community of love that has Christ for its head and the Holy Spirit as its soul. (3) Within you, as often as you desire, Christ himself lives, body and blood, soul and divinity—as truly in you as in pope or priest. (4) Your prayers are never really solitary; each prayer is offered in union with the whole community of Christians, to "Our Father," the Father of each and all of us.

And, marvel of marvels, this fourfold gift is here in this sacred hour: the faith you proclaim, your life in common, Christ within you, your praying together. Such is my encouraging word. There is indeed a challenge here: How well do I carry this fourfold gift into my life outside these sacred walls? Does the discouraging "reality" I sketched above say something to my Christian existence? Important questions. But today let me stress the gift itself. In the striking language of Jesuit poet Gerard Manley Hopkins, "Let [Christ] easter in us."[4] The noun "Easter" becomes a verb; a static reality is transformed into an action, something incredibly active within us, in our living. Easter becomes a way of life, a life of joy in the Lord, joy in ourselves, joy in all others, joy in the world. Yes indeed, my risen sisters and brothers, let Christ easter within us!

Holy Trinity Church
Washington, D.C.
April 30, 2000

10
FROM EASTER EXPERIENCE
TO WORLD-WIDE WITNESS
Third Sunday of Easter (B)

- Acts 3:13–15, 17–19
- 1 John 2:1–5a
- Luke 24:35–48

Today's Gospel is worth looking at closely. It begins with the two disciples rushing back from Emmaus and telling "the Eleven and their companions what had happened on the road, and how [Jesus] had been made known to them in the breaking of the bread" (Lk 24:33, 35). Now Jesus appears to all of these. Notice how the appearance to the two on the road to Emmaus and the new appearance to the disciples gathered together in Jerusalem are very similar. In each case Jesus appears and the disciples do not recognize him; in each case he instructs them by way of the Scriptures; in each case there is a meal that Jesus himself takes; and he departs from them. In that context let's ask three questions. (1) What is the disciples' experience of the risen Jesus all about? What is Luke trying to do? (2) Do we have an experience of Jesus similar to that of those earlier disciples? (3) If we do, what might it say about the last sentence in today's Gospel, "You are witnesses of these things" (v. 48)?

I

First, what is Luke trying to do with this appearance of Jesus? Why does he include it in his Gospel? It is part of what he promised at the beginning of the Gospel. He was addressing a catechumen or neophyte named Theophilus: "I too have decided, after tracing everything carefully from the beginning, to put them systematically in writing for you, most excellent Theophilus, so that you may realize what assurance you have for the instruction you have received" (1:3). Luke is not an eyewitness of the events he narrates, but he has done his homework. His investigation, he says, is complete, accurate, and thorough; and he has organized it systematically, so that Theophilus may rest reassured about the initial instructions he has received. And not only Theophilus: all Christian readers in Luke's time and thereafter.

Now for today's Gospel: How does Luke's account of Jesus' appearance to his followers in Jerusalem reassure his readers that what the Church was teaching about Jesus was true? Well, it begins with doubt, with fear: The people in that house are terrified; they think they are seeing a ghost. It may look like Jesus, but it cannot be; they have seen him die. And remember, there had to be something different about the risen Jesus, about this body that could pass through closed doors. So what does Jesus do, simply to make it evident to his disciples that he is the same person they had come to know before Calvary? First, believe your senses: "Look at my hands and my feet and see that it is really I. Touch me and see; no ghost has flesh and bones such as you see that I have" (Lk 24:39).

Still they are not quite sure. Luke excuses their disbelief, attributes it to their joy—somewhat as he had excused the disciples for sleeping during Jesus' agony in the garden: "They slept from grief" (22:45). So, another proof, a striking proof: "Do you have anything here to eat?" They do indeed; they have just broiled some fish. And Luke says so simply, "They offered him a piece; he took it and ate it in front of them" (vv. 42–43).

Then, as with the disciples on the road to Emmaus, Jesus gives them a short course in Scripture: the Pentateuch, the Psalms, the prophets. "He opened their minds to understand the Scriptures," made it clear to them from the Word of God that he had to die, had to rise, and that forgiveness was to be "preached in his name to all the nations, beginning from Jerusalem" (vv. 44–47). And finally, a significant short sentence: "You are witnesses of all this" (v. 48). Not only have they experienced all this; their task in the Period of the Church is to testify to it. Not only witness; bear witness! Not only see; proclaim! Not only experience; let the world know what you have experienced![1]

II

This leads directly to my second question: Do we have an experience of Jesus similar to that of those earlier disciples? Similar but not the same. We should. One such experience is clear to me as I look out at you. The fact that you are worshiping here at this moment means that Jesus has touched you in some genuine fashion. Each act of faith is part of Jesus' Easter gift to you. Unless you were in contact with Jesus, you could not say, "We believe in one Lord Jesus Christ, God's only Son, born of the Virgin Mary, suffered, died, rose again, will come in glory to judge the living and the dead." A lovely passage in the First Letter of Peter is true of you: "Although you have not seen him, you love him; and even though you do not see him now, you believe in him and rejoice with an indescribable and glorious joy, for you are receiving the outcome of your faith, the salvation of your souls" (1 Pet 1:8–9).

All well and good. But I have in mind a relationship with God closer still. Listen to St. Ignatius Loyola, words put on his lips by a remarkable German theologian, Karl Rahner—words that express accurately what Ignatius himself experienced:

> I was convinced that first, tentatively, during my illness in Loyola and then, decisively, during my time as a hermit in Manresa I had a direct encounter with God.... I am not going to talk of forms and visions, symbols, voices, tears and such things.... All I say is I knew God, nameless and unfathomable, silent and yet near, bestowing Himself upon me in His Trinity. I knew God beyond all concrete imaginings. I knew Him clearly in such nearness and grace as is impossible to confound or mistake.... I knew God Himself, not simply human words describing Him....This experience is grace indeed and basically there is no one to whom it is refused....[2]

A significant declaration for you and me: Knowing God "silent and yet near," knowing Jesus the way you know your best friend: It's not the same kind of knowing you get from books, the way you know George Washington or Joan of Arc. That sort of knowing is knowing *about* someone. Ignatius means you can know God, you can know Jesus, the way you know someone uncommonly dear to you, an intimacy that resembles the closeness of wife and husband. And, says Ignatius, "there is no one to whom [this grace] is refused." It's not reserved for mystics: Julian of Norwich, John of the Cross. It's meant for everyone whom God has shaped in the image of Jesus.

How do we get that way? Not because we are very smart, were educated at Georgetown. We get it by asking for it, by praying for it, by begging for it, by trying to live as Jesus lived, by loving him, by loving all our sisters and brothers as Jesus loves us. By dealing with Jesus as someone alive. The way St. Teresa of Avila dealt with God. In a period of profound frustration, Teresa complained to God, "Why do you treat me this way?" God's reply? "I treat all my friends that way." Teresa's retort? "No wonder you have so few!"

If that's the way you know, you have the assurance St. Luke was talking about to Theophilus. Study is still useful. We should be prepared to do what the First Letter of Peter advises: "Always be ready to make your defense to anyone who demands from you an accounting for the hope that is in you" (1 Pet 3:15). But for your own profound spirituality you will need arguments, proofs, less and less. For the Easter Jesus will be a personal friend. Yes, there may well be dark nights of the soul, periods when the Jesus you know so well seems to have withdrawn from you, when you may even have to cry out from your own crucifixion, "My God, my God, why have you abandoned me?" (Mk 15:34). But it will pass, I promise you; the peace Jesus promised will return to you.

III

Knowing Jesus by faith and as his friends, you will rejoice in my third point. I mean the vocation that is yours, as it was the vocation of the earlier disciples: "You are witnesses of these things" (Lk 24:48). Not that you were there in Jerusalem when Jesus rose from the dead; not that you saw him in his risen flesh. But if your faith is firm and you have a personal relationship with Jesus, then you have experienced the same Christ who joined the two discouraged disciples on the road to Emmaus, instructed them in the Scriptures, and broke bread with them. You have experienced the same Christ who in Jerusalem showed the doubting disciples his hands and his feet, ate a piece of broiled fish in their presence, and told them what the Scriptures had to say about his suffering and dying, about repentance and forgiveness to be proclaimed in his name to all the world. You experience him when you too gather together in his name, when you too listen to him unfolding God's Word to you, when you too break bread with him and share his cup.

Your task and mine, our vocation in virtue of our baptism, is not significantly different from that of Jesus' early disciples. Proclaim the risen Jesus, bear witness to him, tell the world what you have experienced! At times with our lips, more frequently by our lives. But how? Let me share with you a dream of mine—a dream which I believe is God's own dream for every parish that claims the name Catholic. Here let me focus on one parish, Holy Trinity. Three facets to God's dream...and mine.

First, God's dream was what I sketched above. I mean that each of you would not only keep God's commandments, avoid what St. Paul calls "the works of the flesh: fornication, impurity, licentiousness, dissensions, envy, drunkenness, and things like these" (Gal 5:19–21). Over and above that, get to really know Jesus, experience him as a personal friend. I mean listen to him, talk to him, "let your hair down." Thank him for dying for you, for giving you a mind for thinking, a heart for loving. Complain if you feel like it, grumble, grouse. Just don't treat him like a statue with a bleeding heart!

Second, take that personal love for Jesus and share it. Not only with those you like or who like you. Touch it to the child crippled or the girl abused, the adolescent addicted or the AIDS-afflicted, the slow to learn or the swift to hate, the homeless and the hopeless, the lonely and the unloved, yes the racist and the bigot. Not all at once, please! But, as Mother Teresa said when asked by a D.C. politician how she expected to feed the hundreds of hungry in Washington, "One at a time." You know, we 50-or-so million adult Catholics could change the ravaged face of our country.

Third, take that personal love for Jesus and for his images and touch it to all of God's creation, to that ice-cold word "things." Here we face each day a bewitching temptation: what John Paul II called "an excessive availability of every kind of material goods for the benefit of certain social groups" that "makes people slaves of 'possession' and of immediate gratification, with no other horizon than the multiplication or continual replacement of the things already owned with others still better."[3]

At this point I am not advocating a life of poverty; I am simply repeating what is becoming more and more evident: In raping nature, in exploiting an earth God meant for all, we are doing violence to our sisters and brothers. When we see earth, sea, and sky as our playthings, for our use or our pleasure as we see fit, we are mocking the God who looked at His creation and saw that "it was very good" (Gen 1:29); we are turning God's gift into an enemy that can destroy us.

Yes, destroy us. If you want to be fruitfully frightened, read the recent Special Edition of *Time* magazine, "Earth 2000." Discover why only by protecting the environment can we save ourselves; how half the world's wetlands have been lost in the past century and 20 percent of drylands are in danger of becoming deserts; why while we play God with water, 2.3 billion people do not have enough. Listen to

John Paul's declaration: Christians must "realize that their responsibility within creation and their duty toward nature and the Creator are an essential part of their faith."[4] It touches the greed some industrialists say is necessary for our economy, touches the shocking waste that characterizes our culture. Francis of Assisi's love for animals and plants, for Brother Sun and Sister Moon, was not a touching eccentricity; he was simply acting as a Christian. God's creation, all of creation, is a gift—to be revered, to be used not to destroy but to build up—build up God's kingdom.

In summary: Your salvation, my salvation, is linked to three relationships: Do I love God above all else? Do I love each sister and brother as Jesus loves me? Do I touch the "things" of everyday life with reverence, with care, with gratitude?

Have we moved away from Easter, from the risen Christ? Quite the contrary. This is what the risen Christ asks us to be; this is what the risen Christ demands we proclaim with our lips and our lives. Such is our witness to the world; such our testimony that we have experienced the risen Christ. Such is the risen Christian.

Holy Trinity Church
Washington, D.C.
May 7, 2000

11
MY LIFE FOR THE SHEEP?
Fourth Week of Easter, Year 1, Monday

- Acts 11:1–8
- John 10:11–18

Three persons engage this homily on shepherds: Ezekiel, Jesus, and you.[1]

I

First, Ezekiel. Why here? Because he spells out, with powerful strokes, the downside of the shepherd story. It is not specifically about priests. "From Sumerian kings in the third millennium on, rulers of the ancient Near East referred to themselves as shepherd of their people.... Ezekiel delivers a woe oracle"[2] that can set the stage, in a very negative way, for the shepherd who is Jesus and for ourselves as shepherds in his image.

> The word of the LORD came to me: "Mortal, prophesy against the shepherds of Israel. Prophesy and say to them—to the shepherds: 'Thus says the LORD God: Ah, you shepherds of Israel who have been feeding yourselves! Should not shepherds feed the sheep? You eat the fat, you clothe yourselves with the wool, you slaughter the fatlings; but you do not feed the sheep. You have not strengthened the weak, you have not healed the sick, you have not bound up the injured, you have not brought back the strayed, you have not sought the lost, but with force and harshness you have ruled them. So they were scattered, because there was no shepherd; and scattered, they became food for all the wild animals. My sheep were scattered, they wandered over all the mountains and on every high hill; my sheep were scattered over all the face of the earth, with no one to search or seek for them.'"
>
> (Ezek 34:1–6)

This is not an accusation directed against today's bishops and priests. I find it useful as a stimulus to an examination of conscience. As I roam the country with our project Preaching the Just Word, most of the priests I run across do not have to worry about being included in Ezekiel's excoriation. And yet, every so often I am concerned. I was concerned when in a certain diocesan convocation five of the younger priests refused to attend any of the presentations on justice or even the meditations; they attended meals and the Eucharist; their own bishop publicly called it a violation of justice. I am concerned when I hear that a newly ordained priest came to his first assignment and said to the pastor, "I don't do hospitals." I am concerned when I find seminarians glorying in the liturgy for its beauty and majesty, but utterly unconcerned about the liturgy's constant call to social justice, the movement of a congregation from church to world, from altar to people, from Christ crucified on Calvary to Christ crucified at the crossroads of our country. I am crushed when I read of the obstacles put in the way of our relations with people by priests who betray the chastity they freely promised to our Lord. I am devastated when I find thousands of Catholics in my country deserting our churches for the evangelicals, largely because they find no message for their souls in our preaching, nothing that relates God's Word to their actual lives.

II

But that is the downside, fortunately rather rare. Still, "This chapter of Ezek[iel] may have been particularly attractive to John because it concludes with the affirmation that the people will know God in this activity [i.e., the Lord promising to go and gather his scattered sheep and bring them back to good pasture: Ezek 34:30–31]: 'And they will know that I Am *(ego eimi)* the LORD their God, and they, house of Israel, are my people, says the LORD. You are my sheep and the sheep of my pasture and I Am the LORD your God.'"[3] Our primary focus has to accentuate the positive. And the positive is declared in elevated language by Jesus in the tenth chapter of John.

The "good" shepherd is the ideal shepherd, "not simply 'good at' something."[4] How is Jesus ideal or model shepherd? For at least four reasons in John. (1) Ideal or model because it is his Father who has given these sheep to Jesus, and so "no one [even religious leaders acting in God's name, like those of chap. 9] can take them from him."[5] (2) Ideal or model because Jesus says that the relationship between this shepherd and his sheep resembles the relationship between Jesus and his Father: "I know my own and my own know me, *just as* the Father knows me and I know the Father" (Jn 10:14-15). (3) Ideal or model because "He calls his own sheep by name and leads them out, goes ahead of them, and the sheep follow him because they know his voice" (vv. 3-4). (4) Ideal or model because he is ready to lay down his life for his flock.

This is the shepherd who "had compassion" on the crowds "because they were harassed and helpless, like sheep without a shepherd" (Mt 9:36). This is the shepherd who responded with a powerful parable to Pharisees and scribes grumbling because he welcomed sinners and ate with them:

> Which of you, having a hundred sheep and losing one of them, does not leave the 99 in the wilderness and go after the one that is lost until he finds it? When he has found it, he lays it on his shoulders and rejoices. And when he comes home, he calls together his friends and neighbors, saying to them, "Rejoice with me, for I have found my sheep that was lost." Just so, I tell you, there will be more joy in heaven over one sinner who repents than over 99 righteous who need no repentance.
>
> (Lk 15:4-7)

Notice well: Jesus doesn't flail the straying sheep back to the flock; he lays the lost sheep on his shoulders! He carries the weight of the sinner on his own body. Remember the suffering servant in Isaiah?

> All we like sheep have gone astray;
>   we have all turned to our own way,
> and the LORD has laid on him
>   the iniquity of us all.
>
> (Isa 53:6)

III

And what of you—and me? The four facets that make Jesus the ideal shepherd might well model our own shepherding.

First, the basic assumption. The same Father God who gave the whole flock called humanity to Jesus has entrusted a microportion of that flock to you. Parish or diocese, hospital or hospice, seminary or CCD, college campus or chancery, whatever the situation, the people you serve are God's trust to you. However they happen to enter your pasture, by accident or design, right now they are your

sacred preserve. The saint and the sinner, the settled and the straying, the straight and the not-so-straight, the docile and the dissent-
ing, the hale and the hungry, the well-heeled and the wasted, the
faithful and the unfaithful, the prolife and the prochoice, the native
and the stranger, the white and the Native American—all are equally
your sheep. (If the word "sheep" offends, trash it!)

Second, your relationship to these, to your flock, has for model
the relationship of Jesus to his Father. You can say with Jesus, "I know
my own and my own know me, just as the Father knows me and I
know the Father." Dismayingly close, and still our ideal. But not a
sheerly intellectual knowledge, as of a theorem or syllogism. In John,
knowing includes loving. More difficult than the sheer concept; for
how can you actually love all your flock, especially love them as Jesus
commanded, "Love one another as I have loved you" (Jn 15:12)? Not
by a high IQ, only "because God's love has been poured into our
hearts through the Holy Spirit that has been given to us" (Rom 5:5).

Third, as with Jesus, so with you: Your task is to "lead" your
flock, to "go ahead" of them (Jn 10: 3–4). Not tyrannically, not force-
fully, not in pride; not an ordained Milosevic. A leader in Andrew
Greeley's sense: someone who can move the minds and hearts of
men and women. A work of persuasion, a work of grace, effected
through God's gracious gifts to you. Never forget Paul's "fruit of the
Spirit: love, joy, peace, patience, kindness, generosity, faithfulness,
gentleness, and self-control" (Gal 5:22:23). These are God's gifts to
you—for your people.

Fourth, a tough act to follow: Are you ready to die for your
flock? Not so much, in our time, at the pyre with Polycarp, on the
scaffold with John Fisher. Are you prepared to live for your people?
For all its joys, a priest's life is still a crucified life—especially when
priesthood does not enjoy the high favor of the 50s, when priests
often bear the brunt of parishioners' ire with the hierarchy, when
fewer vocations mean extraordinary expectations, less leisure, only
pockets of prayer, even burnouts and dropouts. And still it is the
cross that gives life, God's life, to shepherd and sheep. That is why I
take comfort and strength from a declaration of Jesus that is intimate
to the tenth chapter of John, "I came that they may have life and have
it to the full" (Jn 10:10). "To the full." The Greek word (perisson) is
ever so rich. It means "in abundance," "in profusion," more than just
enough, more than is absolutely necessary. Think of it: God's life
gushing into you and through you into your people, every moment of
every day—largely through the cross you carry.

A final word. Back in 1981, a gifted liturgist and activist, Father Robert Hovda, expressed a facet of the shepherd-sheep relationship that might well be for all of us an insight and an inspiration each day of our lives:

> Where else [other than at Eucharist] in our society are all of us—not just a gnostic elite, but everyone—called to be social critics, called to extricate ourselves from the powers and principalities that claim to rule our daily lives in order to submit ourselves to the sole dominion of the God before whom all of us are equal? Where else in our society are we all addressed and sprinkled and bowed to and incensed and touched and kissed and treated like *somebody*—all in the same way? Where else do economic czars and beggars get the same treatment? Where else are food and drink blessed in a common prayer of thanksgiving, broken and poured out, so that everybody, *everybody,* shares and shares alike?[6]

My brothers in Christ: The crosses that overhang the story of salvation, the story of priesthood, are mind-blowing and soul-searing. But in light of the equalizing, leveling power of our Eucharist, can we continue to question whether our shepherding is of value to anyone, has any power to save?

Queen's House of Retreat
Saskatoon, Saskatchewan
April 26, 1999

12

IF I DO NOT HAVE LOVE, I AM NOTHING
Sixth Sunday of Easter (B)

- Acts 10:25–26, 34–35, 44–48
- 1 John 4:7–10
- John 15:9–17

"Greater love than this no one has: to lay down one's life for one's friends." A remarkable sentence, for three good reasons. First, the sentence stems from the lips and life of Jesus. Second, it is specially suitable for our Memorial Day weekend. Third, it suggests what your life and mine should be like. A brief word on each.

I

First, Jesus. His "Greater love no one has" was not uttered in a vacuum. What Jesus said was especially true of himself. John's Gospel is clear: "God so loved the world that He gave His only Son [gave him to our world, gave him to a crucifying death], so that everyone who believes in him may have eternal life" (Jn 3:16). And the First Letter of John reinforces the Gospel: "God's love was revealed among us in this way: God sent His only Son into the world so that we might live through him. In this is love, not that we loved God but that He loved us and sent His Son to be the atoning sacrifice for our sins" (1 Jn 4:9–10).

You might remember what St. Paul wrote to the Christians of Rome: "Rarely will anyone die for a righteous person—though perhaps for a good person someone might actually dare to die. But God proves His love for us in that while we still were sinners Christ died for us" (Rom 5:7–8). God's own unique Son was born as we are born, died more cruelly than any of us will ever die, so that you and I might have life: God's life now and for ever.

72

Greater love than *this* no one has, has ever had, will ever have: that *God* should freely, of God's own will, passionately choose to die for us! You may recall that when Jesus predicted the suffering and death he was to undergo, the apostle Peter "took him aside and began to rebuke him: 'God forbid it, Lord! This must never happen to you.' But he turned and said to Peter, 'Get behind me, Satan! You are a stumbling block to me; for you are setting your mind not on divine things but on human things'" (Mt 16:21–23).

II

Greater love than Jesus' love no one has. And still, thousands have come close. This long weekend we recall some astonishing facts, some astonishing figures. We honor not only 592,332 Civil War dead, but thousands upon thousands more: 1600 white and black casualties it cost to take Santiago in the Spanish–American War; 116,516 military dead in World War I; 405,399 in World War II; 54,246 in the Korean War; over 56,000 in Vietnam. Theirs was the kind of love Jesus said "is like" loving God (Mt 22:39).

Staggering figures. But even more stunning than the sum total is a fact we frequently forget: None of these thousands was a "dog tag"; each was a person, an individual unique, unrepeatable, shaped by God to live and love and laugh. And the vast majority perished terribly young, before they could enjoy the freedom we take for granted, claim as our birthright.

What motivated them? God alone knows in detail. But letters preserved by families reenact the tears and fears, the courage and love, that mingled with the blood they shed for us, at times for peoples they never knew. Yes, many a nation is a "land of the free" because America has been the "home of the brave." It's a tough love we celebrate, the kind of love that, like Jesus' love, transmutes sheer suffering into sacrifice: the gift of self that others may live. Like Jesus' love indeed; for as our first reading declared, "Love is from God; everyone who loves is born of God" (1 Jn 4:7).[1]

III

A final word: on you and me, on the hundreds of thousands who this evening will share our memory of the Korean War in song, in letters, in tears. Only a relatively few of us are likely to die for those we love. But all of us are asked to live for our sisters and brothers. It's

easy to forget that while we justly mourn our heroic dead, we are surrounded by a dreadful number of living dead. I mean 13.5 million
children hungering below the poverty line in the richest country on
earth. I mean two million behind bars (second only to Russia in our
imprisoning rate), a disproportionate number of them poor, ill-
defended African Americans. I mean the thousands of women physically and sexually abused; the AIDS-afflicted and the drug-addicted;
the aged lonely and the young unloved; the terminally bored and the
ceaselessly pain-racked, who see no point in living.

Our task? If you've studied philosophy, you may recall the
name Descartes—endlessly famous for a swift sentence, "I think,
therefore I am." An insightful activist preacher, William Sloane
Coffin, called that phrase "a bit of surpassing nonsense." What is
much truer, he claimed, is "I love, therefore I am." For, as St. Paul
insisted in an unforgettable passage, "If I understand all mysteries
and all knowledge, and if I have all faith so as to remove mountains,
but do not have love, I am nothing" (1 Cor 13:2).[2] Nothing. I simply
am not.

A resolve, therefore, to those who died in Korea for us the living: We shall try our level best to live for the dying, for those who
have no hope. One child perhaps, one family. With such love each of
us might transform a single acre of God's world.

Washington Court Hotel
Washington, D.C.
May 28, 2000

13
IN A LITTLE WHILE YOU WILL SEE ME
Sixth Week of Easter, Year 1, Thursday

- Acts 18:1–8
- John 16:16–20

> In a little while you will not see me any more,
> and then again in a little while you will see me.
> (Jn 16:16)

If we are not to continue the wonder and puzzlement of Jesus' disciples ["We don't understand what he is talking about"] (v. 18), if we hope to profit spiritually from a perplexing sentence, we must ask two questions. What did Jesus mean? And how does what Jesus meant touch not only his early disciples but all of us who come later?[1]

I

What did Jesus mean: "You will not see me, you will see me again"? To most of the Greek Fathers of the Church the answer was clear: "Jesus will die shortly, and so in a little while the disciples will not see him; but then in a little while they will see him again, because after his entombment he will rise and appear to them."[2] As indeed he did, during the traditional 40 days: he appeared to Mary Magdalene, to two discouraged disciples on the road to Emmaus, to the apostles through locked doors, on the beach for an apostolic breakfast.[3]

A critical question here: Where did he come from? Not from some hidden home in Palestine. He came from the glory of his Father's presence. Here lies a truth that in my undergraduate existence did not creep into a seminary Scripture course. What truth? The risen Jesus did not have to wait 40 days before he "ascended" to his Father, before he entered into glory. Jesus' resurrection included his ascension, and his ascension was an aspect of his resurrection. The moment Jesus rose from the dead, he returned in glory to his Father. St. Jerome recognized this when he declared, "The day of the Resurrection, the day of Christians,...is also called the Lord's Day, because on it the Lord ascended as a victor to the Father."[4]

What we call Jesus' "ascension" is simply that particular appearance from glory when he took his final leave from the community of his followers—his last visible leave-taking. He "would no longer present himself to them in their corporate unity; henceforth his 'presence' to them" would be either through the Spirit promised by his Father or in the breaking of the bread.[5]

II

This leads naturally to you and me, to your people and mine. You see, it is not only Jesus' early disciples who were to experience his twin promise. The Last Discourse "is addressed to all who believe in Jesus and not only to those who were actually present."[6] For millennia after millennia those who follow Jesus will "weep and go into mourning," will experience suffering, will be saddened while "the world" rejoices.

Our own time is no exception. As I speak, something like 1.8 million men, women, and children have watered the roads from Kosova in old Yugoslavia to...nowhere. These are the killing fields, where men are murdered, where women are raped, where children are separated from their parents, where one poor woman's seven sons have been taken from her and she knows not where any of them are. "The ethnic cleansing is bloody and swift, procured by police, military and paramilitaries working together."[7]

But the weeping Jesus predicted is not a faraway experience; it touches all of us fashioned of flesh and spirit. It touches our children— one out of every five stunted in mind and body by a grinding poverty in the richest nation on earth; 13 killed in Colorado by two schoolmates. It touches our African Americans, still scarred by a racism that has simply grown more genteel, more subtle. It touches the scores of dead, the thousands left homeless, by merciless tornados in Oklahoma and Kansas. It touches the AIDS-afflicted and the drug-addicted, the cancer-ridden and the manic-depressive. It touches all who let the dust of death fall from their fingers on the coffin of a dear one.

You and I, my brothers, are no exception to mourning and weeping. Like Jesus, we too are "able to deal gently with the ignorant and wayward" because we too are "subject to weakness" (Heb 5:2). Like Jesus, we too learn "obedience through what [we] suffer" (v. 8). In recent years many priests have been scarred by their commitment to celibacy; few have escaped criticism as celebrants and preachers, even as males. We weep over the divisions in our parishes, the abortions among Catholics, the indifference of all too many of the young. Burnout is no longer rare: fewer priests, greater obligations on those who remain, higher expectations from the laity; less if any privacy, less time to pray, to relax, to prepare homilies, to fill the cup. It is with nostalgia that we recall Cardinal Bernardin's claim back in 1982 that priests "are called to be challengers, enablers, life-givers, poets of life, music makers, dreamers of dreams."

III

All too true; it is simply what Karl Rahner called "the cross erected over history." A cross that would be intolerable, for us and for our people, if we forgot Jesus' second promise: We will see him, he assured us, "and [our] hearts will rejoice with a joy that no one can take from [us]" (Jn 16:22).[8] Christians will "see" Jesus; he promised it. But "seeing" Jesus is not a matter of keen eyesight, seeing Jesus as Peter and John saw him before and after Calvary. It is not primarily a pledge that we will see Jesus in another life, beyond the grave. It means that Christians can experience his continued presence...now. How? As with the apostles, so with us: "God's love has been poured into our hearts through the Holy Spirit that has been given to us" (Rom 5:5); and day after day the body of our Lord can feed our flesh and our spirit. Two incomparable ways in which Jesus is present to us.

That promise is intimately related to an earlier promise of Jesus, a similar promise, in the Last Discourse: "In just a little while the world will not see me any more, but you will see me because I live and you will live" (Jn 14:19). Because Jesus has life, because Jesus is life, we too come alive; we "see" him, experience him, share his life. Stay with that a few moments; it phrases succinctly what it is to be a Christian; what is God's exciting, awe-inspiring gift to us; what is the joy no one can take from those who believe, who trust, who love.

In the midst of ceaseless death, here is the high point of human living. I'm sure you have experienced at some time what it feels like to be so alive that it literally takes your breath away. A last-second basket or a heart transplant, a homily that stirs your congregation, or a First Communion that ignites your parish, an addict or a bedridden woman with new life from your caring—this is human living! Intensify that feeling a thousand times, and you begin to sense what it should feel like when you realize that God's Son is alive in you—when you can exclaim with St. Paul, "It is no longer I who live, but it is Christ who lives in me. And the life I now live in the flesh I live by faith in the Son of God, who loved me and gave himself for me" (Gal 2:20).

In this season of resurrection, this is what our people need to hear from us—to hear convincingly. We are accustomed to thinking of ourselves as "the people of God." And we are. The First Letter of Peter declared it: "You are a chosen race, a royal priesthood, a holy nation, God's own people, in order that you may proclaim the mighty acts of Him who called you out of darkness into His marvelous light" (1 Pet 2:9). But with all that we risk forgetting that, even more profoundly, we are the Body of Christ. "For just as [our physical body] is one and has many members, and all the members of the body, though many, are one body, so it is with Christ. For in the one Spirit we were all baptized into one body...and we were all made to drink of one Spirit" (1 Cor 12:12–13).

Early theologians used to preach with passion, "God became human to make us divine." And we are; for the life of Christ has become our life. In the midst of tears, we rejoice; surrounded by death, we are alive; tormented by the apparent absence of God, we experience the presence of Christ. Believe it, live it, preach it!

Immaculate Heart Retreat Center
Spokane, Washington
May 13, 1999

14

WISDOM IS A BREATH OF GOD'S POWER
Sixth Week of Easter, Year 2, Monday

- Acts 16:11–15
- John 15:26—16:4a

In preparing this homily, I was fascinated by the expression "the Spirit of truth" (Jn 15:26). No problem with "Spirit": clearly the Holy Spirit. But "truth?" I found I had to ask two questions. (1) What sort of truth did Jesus have in mind? (2) How does this sort of truth touch our daily lives? I shall close with (3) a personal prayer.

I

First, what sort of truth did Jesus have in mind? I harked back to my years of philosophy. Remember epistemology, the science of knowing? An idea, a statement, a judgment was true if it was conformed to reality, was in harmony with the real. If I say that George Washington was born in 1732, and it turns out that he was, then my statement is true. And that went back to common Hellenistic usage, where "truth" hovered between "reality," "the ultimately real," and "knowledge of the real."

Now is that the truth Jesus had in mind when he told his disciples, "The Spirit of truth will guide [you] along the way of all truth" (16:13)? The Holy Spirit will see to it that what you know will be conformed to the reality? The best of scriptural scholarship declares this not untrue, simply inadequate.[1] The primary influence on John was not Hellenistic thought; it was Judaism. There "truth" often serves as a synonym for wisdom. Proverbs, for example, commands us to "buy truth" and puts that in parallelism with the command to "buy wisdom" (Prov 23:23). Moreover, "truth" is associated with "mystery," so

79

that to know the truth is to know the plans of God (Wis 6:22); truth speaks of God's plan of salvation as revealed to humans. The two ideas, wisdom and mystery, come together when Jesus declares that he is "the truth" (Jn 14:6): He is Wisdom incarnate and he is the expression of God's mysterious plan of salvation (Col 1:27; Eph 3:4).

The "truth" in question, then, the truth into which the Holy Spirit will guide Jesus' disciples, guide you and me, is far richer than a wealth of sheer factual knowledge. This truth is the wisdom of which the Wisdom of Solomon sang:

> Wisdom is a breath of the power of God,
> and a pure emanation of the glory of the Almighty....
> For she is a reflection of eternal light,
> a spotless mirror of the working of God,
> and an image of His goodness....
> In every generation she passes into holy souls
> and makes them friends of God, and prophets;
> For God loves nothing so much as the man [or woman]
> who lives with wisdom.
>
> (Wis 7:25–28)

And this "truth" is also the "mystery" of which Paul wrote ecstatically to the Christians of Ephesus: "With all wisdom and insight [God] has made known to us the mystery of His will, according to His good pleasure that He set forth in Christ, as a plan for the fulness of time, to gather up all things in him, things in heaven and things on earth" (Eph 8b–10).

II

Second, move from the ethereal to the earthy. Let's focus on wisdom. If the Spirit's "truth" is wisdom, how do we humans, we mortals, go about acquiring it? In Catholic theology, not by a high IQ. Wisdom is a gift, a gift of the Holy Spirit, a gift given at baptism, one of our traditional "seven gifts." Not that you cannot be wise at all without the Holy Spirit, cannot with natural wit judge soundly and deal sagaciously with facts as they relate to life and conduct. I cannot believe that all the wisdom in Cicero's treatise *On Old Age* was shaped with the Holy Spirit perched on his shoulder. I cannot believe that every wise decision of our Supreme Court was inspired by the Holy Spirit. I cannot believe that the Holy Spirit is responsible for every insight in my three-point homilies. I cannot believe that all the wisdom you impart to the Eagles of Gonzaga comes down from "on high." What, then, is the wisdom given at baptism?

I suggest that the baptismal gift of wisdom has to do with what is specifically Christian, the Spirit as enabler of our Christian contemplation, our Christlike activity. Some examples. The gift enables us to savor, to have a taste for, the things of God. Not only to accept intellectually every truth in the catechism, but to relish what we believe, appreciate it, enjoy it. Wisdom repeats the Creed not by rote but with gusto. "We believe!" A cry from the heart: "We believe in Jesus Christ, who died for us, rose for us." Murmured at times with tears: "We believe in the resurrection of the body." Whispered at times in awe: "We believe in life everlasting."

Wisdom gives fresh zest to our hope. It moves us from the hope that is a vague wish ("Dear God, do you think you might... ?") to a lively expectation that, whatever happens, two realities are beyond doubt: The Spirit will often surprise us, and God will always be there.

It is the Spirit's wisdom that enables us to love as Jesus loved, even unto crucifixion. As Romero loved...the six Jesuit martyrs at the University of Central America...the four American women raped and murdered in El Salvador. As Walter Ciszek loved.

It is the Spirit's wisdom that changes the sheer activist into a contemplative in action. I mean someone who looks long and lovingly at the real, someone who finds God and His Christ active not only in all persons but in all things: in every star and blade of grass, in the agitated Atlantic and the graceful gazelle, in the bread that nourishes us and the Pinot Noir that pleasures us. A Thomas Merton, a Teresa of Avila.

It is the gift of wisdom that allows us not only to know *about* God but to *know God*. It makes possible an experiential knowledge of God, the kind of knowledge Ignatius Loyola possessed, the direct knowledge Ignatius was convinced is a grace God refuses to no one.

It is the gift of wisdom that separates two types of theologians. You see, wisdom is, as Cistertian Basil Pennington saw, "the noblest of the intellectual virtues."[2] It makes for mature judgment, a way of looking at God and the universe with God's own eyes. But he added insightfully: When theology "includes a true experiential knowledge of God through that love which is the Holy Spirit and when it contains an affective dimension as well as an intellectual one, [it] is in itself a true wisdom."[3] Such was monastic theology, the theology of a Bernard of Clairvaux, where the aim was not so much knowledge as experience, and the way to experience was not so much the question as desire. It was summed up in the title of a splendid little book by Dom Jean Leclercq, *The Love of Learning and the Desire for God.*[4]

III

I close with a personal prayer. I am profoundly grateful to the Spirit of truth for moving me from the truth of epistemology to the truth that is wisdom. "Not," as Paul confessed, "that I have already reached the goal; but I press on to make it my own" (Phil 3:12). And such is my prayer for you and your apostolates:

> May the Spirit of truth grace us not only to believe and hope and love, but to relish what we believe, joy in our hope, gladden our love with rich laughter. Grace us to find God and His Christ not only in our students and our parishioners, but in every work that leaps from our hands and our hearts. Grace us not only to know about God, but to experience God Himself as Ignatius did. In a word, may the Spirit of truth link our knowledge to love, so that knowing will always lead to loving: loving God above all created idols, loving every sister and brother like another self, loving every work of God's creative hand. Spirit of truth, grace us with *your* truth. Grace us with wisdom.

Our Lady's Chapel
Gonzaga College High School
Washington, D.C.
May 29, 2000

15
FATHERS AND MOTHERS,
RECOGNIZE YOUR DIGNITY!
Seventh Week of Easter, Year 1, Tuesday

- Acts 20:17–27
- John 17:1–11a

Today's Gospel is the first part of a prayer Jesus raised to his Father for his disciples the evening before his crucifixion. It contains a sentence I find particularly appropriate for fathers and mothers who have seen their sons pass happily through the halls of Gonzaga.[1] The sentence runs: "Father, this is eternal life, that they may know you, the only true God, and Jesus Christ whom you have sent" (Jn 17:3).

Why appropriate? Listen to what Jesus is saying. Eternal life, God's life in us now and for ever, consists in this: that we know God our Father.[2] But be careful: In John's Gospel, knowing is not a sheer head trip; for John, genuine knowledge includes love. Naked knowledge, lacking love, is barren. My point is, if you want to know what it means to be a parent, get to know and love God the Father. What it means to be a parent, not only a father. For there is no sex or gender in God. That is why Pope John Paul I, pope for only 34 days, could say in 1978, "God is not only father but even more so mother, who...wants only to be good to us, especially when we are bad."

So then, two stages to my homily. (1) What fatherly and motherly qualities do we find in God? (2) With God as model, what does this say to your parenting, to your fathering and mothering?

I

What is so fatherly, so motherly, in God? God not only knows God's children; God's knowledge is God's love. Listen to the prophet Isaiah.[3] When the Jews returned from exile in Babylon to an impoverished Jerusalem, they cried in discouragement, "The LORD has forsaken me, my LORD has forgotten me." God's response is unexpectedly feminine:

> Can a woman forget her nursing child,
>   or show no compassion for the son of her womb?
> Even these may forget,
>   yet I will not forget you.
> See, I have inscribed you on the palms of my hands.
>   (Isa 49:14–16a)

What is so fatherly, so motherly, in God? God gives good things to God's children. Life, of course, but so much more within life: earth and air, fire and water; an animal kingdom and a vegetable paradise; a mind to imagine, a heart to love, flesh to feel; God's own Son to wear our flesh, to rest within us as our food and drink, God's own Holy Spirit to direct our ways.

What is so fatherly, so motherly, in God? God is faithful. If there is one word characteristic of God in the Old Testament, it is...fidelity. Time and again God's own people proved faithless. Read Psalm 106:

> They forgot God, their Savior,
>   who had done great things in Egypt....
> They had no faith in His promise...
>   and would not listen to the word of the LORD....
> Nevertheless He paid heed to their distress,
>   so often as He heard their cry.
> For their sake He remembered His covenant,
>   and showed compassion in the abundance of His steadfast love.
>   (Ps 106:21–45)

What is so fatherly, so motherly, in God? God is a forgiving God. God is the shepherd who leaves the 99 sheep and goes in search of the single sheep who has strayed, carries him back on His shoulders, has a party for the wanderer. God is the real Father of the prodigal son, the Father who is so prodigal Himself that when the repentant son returns, He runs to meet him, kisses him, throws a Washington-type party for him, "for this son of mine was dead and is alive again; he was lost and is found!" (Lk 15:24). God is behind the declaration of Jesus, "There will be more joy in heaven over one sinner who repents than over 99 righteous persons who need no repentance" (Lk 15:7).

What is so fatherly, so motherly, in God? God's love comes at a cost; God pays a price. The most costly price? Calvary: the death of

God's own Son. And somehow, in ways that escape our feeble human intelligence, whatever happens to us, for good or ill, our tragedies as well as our triumphs, somehow all this touches a sensitive God.

II

Now what about you? What of you as mothers and fathers in God's image and likeness? Simply apply to yourselves what I have said about God.

First, like God, you know your children. But what likens you even more to God, your knowledge is not sheerly intellectual; it is a loving knowledge. For these are not objects "out there" to be admired or regretted; these are the fruits of your love, of your loving relationship. And so, you are the first teachers of your children. Remember the film *Mr. Holland's Opus*? The teacher of Mr. Holland's deaf son says to Holland himself, "The most important teacher your child will ever have is you." First and primary teachers. Not simply because you gave them life; more importantly, because you are the first to show them love. Never cease to show them love.

Second, like God, you know how to give good things to your children. Life, of course; love, indeed; and the wisdom that stems from experience. But also the good things of God's earth, the fruits of your skill, of your time, of your energy. In a special way, a Christian education, a Gonzaga education, that weds a love of learning to a desire for God, touches their hands and their hearts to the needs of the less fortunate, insists that who they are is more important than what they have.

Third, like God, you are faithful. If your children disappoint you, disobey you, even betray you, your love keeps your covenant with them alive. Not easy when drugs and violence destroy families. In extreme situations—schoolchildren murdered by schoolchildren in Littleton, in Paducah, in Jonesboro—fathers and mothers of teenage killers have indeed wept for their wayward sons but have not taken back their love.

Fourth, like God, you somehow, with God's grace, find it possible to forgive what others may have done to your children. Listen to an emotional outburst to the *Washington Post* from the father of a murdered daughter:

> How dare the [Supreme Court] speak for me, my family and my murdered daughter [Lisa] when it says: "Only with finality can the victims move forward knowing the moral judgment will be

carried out.".... If they are referring to the victims' families, what about all those who are opposed to the death penalty, such as myself and family members belonging to the national organization Murder Victims Families for Reconciliation and those countless others, who remain silent but don't want any more killings? ...My daughter would not have wanted to see anyone killed, and especially not in her name.[4]

Fifth, like God, your fathering and mothering costs you. You know that, experience it, too intimately for me to describe. Your loving exacts a price—a cross that is never quite lifted from your shoulders. Never far from my own mother's mind and heart for almost three decades was the cancerous dying of my father and only brother within three weeks of each other. And yet, always hovering above you is the twin promise of Jesus, "You have pain now; but I will see you again, and your hearts will rejoice, and your joy no one will take from you" (Jn 16:22).

Dear mothers and fathers: Back in the fifth century a remarkable pope, Leo the Great, closed a Christmas sermon with these words: "Christians, recognize your dignity! You share in God's own nature. Bear in mind [the Christ] who is your head and of whose body you are a member. Through the sacrament of baptism you have become a temple of the Holy Spirit."[5]

May I say something similar to you this evening? Fathers and mothers, recognize your dignity! You are not merely slaving dads and soccer moms. You are images of God's own fathering, God's own mothering. Like God, with God, you brought new life to this earth. You nurtured that life, spirit and flesh, from helpless infancy to reasonable maturity, in sorrow and joy, through ecstasies and calvaries. And whatever has happened since then, there should be a joy no one, nothing, can take from you: As mothers and fathers, your life has been Godlike, your life *is* Godlike. Recognize your dignity!

Our Lady's Chapel
Gonzaga College High School
May 18, 1999

16
RENEW THE FACE OF THE EARTH: PENTECOST 2000
Pentecost Sunday

- Acts 2:1–11
- Leviticus 25:8–12, 17–19
- John 4:5–42
- Luke 4:16–21

We gather here for a unique event. A celebration. A prayer celebration. A jubilee celebration. An ecumenical celebration. A celebration of the Christian churches of North-Central Alabama. To address your unity and your diversity is, I confess, an intimidating task. Fortunately, the Gospel just proclaimed from Luke suggests a theme that is indeed provocative but should capture every Christian mind and heart..

The key word is *justice*. Not that Jesus uses it here. Still, his swift summary of his mission, of the reason why he borrowed our flesh and pitched his tent among us—good news for the poor, freedom for captives, sight for the blind, relief for the oppressed—is the justice he inherited from his Jewish ancestry, the justice that recaptures the Jubilee in Leviticus, the justice he preached and lived as the supreme Servant of Justice. This is the justice demanded by Pentecost 2000, the justice demanded by the Holy Spirit who has descended upon each and all of you.

To grasp why all this is so, you need to focus on three realities: (1) the difference between our justice and God's; (2) what God's justice, biblical justice, demands of us in concrete human living; (3) how God's justice, biblical justice, touches the unity we seek in community.

I

First, the word *justice*. In our American culture. In ethics and in law, we are just when we give to someone what he or she

87

deserves. When an employer pays a salary adequate for human living, for the worker and the family, and workers perform what their free contract demands. When a judge or jury hands down a decision not from prejudice but in harmony with the evidence. When our President after the Oklahoma City bombings declared, "We will bring the criminals to justice." We will see that they are punished as they deserve.

Such justice, human justice, giving people what they deserve, is itself demanded by God's Word. Exodus is rich therein: "When you bear witness in a lawsuit, you shall not side with the majority, so as to pervert justice; nor shall you be partial to the poor in a lawsuit" (23:2–3). "You shall take no bribe, for a bribe blinds the official, and subverts the cause of those who are in the right" (23:8). "If you take your neighbor's cloak in pawn, you shall restore it before the sun goes down; for it may be your neighbor's only clothing to use as cover; in what else shall that person sleep?" (22:26–27).

And we can recognize obvious injustice, sometimes somewhat late. The Dred Scott decision, that declared slaves to be property. Laws that were racially inspired. Legal systems that keep the poor imprisoned for months before they can come to trial. The sweatshops that condemn children and women to inhuman hours, inhuman work, inhuman salaries.

My point? God's Word, biblical justice, while sensitive to all that, raises justice to a level higher still. That higher level of justice is summed up in an unforgettable word: fidelity, faithfulness. Fidelity to what? To relationships. What relationships? Three. To God, to people, to the earth.

To God. It is the commandment from Mount Sinai: "I am the LORD your God....You shall have no other gods before me" (Exod 20:2–3). More than that, the high command in the Old Law and the New: "You shall love the LORD your God with all your heart, with all your soul, with all your mind, with all your might" (Deut 6:5; Mt 22:37). Not to love God above all human idols, not to love God with every fiber of our being, is a sin against justice. Those words from the Lord God and His Christ are not counsels, suggestions, pretty pieces of practical advice. These are commands. The love relationship between God and ourselves, between Jesus and us, is so intimate to human living that not to live it is to destroy or impair the primary reason God fashioned each one of us. That is the supreme injustice. What is new in biblical justice? The most momentous four-letter word in history: love. No human law, no philosophical ethic, can command love. God does.

To people. Here a command Jesus borrows from the Torah, from the book called Leviticus: "You shall love your neighbor as yourself" (Lev 19:18; Mt 22:39). But Jesus takes it a giant step forward. Your "neighbor" is not only the man or woman next door. On this Jesus was terribly strong: "You have heard that it was said, 'You shall love your neighbor and hate your enemy.' But I say to you, Love your enemies and pray for those who persecute you, so that you may be children of your Father in heaven; for He makes His sun rise on the evil and on the good, and sends rain on the righteous and on the unrighteous" (Mt 6:43–45). St. Paul insists that the way you fulfil God's law is by loving (Rom 13:10). The First Letter of John declares that "the whole law is summed up" in that "single commandment" (Gal 5:14; see Jas 2:8). The neighbor is simply every human person, everyone shaped by God in the image of Jesus.

Love them "as yourself"? Not a psychological balancing act: As much or as little as I love myself, that much or that little love I am to lavish or trickle on others? No. I am to love every man, woman, and child like another I, another self, as if I were standing in their shoes, especially the paper-thin shoes of the less fortunate, the downtrodden.

To the earth. I mean care for God's nonhuman creation. This is something of a newcomer on the Christian scene. Down the centuries most Christians have taken very literally what seemed to be God's clear demand to our first parents, "Fill the earth and subdue it; and have dominion over the fish of the sea and over the birds of the air and over every living thing that moves upon the earth" (Gen 1:28). It took us centuries to realize that God's command does not mean God has given humankind unrestricted power to do with the earth what we will. It is not exploitation that is the mandate given humanity in this section of Genesis; it is reverential care. The Psalmist had it right: "The earth is the Lord's, and all that is in it" (Ps 24:1).

In summary: God's plan of salvation is a matter of relationships. Salvation takes place within a single, all-embracing community. I shiver when I realize it: My salvation depends on fidelity to three relationships, on my response to three questions: Do I love God above all else? Do I love each sister and brother as Jesus loves me? Do I touch each "thing" (that ice-cold word) with the reverence God asked of humankind at its birthday?

II

Such is God's justice. But what does God's justice, biblical justice, demand of us in the concrete? Take each of the relationships
and bring it down to earth.

Our relationship to God. Most of us do well with belief, accepting what God has revealed to us. The Sunday Creed is a splendid
example. Yes indeed, I believe in God the Father, Maker of heaven
and earth. I believe in Jesus Christ, His unique Son, as truly God as is
the Father; the God who, the early liturgy sang,

> though he was in the form of God,
>> did not regard equality with God as something to be exploited,
> but emptied himself,
>> taking the form of a slave,
>> being born in human likeness.
> And being found in human form,
>> he humbled himself,
>> and became obedient to the point of death—
>> even death on a cross.
> Therefore God also exalted him,
>> and gave him the name
>> that is above every name,
> so that at the name of Jesus
>> every knee should bend,
>> in heaven and on earth and under the earth,
> and every tongue should confess
>> that Jesus Christ is Lord,
>> to the glory of God the Father.
>
> (Phil 2:6–11)

You and I believe that, and so much more. Believing it, we
know a good deal *about* God. What God asks of us is to *know God,
know Jesus*. Not a vision, not an apparition. Simply a personal relationship, the way a wife and husband know each other, a mother her
child. This is the kind of knowing that is not purely a head trip; to
know in this way is to love. And St. Ignatius Loyola claimed that this
kind of knowledge, relating to God, to Jesus, to the Holy Spirit as
person to person, in wondrous intimacy, is a grace God does not
refuse to anyone, does not refuse to you. But you have to want it,
desire it, yearn for it, pray for it.

Our relationship to people. God's justice takes us to the most
vulnerable in our society: our children. Do you know how many
children live below the poverty line? 13.5 million; one child out of

every five—in the richest nation on earth.[1] Not the genteel poverty of Jesus, Mary, and Joseph in Nazareth. No. The kind of poverty that mangles minds and batters bodies, that leads to AIDS and drug abuse, to ignorance and violence. Our response? Three examples.

God's justice takes us to the poor. Theologian Jon Sobrino has expressed it briefly and pungently: "When the Church has taken the poor seriously, it is then that it has become truly apostolic. The poor initiate the process of evangelization. When the Church goes out to them in mission, the paradoxical result is that they, the poor, evangelize the Church."[2] Very simply, the poor are not just recipients of apostolic ministry; they are our teachers and educators...if we have eyes to see, ears to hear.

Is it an impossible dream to hope that every family in Birmingham with a fair share of God's good gifts might choose one child, lift that child from its slavery? It would take so little: a wheelchair here, a scholarship there, bread that nourishes, decent clothes, even a warm shoulder on which to rest.

God's justice takes us to the AIDS-afflicted. Countless Americans who claim to be people of compassion see in AIDS God's plague on the promiscuous: God is giving to the AIDS-afflicted simply what they deserve. Fidelity to relationships, to our covenant with God cut in the blood of Christ, calls for an attitude expressed by Cardinal Joseph Bernardin of Chicago in a 1986 pastoral letter:

> God is loving and compassionate, not vengeful. Made in God's image, every human being is of inestimable worth, and the life of all persons, whatever their sexual orientation, is sacred and their dignity must be respected. The Gospel reveals that while Jesus did not hesitate to proclaim a radical ethic of life grounded in the promise of God's kingdom, he never ceased to reach out to the lowly, to the outcasts, of his time—even if they did not live up to the full demands of his teaching.[3]

In my efforts to live God's justice, it would help immeasurably if, like Mother Teresa in the slums of Calcutta, I too would cradle in my arms one of God's little images born with so dread an affliction.

God's justice takes us to our African American sisters and brothers. Their cry still echoes the cry of Yahweh to Pharaoh, "Let my people go!" (Exod 10:3). Rather than listen to cold statistics, listen to black Sister Thea Bowman, stricken with breast cancer and bone cancer, racing her wheelchair across the country to spread her gospel of love. Listen to her as she spoke her mind passionately in 1989 to the bishops of the Catholic Church in the United States:

> Despite the civil-rights movement of the '60s and the socio-educational gains of the '70s, blacks in the '80s [yes, blacks in 2000] are still struggling, still scratching and clawing as the old folks said, still trying to find home in the homeland and home in the church, still struggling to gain access to equal opportunity.
>
> A disproportionate number of black people are poor... more than a third of the black people that live in the United States live in...the kind of poverty that lacks basic necessity.
>
> I'm talking about old people who have worked hard all their lives and don't have money for adequate food or shelter or medical care.
>
> I'm talking about children who can never have equal access and equal opportunity because poverty doomed them to low birth weight and retardation and equal opportunity for education....
>
> One of every 21 black males is murdered. A disproportionate number of our men are dying of suicide and AIDS and drug abuse and low self-esteem.[4]

As I crisscross our country with my project Preaching the Just Word, I find that racism is not dead; it has gone undercover. Hate has a new face clean-cut, a new voice softer-spoken, has learned how to sell itself more effectively. As of 1998, 254 hate sites operated on the Internet. Notes a member of Klanwatch, a project of the Southern Poverty Law Center: "Instead of saying, 'The dirty Mexicans are stealing our jobs,' they say, 'We are overwhelmed by immigration.'"

Our relationship to God's nonhuman creation. I mean the four ancient elements: fire, air, water, and earth. I mean everything that is not God or the human person. I mean all the "things" we see and hear and touch and taste and smell. What is demanded of each and all of us? We must realize, with John Paul II, "that [our] responsibility within creation and [our] duty toward nature and the Creator are an essential part of [our] faith."[5]

Less than a decade ago (1992) the Union of Concerned Scientists issued a declaration that said in part: "Human beings and the natural world are on a collision course. Many of our current practices put at serious risk the future that we wish for human society and the plant and animal kingdoms, and may so alter the living world that it will be unable to sustain life in the manner that we know."[6]

Although the United States has only 4.7 percent of the world's population, Americans use an astonishing amount of the world's resources and generate a large percentage of the world's waste. Americans produce 21 percent of all goods and services, including most of the world's weapons. We use 33 percent of the world's processed energy and mineral resources, and produce at least 33 percent of the world's pollution.

The average U. S. citizen, when compared to the average citizen of India, uses: 50 times more steel, 56 times more energy, 170 times more synthetic rubber and newsprint, 250 times more motor fuel, 300 times more plastic. One percent of the nation's population owns about 80 percent of the country's property and controls 90 percent of its wealth.[7]

In a Christian vision, God intended our earth for all God's children. And so we who accept this owe our less fortunate fellows a frequent examination of conscience: Am I an overconsumer? Do I needlessly replace what I have with something better? Do I waste—paper, food, clothes, gas, even time? I suspect that, in your Birmingham as in my Washington, we could feed all our hungry poor each day with what we throw away at home and in restaurants. Little is safe from economic plunder. Rain forests, trees, green acres—we pillage and we rape. In an article entitled "The Killing Fields," the author writes vividly: The sites designated for wildlife's preservation "are becoming an abattoir [a slaughterhouse], almost as if someone had let a serial killer into Noah's ark."[8]

III

My third and final question: How does God's justice, biblical justice, touch the unity we seek in community? The fact is, we who believe are still divided. On serious issues: papal power, sacraments, the Lord's Supper, contraception, abortion, many another. Or, as our teenagers say, "whatever." Let me take you back to the Second Vatican Council, concluded 35 years ago. In its Decree on Ecumenism the council has a highly practical suggestion:

Cooperation among all Christians vividly expresses that bond which already unites them, and it sets in clearer relief the features of Christ the Servant. Such cooperation, which has already begun in many countries, should be ever increasingly developed, particularly in regions where a social and technical revolution is taking place. It should contribute to a just appreciation of the dignity of the human person, the promotion of the blessings of

peace, the application of gospel principles to social life, and the
advancement of the arts and sciences in a Christian spirit.
Christians should also work together in the use of every possible
means to relieve the afflictions of our times, such as famine and
natural disasters, illiteracy and poverty, lack of housing, and the
unequal distribution of wealth. Through such cooperation, all
believers in Christ are able to learn easily how they can understand each other better and esteem each other more, and how
the road to the unity of Christians may be made smooth.[9]

A remarkable statement. The council was not downplaying doctrine. It was aware of an old slogan, "doctrine divides, service
unites." Today that slogan finds rare voices. Truth matters. It is not
insignificant for Christianity whether or not Jesus Christ is divine as
the Father is divine. Not insignificant whether or not Jesus Christ is
actually present in the Eucharist, body and blood, soul and divinity.
But what the council recognized with uncommon clarity is this: If we
can learn to work together as sisters and brothers in bringing God's
justice, Jesus' justice, to realization, this collaboration may smooth
the way to an even more perfect unity.

Recently a sympathetic Protestant said to a Catholic friend, "If
you Catholics could get your act together, you'd be dangerous." Let
me expand on that: If we *Christians* could get *our* act together, we'd be
doubly dangerous. All of you remember Jesus' prayer to his Father
before his passion, his prayer for all who believe: "that they may be
one, just as we are one, I in them and you in me, that they may
become completely one. Thus the world may come to know that you
sent me and that you loved them even as you loved me" (Jn 17:22).

Yes, we are not completely one in doctrine; here Christians
have been struggling since blessed Peter's time. And still what
Vatican II declared remains true: "all those justified by faith through
baptism are incorporated into Christ," are therefore sisters and
brothers in Christ.[10] Is it not, therefore, our sacred obligation to act
as sisters and brothers? Concretely, as ministers of God's justice to
our world? As far as possible, to collaborate, literally to "work
together." I am not downplaying all separate organizations; Catholic
Charities Inc. and Protestants for the Common Good have valid reasons for existing. What we dare not do as ministers of God's justice is
act as competitors, much less as enemies.

We have Jesus' solemn word for it: The closer our unity, the
more intimately we labor as brothers and sisters in fidelity to God, to
God's people, and to God's earth, the more likely are men and
women to recognize two realities: that the Father has sent Jesus and

that the Father loves them as He loves His own Son. Can you imagine a richer reward for acting like sisters and brothers? Since we cannot do this by our weak human powers, I ask you, this blessed day of Pentecost, to pray aloud, passionately, after me:

Come, Holy Spirit,...fill the hearts of your faithful...fill my heart...and kindle in us...kindle in me...the fire of your own Pentecost love.... Send forth your Spirit, O Lord,... and renew the face of the earth.... Renew Alabama.... Renew Birmingham.... Renew us.

Civic Center
Birmingham, Alabama
June 11, 2000

ORDINARY TIME

17

BRING THE HOMELESS POOR
INTO YOUR HOUSE?
Sixth Sunday of the Year (B)

- Leviticus 13:1–2, 44–46
- 1 Corinthians 10:31–11:1
- Mark 1:40–45

It may sound strange, but I am terribly pleased that our first and third readings today focus on a leper. Let me tell you why in three stages. First, the leper as Leviticus describes him. Second, the leper as Jesus cures him. Third, the leper who calls out to us today.

I

First, the leper in Leviticus. This section of Leviticus is not concerned with what we know as Hansen's Disease.[1] It deals with various diseases of the skin, focuses on those diseases that made for impurity under the Mosaic law. Not every skin disease deserved such censure; only those regarded as infectious. Hygiene did enter the picture, but more important was "the lack of bodily integrity necessary for the worship of Yahweh." This is why the so-called leper was not only ostracized, banished from society; he was barred from worshiping with the community.

It was the priest who had to examine those suspected of an infectious disease. Leviticus describes the examination in minute detail—details that go on for 44 verses, details that end with three dread sentences: "The person who has the leprous disease shall wear torn clothes and let the hair of his head be disheveled; and he shall cover his upper lip and cry out, 'Unclean, unclean!' He shall remain unclean as long as he has the disease; he is unclean. He shall live alone; his dwelling shall be outside the camp" (Lev 13:45–46).

It was the priest who determined whether the disease was active or inactive. Not as a physician, for the priest did not prescribe treatment. Rather as a judge and interpreter of the law. His favorable decision was required before the leper could undergo purification rites and reenter the community, Meanwhile the poor fellow had to remain outside the city, had to warn the unsuspecting of his condition—by his torn garments, his long disordered hair, his covered beard, his repeated cry, "Unclean!"

II

Turn now to Jesus. In his company this evening, we meet a "leper" in person, a man with one of the repulsive scaly-skin diseases described in Leviticus. At his plea, "If you want to, you can make me clean" (Mk 1:40), Jesus is deeply stirred; Mark tells us he was "moved with pity, with compassion" (v. 41). And so Jesus heals him. But notice how Jesus heals him. Not simply words, "Be made clean." Jesus "stretched out his hand and touched him" (v. 41). A man himself, Jesus touches a man with an infectious disease. Only then does he send him to the priest to confirm what he has done.

That very human gesture, that comforting touch, is supremely important in the ministry of Jesus. It illustrates splendidly why the Son of God took our flesh and walked our earth and died our death. Not primarily to heal diseases. More importantly, to make all relationships right: our relationship to God, to one another, to the earth. Take the leper. Here is one of God's children with a disease that not only disfigures him; it ostracizes him from other citizens, removes him from his family, separates him from his synagogue. He is a pariah, an outcast, not fit to mingle with his fellows, only with other outcasts. In healing him, Jesus restores him to his fellow Jews, to his wife and children, to his worshiping community.

This is what we call biblical justice, the justice that pervades the Old Testament and the New: restoring right relationships. Not simply our earthbound justice—giving every man, woman, and child what they deserve, what they can claim from us as a strict right, because it can be proven from ethics or has been written into law. Over and above that, being faithful to relationships—relationships that stem from a covenant with God—for a Christian, a covenant with Christ cut in the blood of Christ.

Now that the Super Bowl is over and Michael Jordan is rewiring the Wizards,[2] lounge back some snowbound evening and page through the Gospel of Mark. Don't stop with the leper in today's reading; read on. Look for the other "little people": the children, the women, the disabled, the possessed, those lumped together as "sinners." Yes, Jesus destroys a paralysis, commands the paralytic to walk. But even more importantly, Jesus makes him right with God, forgives his sins. And ever so touchingly, Jesus restores him to his family: "Take your mat and go to your home" (v. 11). Another relationship reestablished.

Take the demonized man howling among the tombs and on the mountains. Not only does Jesus restore him to his "right mind" (5:15). When the man wants to stay with him, Jesus refuses: "Go home to your friends and tell them how much the Lord has done for you" (v. 19). And so it goes, straight through Mark.

And if you move through Mark, you discover the cost of biblical justice, of struggling like Jesus to make all relationships right. The cost is a cross. Not only true of Jesus. "If any want to become my followers, let them deny themselves and take up their cross and follow me" (8:34).

III

Finally, move from Jesus' dear land to our own. What might Leviticus' leper and Jesus' leper suggest to you and me today? Let me try something unusual on you, ask you to fly with me as I give free rein to my imagination. I shall not talk about real, unmistakable leprosy. Only several thousand suffer from Hansen's Disease in the States. Let's look at the men and women who may not be physically scarred but are still today's outcasts, the pariahs, ostracized from human society, separated from their families, even at times from our churches. I mean...the homeless.

I am not speaking of the small number who *want* to live apart from us, *want* to huddle around a fire in the slums, *want* to sleep on park benches, behind bushes, on warm grates. I mean the 700,000 who don't want to be homeless. I mean people with part-time or low-paying jobs who cannot find affordable shelter; having a job is no longer a guarantee against homelessness. I mean the mentally unbalanced prematurely released from asylums. I mean the substance abusers unable to obtain treatment.[3] Add to them the million young runaways who sleep on America's streets each night, all too many of them prostituted or angel-dusted. Add to them so many of the elderly (not all) for whom a nursing home is hardly a home, who watch and wait for a son or daughter, a relative, a friend, anyone to spend one hour with them.

Take another segment of our population, not ordinarily listed as homeless. I mean immigrants in detention. In 1999 there were over 200,000 in varying lengths of detention; by the end of 2001 there will be over 302,000. For lack of bed space in facilities owned and operated by the U.S. Immigration and Naturalization Service, 60 percent of detainees, three out of five, are currently housed in city and county jails. Once there, they are routinely housed with inmates held on criminal charges or those with criminal histories. In remote areas contact with attorneys is difficult, language always a problem. In San Pedro, California, a husband and wife were held in separate units for 16 months, never allowed to visit each other or write directly; while in custody, they lost their home; their three children, the oldest 15, were left to fend for themselves in Los Angeles.

Listen to a Jesuit friend of mine. He helps the Jesuit Refugee Service with English and Bible classes in a detainee center in New Jersey:

> There are no windows; they never breathe fresh air or see the light of day, except through one skylight. One woman has been there for almost three years. It would break your heart to see them. They have such a lost and hopeless look on their faces....
>
> When one of the English teachers failed to erase the board after her last class, the INS people interpreted this as disruptive of good order, canceled the English classes until further notice, and sent a monitor in to observe the Bible classes the following night. The Gospel reading for the following Sunday was Matthew 25:31 ff., including "I was in prison and you visited me." The INS regarded this and some of the questions for reflection as disruptive. The Bible Study was canceled too.[4]

Subsequently, INS officials "claimed that in programs like the Bible study and English classes [Jesuit Relief Service] volunteers were offering 'unreasonable hope to detainees' and teaching them 'to think on their own.'"[5]

Why this excursion into the homeless? Not to condemn HUD and INS; their tasks are monumental, their resources limited, the perils from terrorism never far away. Still, there are areas of injustice here. There is much that cries for correction, for improvement. But little will change unless we keep alert, aware of what is happening outside our personal and parochial preserve. Little will change until we see the homeless not as cases but as faces, each a person precious to God, each a someone, each a brother or sister. Little will change unless we realize that politics and religion are not two utterly separate compartments of human living, that when politics touches a moral issue, politics is touching your Christian turf and mine. When a man on death row in Texas appealed his conviction because his court-appointed attorney had fallen asleep during the trial, and the appeals judge rejected the appeal on the ground that our Constitution gives a defendant the right to an attorney but not the right to have him awake, you and I had every right to cry "Shame!" Similarly, when 700,000 of our brothers and sisters cannot find a home to which their human dignity entitles them, we do right to cry out to our public servants in agonized protest. When thousands of immigrants, many fleeing persecution, are lodged with criminals, when some are refused Bible study because a sentence from the lips of Christ offends the political sensibilities of an INS district director, how dare I keep silent?

Not mine to tell any of you here what precisely is your role in such issues. I know from rich experience how deeply God's justice is rooted in your worshiping community, how consistently you struggle to ease the hurts of your sisters and brothers. What, then, am I asking of you? Perhaps to broaden the range of your justice experience; perhaps come together more frequently to share your knowledge and wisdom, the hurts and agonies of the homeless and hopeless; perhaps even listen to their stories from the very voices of the victims. Above all, listen to what God might be saying to you—the God who took our flesh and blood, our mind and heart, to begin making all relationships right. Listen long to the Lord speaking to all of us through Isaiah (58:6–9):

> Is not this the fast that I choose:
>   to loose the bonds of injustice...?
> Is it not to share your bread with the hungry,
>   and bring the homeless poor into your house;
> when you see the naked, to cover them,
>   and not to hide yourself from your own flesh?
> Then your light shall break forth like the dawn,
>   and your healing shall spring up quickly;...
> Then you shall call, and the LORD will answer;
>   you shall cry for help, and He will say, Here I am.

Holy Trinity Church
Washington, D.C.
February 13, 2000

18
MY TEACHER, I WANT TO SEE AGAIN
Eighth Week, Year 1, Thursday

- Sirach 42:15–25
- Mark 10:46–52

Preparing this homily,[1] I made an early error. Which reading would be the focus: Sirach or Mark? The beauty and harmony of creation or the blindness of Bartimaeus? A prayer to our Lady followed: "Remember, O most gracious Virgin Mary, that never was it known that anyone who fled to thy protection, implored thy help...," and suddenly there it was. Help indeed. Not *which* reading...both. What we preachers of justice need every so often is to regain our sight, to "see again" (Mk 10:51), to see with fresh sight what is before our eyes, God's creation and what we have done with it, done to it.

And so, three stages, three questions. (1) What does it mean to see, to regain our sight? (2) What is it we *want* to see? (3) What is it we *ought* to see but perhaps shudder to see and don't really see?

I

First, what does it mean to pray with Bartimaeus, "My teacher, I want to regain my sight; I want to see again"? I take you back to an extraordinary experience of mine 27 years ago. The place: Sedona, Arizona; the Spiritual Life Institute of America. The man: Discalced Carmelite William McNamara. The insight: contemplation. Not contemplation as mystical experience; contemplation as "a long loving look at the real."

[Contemplation is] experiential awareness of reality and a way of entering into immediate communion with reality. Reality? Why, that means people, trees, lakes, mountains....You can

study things, but unless you enter into this intuitive communion with them, you can only know about them, you don't know
them. To take a long loving look at something—a child, a glass
of wine, a beautiful meal—this is a natural act of contemplation, of loving admiration.... To be able to do that, there's the
rub. All the way through school we are taught to abstract; we
are not taught loving awareness.[2]

Contemplation, then, is simply seeing things as they actually
are. It's the whole person reacting to the real. Not only eyes and
mind—emotions and passions, touch and taste and smell. It's God's
injunction in Psalm 46, "Be still, and see that I am God" (Ps 46:10).
It's Teresa of Avila gorging a roast partridge. The nuns are scandal-
ized. Teresa laughs: "At prayer time, pray! At partridge time, partridge!" It's philosopher Jacques Maritain insisting that the
culmination of knowledge, the high point of knowing, is not the concept but the experience: Man, woman, "feels" God.

Our prayer, time and time again: "My teacher, I want to regain
my sight; let me see again."

II

Second, what is it we *want* to see, pray to see? We could begin
with Sirach, with what in his lyric poem he called "the works of the
LORD" (Sir 42:15). His is an invitation to praise the Lord for His awesome power in creation: light and darkness, moon and stars, snow
and rain, clouds and hail—everything that does God's will unfail-
ingly. Then he goes on to praise Israel's great ancestors: patriarchs
Moses and Abraham; judges like Samuel; kings like David and
Solomon; prophets like Elijah and Elisha, Isaiah and Ezekiel.

We are more fortunate than the son of Sira. He lived during
the third and early second centuries before Christ. We are in a position to see him for whom Sirach and his ancestors mutely yearned.
We can actually know and love God's unique Son. True, we do not
see him in the flesh as Bartimaeus did when he regained his sight.
But remember, even for Bartimaeus the grace of graces was not the
miracle of eyesight. "Your faith," Jesus told him, "your faith has
made you well" (Mk 10:52). He saw with his faith, with his trust,
before he saw with his eyes.

Like Bartimaeus, most of us can hardly avoid praying time
and again, "I want to regain my sight." I mean the sense of wonder
with which we were born, the sense of wonder that dulls with

priestly routine. I mean the "loving look at the real" that made our first Communion a memorable moment of wonder, ordination day an awesome glimpse into playing Christ for others, our first Mass so exhilarating an experience. I mean those occasional insights into our priesthood, as when we saw with poet Gerard Manley Hopkins how

> ...Christ plays in ten thousand places,
> Lovely in limbs, and lovely in eyes not his
> To the Father through the features of men's faces.[3]

Yes, dear Lord, I want to regain my sight.

III

Third, what is it we *ought* to see but perhaps shudder to see and don't really see? Earlier in this retreat you faced a number of justice issues in your own back yard, scotch-taped them to your conference wall. And you did well to record those injustices. For, as gifted Protestant preacher John Buchanan remarked perceptively five years ago, "Part of what the preacher is about is knowing what the issues are, the questions being asked, which define a culture in a given time and place. The preacher must read and listen and see and participate in the world in which the congregation lives."[4]

But even these can become abstractions. For several moments, broaden your vision and make it even more dismayingly concrete.

The Children's Defense Fund has just issued its annual report, *The State of America's Children Yearbook 1999.*[5] Did you know that in the next half hour "200 children will drop out of school; 45 children will be born into poverty; five children will be arrested for violent crime; and one child will be wounded by gunfire"?[6]

Let's get even more specific about America's children. "1 in 2 never completes a single year of college; 1 in 3 is born to unmarried parents; 1 in 4 is born poor; 1 in 5 lives in a family receiving food stamps; 1 in 7 has no health insurance; 1 in 8 never graduates from high school; 1 in 12 has a disability; 1 in 24 lives with neither parent; 1 in 60 sees his or her parents divorced in any year; 1 in 137 will die before his or her first birthday; 1 in 620 will be killed by guns before age 20."[7]

Does it trouble you that among industrialized countries the United States stands first in defense expenditures and last in protecting our children against gun violence? Does it agonize you that our country stands first in health technology and 18th in infant mortality? Does it shock you that our country is first in the number of millionaires and billionaires and 17th in efforts to lift children out of poverty?[8] Does it tear your heart that in our "land of the free" the younger you are the poorer you are?

The danger? A response all too familiar, all too frequent: "It's not my problem." If such is my response, then my eyes have not really been opened; I do not yet see. A priest's "long loving look at the real" is not limited to Our Lady of Fatima Church, to the Diocese of Spokane, to the Society of Jesus. It is a response to whatever is real—especially the real that cloaks man's inhumanity to man, that claims God's creation for a privileged few. Not in an unreal yearning to solve the world's problems. Rather a profound realization that the ills of our world, from poverty and racism in our own land to the killing fields of Kosovo, make demands not only on governments and diplomats. They call for the compassion of Christians. They plead to our people to recognize with St. Paul that "if one member of [Christ's] body suffers, all suffer together with it" (1 Cor 12:26). They beg the ordained to see in the Eucharist we offer an incomparable power to change hearts from Spokane to Kosovo. Impossible, you say? Only if our eyes are still blind, our faith void of vision.

Immaculate Heart Retreat Center
Spokane, Washington
May 27, 1999

19
WATER, WILDERNESS,
AND GRIZZLY BEARS
Eighteenth Week, Year 1, Thursday

- Genesis 1:11–12
- Matthew 5:1–12

What have water, wilderness, and grizzly bears in common? I had no idea before last week, did not even ask the question. But the question became terribly real when I decided to speak to Montanans on one aspect of biblical justice: our relationship to the realities we call so abstractly "material creation."[1] Let me put it all together in three stages, with three questions. (1) What does material creation have to do with biblical justice? (2) How does Montana fit into this divine scheme of things? (3) Is there a spirituality that can undergird our preaching in this area?

I

First, a word on material creation and biblical justice. What do I mean by material creation? I mean the four elements: earth and air, water and fire. I mean our national bird, the bald eagle that isn't bald at all. I mean the salmon swimming upstream 2,000 miles to lay its eggs. I mean the deer of North America: white-tailed, mule and caribou, elk and moose. I mean the Giant Sequoias that live for thousands of years and grow higher than 30-story buildings. I mean the plants that supply us with food for eating, lumber for building, fuel for burning, drugs for healing, oxygen for breathing. I mean everything that is not God or the human person.

What have all these to do with biblical justice? Remember what biblical justice is: a relationship, always a relationship. Not only to God, loving Father, Son, and Spirit above every idol of earth. Not

108

only to people, loving each man, woman, and child, even a bitter enemy, as an image of God, like another self, another I. With all that, a relationship to all that is not God or people. A relationship that makes demands on us, calls for a fidelity similar to that we show to the divine and the human.

You see, for centuries Christians have left an unfortunate impression on our world. A misinterpretation of Genesis 1:28. A conviction that we humans, alone shaped in God's image, have a mandate to make all that is not human serve our plans and our purposes, our pleasures and our wants, our wills and our whims. We have only recently realized that God's command to "have dominion" is not a license to despotic subjugation; it is a call to reverential care. Biblical scholars, theologians, even church documents have been slow to recognize this.

Why? Lutheran theologian Joseph Sittler insisted that our basic ecological error is that we Christians have separated creation and redemption. The reason why we can worship nature in Vermont and at the same time manipulate nature in New York is that, in our view, the redemption wrought by Christ leaves untouched the creation wrought by God. And once we wrench redemption from creation, once we put nature "out there" and grace "in here," as long as we omit from our theology of grace humans' transaction with nature, it is irrelevant to Christians whether we reverence the earth or ravish it.[2]

No longer, good friends. Back in 1990, John Paul II called for a world's address to exhaustion of the soil, to uncontrolled deforestation, a serious look at life styles, consumerism, instant gratification. He commended contemplation of nature's beauty, recognition of its restorative power for the human heart. He made bold to assert that Christians "must realize that their responsibility within creation and their duty toward nature and the Creator are an essential part of their faith."[3]

II

Second, how does Montana fit into this divine scheme of things?[4] Three ways: water, wilderness, grizzly bears.

Water. Behind water lies ASARCO: American Smelting and Refining Company. ASARCO wants a permit to build an enormous underground copper/silver mine. Where? Near Noxon in northwest Montana, roughly 15 miles from the Idaho border, 25 miles upstream of Idaho's largest fresh-water lake. The ore body would be mined 24 hours a day, every day, for 30 years.

The problem? Water quality. ASARCO plans to treat mine wastewater using unproven, experimental technology and discharge three million gallons per day into the lower Clark Fork River. According to the EPA, this discharge will consume all of the allowable pollution in the lower Clark Fork River, thereby precluding other forms of growth and development in the area. The two water treatment systems proposed require frequent monitoring and inspection by a state regulatory agency that requires only one inspection a year and does not have sufficient or properly trained personnel.

Wilderness. The vast majority of Montanans want to preserve the unique spaciousness of this state, protect its great expanses of wild lands, the critical watersheds, the marvelous free-roaming wildlife habitat. The ecological, economic, and spiritual values of these roadless areas are immeasurable and merit permanent protection as wilderness. Since this is public land, it is for the Congress to determine its disposition. But for the first time in a quarter century not a single member of the Montana Congressional delegation has introduced a bill to protect the wild land base.

Grizzly bears. There is serious talk of taking the grizzly off the threatened list, therefore no longer needing protection. But grizzlies are dwindling and could disappear. Their habitat is disappearing steadily through logging, road building, sprawling subdivisions, and development by the oil and gas and recreation industries. Grizzlies are dying regularly at the hands of humans. "Delisting the grizzly," we are told, "would loosen habitat protections that are keeping the entire Yellowstone ecosystem patched together in the face of tremendous pressures."[5]

III

A third point: What does all this demand of us? Not a solution in a 15-minute homily. As preachers of justice, our task is to help people to recognize, understand, value, and live the various relationships they have: to God, to people, to earth. To help heal the ruptures that alienate, that destroy those relationships. I have focused on restoring or reanimating the relationship that links us to God and the material creation God looked at and saw "it was very good" (Gen 1:31). To be effective in this mission, what you and I need (and our people with our help) is a conversion. Not necessarily a sudden, swift, instantaneous turnabout; more like the long-term process that theologian Bernard Lonergan has so cogently left us.[6]

What precisely does this conversion involve? Four precepts that touch intimately your water, your wilderness, your grizzly bear—and much else. (1) Be attentive: Focus on the full range of your experience. (2) Be intelligent: Inquire, probe, question. (3) Be reasonable: Marshal evidence, examine opinions, judge wisely. (4) Be responsible: Act on the basis of prudent judgments and genuine values. This last includes being in love: wholehearted commitment to God as revealed in Jesus Christ.

Involved here are three conversions: intellectual, moral, and religious. Stay with me here. This is not an abstract lecture; it is a spiritual adventure.

An intellectual conversion? Yes. Get rid of a misleading myth about human knowing: that to know is to see, hear, touch, taste, smell, feel. To know our world meaningfully is not the sense experience of an individual, yours or mine or anyone else's. It is the external and internal experience of a community, continually checking and rechecking its judgments. It is the experience of your parish, of your diocese, of your state.

A moral conversion? Yes. We must shift our criteria for decisions and choices from satisfactions to values. Opt for the truly good, even for value against satisfaction when they conflict. Root out the biases in ourselves, in culture, in history. Listen to criticism; learn from others.

A religious conversion? Yes. When does that occur? When we fall in love—unqualified self-surrender. Loving with all our heart, all our soul, all our mind, all our strength. It means accepting a vocation to holiness. It is God's love flooding our hearts through the Holy Spirit given to us. It involves replacing the heart of stone with a heart of flesh, then moving gradually to a complete transformation of all my living and feeling, my thoughts and words, my deeds and omissions.

This is not ivory-tower stuff. It keeps our spirituality from being reduced to more and more prayer, fidelity to daily meditation, resistance to temptations, avoidance of the near occasions of sin, the Psalmist's "clean heart" (Ps 51:10). It has to do with truth, with values, with love, with suffering, with a transformation not only inside me—a transformation of my relationship to God, to people, to the earth, to culture and history.

Awesome? Yes indeed. But only through such transformation can God's creative dream for community, for the kingdom, be realized. Here, for me, is a type of conversion that is crucial for a profound spirituality of biblical justice. Why? Because its high point, religious conversion, is conversion to a total being-in-love: in pursuing truth, in realizing human values, in orienting me to the universe. It is a conversion that develops through all my life. It involves my relationship not only to God and people but to the earth that sustains me; involves not only my spiritual soul but my mind and heart, my emotions and passions. It is critical not only for individual holiness but for building community, for the Church's mission to promote the human family, the Church's redemptive role in human society.

How sum it up? Start with biblical justice, fidelity to relationships that stem from our covenant with God in Christ: loving God above all idols, seeing in each flawed human an image of Christ, touching every facet of earth and sea and sky with reverence. Link that to life within the Body of Christ, a life of faith and hope and love, life in ever-widening communities (parish, diocese, universal church) for the building of the human family, life nourished by the body and blood of the risen Christ. Introduce into that complex a ceaseless, never-ending conversion to a communal search for an intellectual value called truth, a communal opting for what is truly good against self-satisfaction, a communal self-surrender to Love incarnate.

With such a spirituality we might begin edging back to storied Eden, to that brief shining moment when humanity was at peace with God, humans at peace with one another, humans at peace with the rest of God's creation. It is still a dream divine. And if the kingdom is not yet what God had in mind, it just might stimulate our search together for a spirituality that makes us more attentive, more intelligent, more reasonable, and more responsible. In a word, more Christlike.

Given a diocese so Christlike, Montana may continue to exult in wondrous waters, in exhilarating wilderness, yes in its grizzly bear.

St. Mary Catholic Community
Helena, Montana
August 5, 1999

20
YOU GIVE THEM SOMETHING TO EAT
Eighteenth Week, Year 2, Monday

- Jeremiah 28:1–17
- Matthew 14:13–21

"*You* give them something to eat" (Mt 14:16). The words of Jesus intrigue me. Five thousand men, not counting women and children, all of whom had followed him on foot to a deserted place: Give them something to eat? Do you wonder that the disciples objected, "We have nothing here but five loaves and two fish" (v. 17)? I don't know what Jesus expected them to do. One Scripture scholar says, "Jesus trains the disciples to have self-confidence, to show initiative, to be leaders."[1] Perhaps. Whatever it was, this eucharistic liturgy that focuses on Jesus feeding thousands of the hungry brings Dorothy Day to my mind. We are told that Dorothy "could not go to Communion and be insensitive to the reality that someone was hungry; she could not enjoy the warmth of eucharistic consolation and know that she had a blanket while her brothers and sisters did not; she could not 'go to the altar of God' and be aware that someone was sleeping over a grate on the sidewalk."[2]

This evening, as we continue to mull over biblical justice and the injustices in our own areas,[3] let me take the disciples' problem a step further, expand the hunger of the 5,000-plus, move it to the hungers of America's children, move it to Jesus' command today, "*You* give them something to eat." I shall begin with some troubling statistics, go on to some pertinent biblical principles, and end with some suggestions that touch on our response to "*You* give them something to eat."

I

First, some troubling statistics. A week ago last Saturday, Marian Wright Edelman, founder and president of the Children's Defense Fund, wrote a strong piece for the Op-Ed page of the *New York Times*. Her context was the theme of the Republican National Convention's opening night, "Leave No Child Behind"—actually the trademark of her Children's Defense Fund. Under the title "There's No Trademark on Concern for Kids," she said in part:

> While the nation enjoys the greatest prosperity in history, tens of millions of children are being left behind: 13.5 million live in poverty, 12 million have no health insurance, 5 million are alone every day after school lets out. And more than 4,000 each year pay the ultimate price for adult irresponsibility: they are killed by guns.
>
> Millions more receive substandard education in crumbling schools without enough books, equipment or teachers. Or they are eligible for Head Start or child care assistance when parents work, but receive neither. Or they are abused or neglected or are languishing in temporary foster homes, waiting for adoption....
>
> It is not only morally wrong but economically foolish to allow one in five American children to live in poverty. How would we feel about a family that kept four of its five children well fed, well clothed and well educated, but let the fifth go hungry and without health care or good preparation for the future? The acid test for parties or politicians claiming the mantle "Leave No Child Behind" is what they will actually do.[4]

II

Pungent statistics. But what do they boil down to? In a word: injustice. Why injustice? Because these 13.5 million hungry children live in our own country, a country bountifully blest with the riches of this earth. Among industrialized countries America is first in military technology, first in military exports, first in defense expenditures, first in Gross Domestic Product, first in the number of millionaires and billionaires, first in health technology; and yet America is 14th (14th in 25) in the proportion of children in poverty, 16th in living standards among our poorest one-fifth of children, 16th in efforts to lift children out of poverty, 18th in the gap between rich and poor children.[5]

The point is, 13.5 million children are not receiving the food to which they have a strict right, a right that stems from the fact that they are as human as you and I, are part of a family, the human family. It is a right strengthened by the fact that the food they need is available; America is not a starving Sudan. Father Bryan Hehir phrased the issue incisively: "Children are the supreme test of our moral vision. They are because they are so vulnerable. In a sense they stand as a crystallization, as an example, as a kind of eternal symbol of our responsibility for each other, since they are so dependent upon us."[6]

That conclusion stems from sheer reason, what philosophers call ethical justice. Even more importantly for Christians, here is a frightening failure in fidelity, in a responsibility that stems from our covenant with God cut in the blood of Christ. It is a type of injustice whose ancestry pervades the Prior Testament. Take the words of the Lord through Isaiah:

> Is not this the fast that I choose:
> to loose the bonds of injustice?
> Is it not to share your bread with the hungry,
> and bring the homeless poor into your house?
> If you offer your food to the hungry
> and satisfy the needs of the afflicted,
> then your light shall rise in the darkness
> and your gloom be like the noonday.
> (Isa 58:6–7, 10)

That command of God to Israel finds a striking conclusion with the promised words of Jesus at the Last Judgment: "Come, you that are blessed by my Father, inherit the kingdom prepared for you from the foundation of the world; for I was hungry and you gave me food..." (Mt 25:34–35). Why the connection? The Letter of James could scarcely be clearer: "What good is it, my brothers [and sisters], if you say you have faith but do not have works? Can faith save you? If a brother or sister is naked and lacks daily food, and one of you says to them, 'Go in peace; keep warm and eat your fill,' and yet you do not supply their bodily needs, what is the good of that? So faith by itself, if it has no works, is dead" (Jas 2:14–17). And the First Letter of John is uncompromising: "If anyone has this world's goods and sees his brother in need and closes his heart against him, how does the love of God remain in him?" (1 Jn 3:17).

III

Finally, pertinently, what in the concrete is demanded of Americans? On one level Marian Wright Edelman had no doubts: "The acid test for parties or politicians claiming the mantle 'Leave No Child Behind' is what they will actually do."[7] On the earned-income tax credit, the minimum wage, Head Start, child care, and much else. But what of us who have been commissioned by baptism and/or ordination to proclaim the gospel, to live out Jesus' own mission "to preach good news to the poor, proclaim release for prisoners and sight for the blind, send the downtrodden away relieved" (Lk 4:18)? Specifically, how might Jesuits respond to Jesus' directive, "*You* give them something to eat"? Several suggestions.

First, let me go out on something of a limb. I suggest that we apply to the crisis of hunger—not only hunger in America but the world-wide crisis of hunger—what Father General Pedro Arrupe wrote to the whole Society in 1980 when he created the Jesuit Refugee Service:

> ...this situation constitutes a challenge to the Society we cannot ignore if we are to remain faithful to St. Ignatius' criteria for our apostolic work.... In the *Constitutions* St. Ignatius speaks of the greater universal good, an urgency that is ever growing, the difficulty and complexity of the human problem involved, and the lack of other people to attend to the need (*Constitutions* 623). With our ideal of availability and universality, the number of institutions under our care, and the active collaboration of many lay people who work with us, we are particularly well fitted to meet this challenge and provide services that are not being catered sufficiently by other organizations and groups.... St. Ignatius called us to go anywhere we are most needed for the greater service of God.... God is calling us through these helpless people.[8]

I dare to hope that one day soon the Society of Jesus will list hunger as a challenge "we are particularly well fitted to meet," a service "not being catered sufficiently by other organizations and groups."

Second, the Maryland Province is not insensitive to Christ's command, "You give them something to eat." The "Province Ministries" booklet is rich proof: the McKenna Center at St. Aloysius, Gonzaga kids manning McKenna's Wagon, the Urban Service Team in Camden, the Ignatian Volunteer Corps, Loyola College students reaching out to the needy, St. Ignatius Loyola Academy, and much else. Impressive, each one. A question: If not actually involved, do I actively encourage those who are? Do I seek support for them—moral, financial, spiritual? Or do I simply admire from a distance?

Third, in preaching or proclamation, does hunger ever enter in? Do I know how many children are hungry in my parish, in my area, in my city? If I do know, do I care, do I agonize? If I do care, if I do agonize, do I share my knowledge, my anguish, with my people, with my friends, with young students searching for a challenge?

Fourth, do I ever allow myself to experience hunger, to taste a child's hunger? Try to sleep without having eaten that day? Not terribly difficult, because I know that the banana, the "eggs once over," Maxwell's "good to the last drop" will be there for the taking. But still, an awareness, a gnawing sense of what America's left-behind children are enduring day after day.

My brothers in Christ: This plea of mine, "*You* give them something to eat," is not simply a call to action. Undergirding the action must be a spirituality. For all too long and for all too many, spirituality has been identified with our interior life, what goes on inside of us, what is a profoundly private experience. A holistic spirituality includes both the inner experience of God and its outward expression in relationships. That is why I was delighted to discover some years ago a definition that attracts me mightily, a definition that sums up our retreat/workshop succinctly: Spirituality is a "process of being conformed to the image of Christ for the sake of others."[9]

For the sake of others. Horace McKenna's slogan, SOME: "So Others May Eat."

Loyola Retreat House
Faulkner, Maryland
August 7, 2000

21
WHAT MORE TO DO FOR MY VINEYARD?
Twenty-seventh Sunday of the Year (A)

- Isaiah 5:1–7
- Philippians 4:6–9
- Matthew 21:33–43

Today's readings—I wonder if they have stayed with you. Why? Because they are so important for the parish renewal that begins today. Because time is so precious and so short, I shall focus on the reading from Isaiah.

I

The reading from Isaiah is a parable. What is a parable? It's a story: a fictitious story, not real, made up, imagined, to bring out a moral or spiritual truth. Now this parable in Isaiah is a masterpiece. A masterpiece of literature. A masterpiece of morality. A masterpiece about love—love lavished but not returned. Listen to the story.[1]

A man owns a vineyard; it is very dear to him. He lavishes extraordinary care on it. He digs it, clears it of stones, plants it with choice vines, builds a watchtower in the midst of it, hews out a wine vat in it. "What more was there to do for my vineyard that I have not done in it?" With such preparation, he expects his vineyard to yield splendid grapes. What does it actually yield? Rotten grapes; stinking grapes. What will he do now? He threatens to remove the hedge that surrounds it, break down its wall, let it be trampled down. He will make it a waste, overgrown with briars and thorns. He will not even let it be rained upon.

What is the lesson, the truth, the reality within the parable? Start with the vineyard's owner: Who is he? Yahweh, God, the Lord. Then what is the vineyard? The house of Israel, the people of Judah.

What was so wondrous about its planting? Israel was a people of God's own planting, God's special choosing, God's special care. It was God's "pleasant planting." He had lavished love upon it. What did the Lord have a right to expect from His people? Justice—the rights of the poor defended. What did Israel actually bring forth? Social crimes, violence, bloodshed. What might the Lord have expected? Righteousness. What did His people actually produce? An outcry, the cries of the exploited poor.

At that time, Israel had a social order that let the powerful grow rich at the expense of the weak. A single vivid sentence:

> Ah, you who join house to house,
>   who add field to field,
> until there is room for no one but you,
>   and you are left to live alone
>   in the midst of the land!
> (Isa 5:8)

Where did God's people place their trust? Not in God. In things other than God: magic arts, foreign powers, earthly wealth, military might, idols. How did God react? A frightening sentence, in the very human language of the prophets: "Therefore the anger of the LORD was kindled against His people, and He stretched out His hand against them and struck them; and their corpses were like refuse in the streets" (Isa 5:25). It is the strong language of the prophets. We would say, God left them to their own folly; God left them where they wanted to be left, to what they could achieve by their own wits, their own might. The result? Disaster.

II

Today we begin a parish renewal. To renew—what does it mean? St. Paul told the Christians of Philippi what it means in very general terms: "Beloved, whatever is true, whatever is honorable, whatever is just, whatever is pure, whatever is pleasing, whatever is commendable, if there is any excellence and if there is anything worthy of praise, think about these things" (Phil 4:8).

You see, Jesus too has a parable about a vineyard. You will find it in the Gospel of John, chapter 15. In Jesus' parable the vineyard is somewhat different from the vineyard in Isaiah. In Jesus' parable *you* are the Lord's vineyard—but not the whole vineyard. Recall Jesus' words the night before he died for us: "I am the vine, you are the branches. If you remain in me and I in you, you bear much fruit, for apart from me you can do nothing. If you do not remain in me, you are like a branch, cut off and withered, which they collect and throw into the fire to be burned" (Jn 15:5–6).[2] The point is, "the branch gets its life from the vine, that is, the disciple gets his [or her] life from Jesus."[3]

You and I are alive in Christ only if we are in Christ and he is in us. His life began in us at baptism, when, as St. Paul sang, "In the one [Holy] Spirit we were all baptized into one body...and we were all made to drink of one [Holy] Spirit" (1 Cor 12:13). But this body of Christ that is the "we" of Christians, this body, like our physical body, has to grow; but to grow it has to be nourished. And it is.

How is this body of Christians nourished? Nourished wondrously by the very flesh and blood of our Lord Jesus Christ. What we call "Communion." Communion: union with—with Jesus and with one another. Right here there is a division in the body of Christ. Do you know how many Catholics in this country celebrate the Eucharist, receive Christ in Communion, at least two Sundays a month? Thirty percent. Three out of every ten Catholics. A first facet of our renewal? One hundred percent of St. Augustine parish feeding each week on the flesh and blood of Christ. How important is it? Meditate on the words of Jesus:

> I myself am the living bread that came down from heaven. Whoever eats this bread will live for ever. And the bread that I shall give is my flesh for the life of the world.... Let me firmly assure you, if you do not eat the flesh of the Son of Man and drink his blood, you have no life in you. Whoever feeds on my flesh and drinks my blood has eternal life. And I shall raise him up on the last day. For my flesh is real food, and my blood is real drink. Whoever feeds on my flesh and drinks my blood remains in me and I in him.
>
> (Jn 6:51–56)

This is the food that changes us into Christ, deepens and expands our likeness to him. This is the bread that makes us alive in Christ, makes it possible for us to believe what we cannot see, hope for what is still not ours, love one another as Jesus has loved us. Here, in the Eucharist, the branches, you and I, live off the vine, off Jesus, more richly than anywhere else.

In a political campaign an indispensable move is to get the people to the voting booth, get them to vote. In a Catholic renewal a move we dare not disregard is to get Catholics to the church, get them to receive the body and blood of their Savior. Hard to believe, isn't it? We have to implore, have to beg, our sisters and brothers to receive the bread that can give them life—God's life now, God's life for ever. "If you do not eat [my] flesh and drink [my] blood, you have no life in you." This is not some off-the-wall idea of mine; this is Jesus talking!

III

A third point: For a Catholic renewal, it is not enough to receive—even to receive Jesus into our bodies. With Jesus within us, we should be on fire to give. Not just money in the collection. Like Jesus, to give ourselves.

There are unnumbered ways in which we can give ourselves. You may remember Dorothy Day, Communist turned Catholic. She lived with the poor, the downtrodden, the refuse of humanity, in downtown New York—shared their slums, their food, their filth, their roaches, their loneliness. Why? Because she was convinced that the gospel, God's good news, has *not* been preached to the poor. Words perhaps, but not our lives.

Only a small number are called to be Dorothy Days. But all of us are called to give of ourselves as God gives us to give. The bedridden and the houseridden have a significant role to play: a wedding of prayer and suffering that rises up to heaven like incense, is incredibly effective if it is your sharing in the cross of Christ. The more active among us cannot leave justice and peace to the parish committee. Let your imaginations soar. Imagine that tomorrow morning 1,200 of you come to St. Augustine's for Mass. You are met at the church doors by the liturgy committee. The chairperson announces to you, "You don't have to attend Mass this morning: We did it for you." Absurd, of course; but many Catholics, perhaps most, leave Catholic action to committees—not only peace and justice but education and RCIA, engaged encounter and marriage encounter, catechetical instruction and preparation of converts, whatever. No committee can do our "Christian thing" for us.

And finally for this afternoon, there is the American Church's perhaps most pressing challenge: how to fashion a genuinely Catholic parish out of many cultures. In your situation, not only the mix of Anglos and Hispanics among you but the descent upon you of New Yorkers and Jerseyites, Irish and Italians, Poles and Germans. And the new stranger in America, the immigrant, eyed with suspicion from east coast to west. A challenge indeed, for hospitality is not simply doughnuts and coffee after Mass. Hospitality is a loving welcome to every new parishioner, because each of them is part of the same Body of Christ as you are, a body wherein, as St. Paul declared, no one can say to any other, "I have no need of you" (1 Cor 12:21).

I do not come to you with an instant solution; there is no such thing. I simply submit that the first years of your new millennium present you with an awesome opportunity to be literally "catholic." I mean universal, wonderfully open to all that is human, hands and arms outstretched especially to the lonely and the unloved, to the outcast and the despised, to the children who are the most vulnerable of Americans. For this is to love as Jesus loved.

Good friends, your vineyard, Christ's vineyard, is growing here in Richmond. Whether in the coming millennium it will yield a harvest worthy of Christ or the rotten grapes of Isaiah's vineyard will depend in large measure on you, on the depth of your faith and love, on your enthusiasm, on the way you dig and plant and build. In this most Catholic of adventures, I promise you not earthly success but the joy that comes from carrying the cross of Christ...with Christ and with one another.

> Saint Augustine Parish
> Richmond, Virginia
> October 2, 1999

22
JUSTICE AND LOVE SHALL PREVAIL
Twenty-seventh Week, Year 1, Friday

- Joel 1:13–15; 2:1–2
- Luke 11:15–26

To close this retreat/workshop,[1] I find the passage from the prophet Joel unexpectedly pertinent. So then, a word on Joel, then a word on you and me.

I

Joel as a person? Nothing in the three chapters to even begin a biography. Scholars have admirably concluded that "the book was written after the rebuilding of the Temple in 515 and before the destruction of Sidon in 343...."[2] Far more important is a set of facts and a message.

The facts? A locust plague and a drought. A plague and a drought that first devastated the countryside and the crops, with a direct effect on worship in the Temple. Immediately affected are the harvesters, the farmers, the cultic personnel. All these Joel urges to lament.

> Be dismayed, you farmers,
>   wail, you vinedressers,
> over the wheat and the barley;
>   for the crops of the field are ruined...
> surely, joy withers away
>   among the people.
> Put on sackcloth and lament, you priests;
>   wail, you ministers of the altar.
> Come, pass the night in sackcloth,
>   you ministers of my God!

> Grain offering and drink offering
>> are withheld from the house of your God....
> Is not the food cut off
>> before our eyes,
> joy and gladness
>> from the house of our God?
>>> (Joel 1:11–13)

Then, using the metaphor of an army, Joel describes the ravages wrought by locusts on the city.

> Before them peoples are in anguish,
>> all faces grow pale.
> Like warriors they charge,
>> like soldiers they scale the wall....
> They do not jostle one another,
>> each keeps to its own track;
> they burst through the weapons
>> and are not halted.
> They leap upon the city,
>> they run upon the walls;
> they climb up into the houses,
>> they enter through the windows like a thief.
> The earth quakes before them,
>> the heavens tremble.
> The sun and the moon are darkened,
>> and the stars withdraw their shining.
>>> (Joel 2:6–10)

The pivotal point of Joel's book? The message. "Then the LORD...had pity on His people" (2:18). The locusts are removed and the drought disappears. But not as "inevitable phenomena in the rhythm of nature. They are saving acts of Yahweh and 'proof' that Yahweh is in the midst of Israel as a savior."[3] At the darkest moment in Israel's situation, in response to their grief, to their repentance, to their weeping and fasting, to the rending of their hearts rather than their clothing, the Lord declares:

> My people shall never again
>> be put to shame.
> You shall know that I am in the midst of Israel
>> and that I, the LORD, am your God and there is no other.
>>> (Joel 2:26–27)

God will be in Israel's midst, and Israel will recognize it— recognize that there is only one God: Israel's God. Not only that.

The presence of Yahweh involves a charismatic outpouring of God's spirit. Israel's sons and daughters shall prophesy, Israel's old men shall dream dreams, Israel's young shall see visions (2:20; 3:1 in the Hebrew).[4]

II

So much for Joel. The neuralgic question: What might Joel's experience say to us as we hasten to our third Christian millennium? Not only to ordained priests; to everyone baptized into Christ. What might Joel be saying to us and to our people?

I suggest, perhaps rashly, that on the eve of our third millennium we American Catholics may be sharing griefs similar to those of Joel's Israel. Only in a metaphorical sense are they locusts and drought. But they may well be potentially more threatening, more devastating.

I am not denying the remarkable results of Vatican II: the liturgy as community at worship, the heightened role of the laity, the Church as servant especially of the poor and the downtrodden, a fresh vision of religious freedom, recognition of Protestant churches as communities of grace—and ever so much more. But in the context of Joel's Israel, we are forced to face some frightening facts and listen once again to God's message.

Facts.[5] Take simply our own United States. The most powerful source of grace is the Mass, our Eucharist, our supreme act of community worship. And yet, what proportion of our Catholics worship regularly, receive Christ in Communion fairly often? Twenty-five percent; one out of every four. Hispanics/Latinos will soon dominate our Catholic population; and yet, those who call themselves Catholics have dropped from 78 percent in the early 70s to 67 percent today.[6] Priests are in desperately short supply. Forty-eight thousand priests left between 1964 and 1986. One-priest parishes with missions are the rule rather than the exception; "two-thirds of American parishes have only one (aging) priest and thirteen percent of them have no resident pastor at all."[7]

For all our Catholic identity, we are dreadfully divided. "Currently...there are over three hundred traditionalist communities across the United States,"[8] with their own liturgies, their selective rejection of Vatican II, at least one with its own seminary. We have Opus Dei Catholics and Catholics for Free Choice; Mother Angelica Catholics for simple obedience and cafeteria Catholics picking and choosing what they want to believe. William Bausch put much of the problem in a typically engaging sentence: "Once we were large-families, fish-on-Friday, missal-toting, novena-going, medal-wearing, fasting-from-midnight, ember-day Catholics who knew who we were."[9] Today, how would you phrase in a single sentence the identity of American Catholicism?

On the edge of our third millennium we face our own locust problem, our own drought. A homily dares not solve complex issues. But this I do say: We need not end this retreat/workshop with the pessimism of Joel's Israelites: "Is not joy and gladness cut off from the house of our God?" What is God trying to tell us? Cardinal Carlo Maria Montini of Milan strikes a splendid opening note, an optimistic prelude:

> For some, changing the calendar year from 1999 to 2000 has little religious significance; but for believers such a change signals a desire to renew hope and courage according to the apocalyptic dimension of the Gospels. We should not expect some big change in human history as we celebrate the new millennium. The year 2001 will not offer significant differences, other than a chance to seek essentials, to listen to the voice of the Holy Spirit, to regain an awareness of the great and essential change in human history brought forth by the coming of Jesus Christ. Yes, changes will occur, since we live daily in this change; every prayer well uttered is this change—all brought about by the life, death, and resurrection of Jesus. The meaning of things has been changed. Every moment, this present moment, brings with it the presence of a new humanity, and we can look at everything in a different way. We can work for justice and love with a certainty that justice and love shall prevail, assured that it is already in the present order of things. In the kingdom of God, the days of forgiveness and love have begun and this order shall be for ever. God's glory shall be revealed day after day.[10]

The message? As for Joel, so for us: "Every moment, this present moment,...we can look at everything in a different way. We can work for justice and love with a certainty that justice and love shall prevail, assured that it is already in the present order of things." At the darkest moments in our situation, in response to our grief, to our repentance, to our frustration, to our suffering, to the rending of our hearts, the Lord declares...what? Not "My people shall never again be put to shame." Simply, "Know that I am in your midst."

The nerve-racking question, of course, is: Do you believe it? Do you actually see God's glory revealed day after day? Even in crucifixion? Especially in crucifixion? The Church's crucifixion and your own? Do you?

Fatima Retreat House
Indianapolis, Indiana
October 8, 1999

23
HANDS CUT OFF?
Twenty-ninth Sunday of the Year (A)

- Isaiah 45:1–6
- 1 Thessalonians 1:1–6
- Matthew 22:15–21

Late last January, in the early stages of this homily, I glanced at the front page of the *New York Times*. A picture in living color caught my eye, cut my heart. The place: Freetown in Sierra Leone, West Africa. The background: civil war, brutish, savage, barbarous, inhuman. The picture: a young man, quite normal-looking, except for one thing: His hands had been cut off. Cut off at the wrists. Cut off by a machete. Cut off by another human being. He had begged his captors, the rebels, to kill him. No, they replied; we want to send a message—to your people, to your president.[1]

I was afraid I would be sick. How blest we are, I mused, in our United States! Even the most cruel of our criminals would not do something so uncivilized. Perhaps. Still, I could not help but see in that picture a metaphor. A metaphor for what we are doing to millions of our children. In a sense, cutting their hands off. How? Making it difficult or impossible for them to touch the better things in their world: to experience the life of the mind, to turn the pages of a book, to build sand castles real or imagined, to write a discovered word on a blackboard, to strum a guitar, to dunk a basketball outside the concrete jungle, to finger a Mackintosh, to take the Lord's body in spotless hands.[2]

I

Is this exaggerated? Not if you cast a clear eye on the facts. Not if you move the metaphor to the grim reality. We recall somewhat casually that one out of five children in the United States grows up below the poverty line. This is more than another unfortunate tragedy, an isolated statistic. Do you know what poverty does to the mind of a child?

Take my little friend Peter. His iron is low, and that slows his ability to solve problems, distracts his attention, keeps him from concentrating. His growth has been stunted, and so he scores lower than others on several tests of academic ability. His family has had to move again and again, and this has disrupted his schooling, even made him drop out for a while. Cold, dampness, mold, allergies cause all sorts of respiratory diseases like asthma, take him from school. Crowding at home, and accompanying stress, interfere with his homework. In his home water is leaking, paint is peeling, plaster is falling, lead is poisoning. He attends one of the poorest inner-city schools, and so his level of achievement is lower than that of a friend in a suburban school with the latest in machines and the best in teachers. His family cannot afford to buy him exciting magazines and books, maps and encyclopedias. He has several responsibilities at home, including younger siblings to care for, and must work more than 20 hours a week to help the family eat. His parents cannot afford a computer. When college beckons, he simply will not be able to pay for it, even with financial assistance from the institution.[3]

Very simply, Peter is not "ready to learn, ready to succeed." And Peter is not alone; he has 14 and a half million brothers and sisters in deadening situations similar to his—14,500,000.

II

So what can we Catholics do about it? Let's start with the school. Not only the parochial school that accepts Catholics and non-Catholics, but the public school as well. Here a tough question raises its head: Why should parochial schools educate non-Catholic children? And why should Catholic parents improve public education, especially if they have no children suffering therein? As with the homeless poor, so with the poorly educated: We care for them not because *they* are Catholic but because *we* are Catholic. What our loving God said to Jacob and Israel, the same God says to each child:

> Thus says the LORD,
> He who created you, He who formed you:
> Do not fear, for I have redeemed you;
> I have called you by name, you are mine.

When you pass through the waters, I will be with you;
    and through the rivers, they shall not overwhelm you;
when you walk through fire you shall not be burned,
    and the flame shall not consume you....
You are precious in my sight,
    and honored, and I love you.

(Isa 43:1–4a)

Each child born into this world is precious to God. And each Catholic should repeat what a loving Jesus said when his disciples wanted to keep little children from bothering him: "Let the little children come to me, and do not stop them; for it is to such as these that the kingdom of heaven belongs. And he laid his hands on them" (Mt 19:14–15).

We care for each child, particularly the disadvantaged, because each, baptized or not, is an image of Jesus. If the mind of a child is imperiled, it should call forth from us the same compassion we lavish on a child with muscular dystrophy. And if we take such children into our schools, it is not primarily to make them Catholic; it is to bring out the human that is hidden within, to ready them for a life of dignity, to help them shape ever so fully their likeness to the Lord who fashioned them.

III

Concrete suggestions for a Catholic homilist? In my project Preaching the Just Word, we do not expect that a ten- or fifteen-minute homily will solve complex social problems, will give politicians and educators a ground plan for improving their schools. What we do expect is that a powerful homily will raise awareness, raise consciousness, in the pews. Specifically, we recommend that, once a well-informed preacher has laid out certain issues of justice, a parish will gather substantial numbers of parishioners together to put flesh on those bones, to begin the process by asking three questions: (1) What are the justice issues that clamor for immediate attention, for drastic reform, in our area? (2) What resources can we command to attack these issues? (3) Since we cannot do everything, what in the concrete shall we do?

The justice issues are discouragingly many, but here, today, the emphasis is on education. Who, within these parish lines, are the children not "ready to learn, ready to succeed"? Where does the problem lie? Overcrowded buildings, substandard science facilities, faulty air conditioning, external noise? Here, researchers tell us, are causes behind low achievement and bad behavior.[4]

Resources? Many Catholic dioceses, even some parishes, are blessed with CEOs in business and hospitals, with doctors and dentists, with builders and architects, with lawyers and judges, with politicians and social activists, with educators and scientists. Is it an impossible dream to harness these competences, to link them with their non-Catholic colleagues, so as to forge a unified force to save the minds of our children? What Habitat for Humanity is doing for decent housing—itself a crucial first step for readiness to learn—can we not expand to touch all that goes on within that habitat, within that environment?

Idealist, visionary, dreamer that I am, I look forward to a new millennium where a Catholic family of even modest means will assume responsibility for a poor family, irrespective of race or religion. Not to take over; simply to help preserve, help improve, the minds of its children. One example. Reliable research has revealed how utterly important it is for children's mental development to have their mothers hold them, caress them, read a book to them. But what to do when a mother cannot afford books? So many of our more fortunate families have them in abundance.

Have I wandered from today's liturgical readings? Not entirely. St. Paul is writing to the Christians of Thessalonica, a port city in Macedonia, a thriving commercial center. He is convinced that their Christian life takes place under the providence of God. In that context he tells them how he constantly remembers in prayer to God three aspects of their Christian living: their active faith, a dynamic faith because what they believe they express in life; their manifested love, expressed in actions that at times are quite difficult; and their steady hope, their patient expectation, despite the tribulations of the age, that Christ will indeed return (see 1 Thess 1:3).[5]

It is precisely these free gifts of God—dynamic faith, manifested love, and steady hope—that urge our Catholic families today to look beyond their individual households, despite the tribulations that trouble them, and to extend their hands to hands that are cut off from so much that makes life human, livable, enjoyable. Yes, good friends in Christ, join today's children's crusade. Help make one child "ready to learn, ready to succeed."

Children's Defense Fund Sunday
October 17, 1999

MEMORIALS OF SAINTS

24

FROM BOSCO THROUGH BELO
TO GONZAGA
Memorial of St. John Bosco

- 2 Samuel 15:13–14, 30; 16:5–13a
- Mark 5:1–20

Today's Eucharist should be uncommonly precious to Gonzaga. Why? Because it honors a Salesian saint whose primary activity was education: the education of the young. With time pressing, let me speak swiftly of three pertinent persons: the Salesians' inflexible founder, a courageous contemporary Salesian, and today's Gonzaga educator.

I

First, the inflexible founder, Don Bosco. More formally, John Melchior Bosco. The context is risorgimento Italy of the 19th century. Don Bosco's vision for his congregation? The education of young boys, specifically the poor and the abandoned.[1] Concretely, Don Bosco's singleminded vision was the boarding school for adolescents of high-school age, both trade and academic students.

Boarding schools had suffered their worst decline in the latter half of the 18th century. Harsh polemics had assailed the Jesuit system of education, the private high schools of that type. The charge? They did not prepare their students for real life. The atmosphere was so secluded that when they were thrown on their own resources, they risked losing their faith and proving useless to society. In Enlightenment thinking, education should conform the student to nature.[2]

In Don Bosco's time the situation had changed; boarding schools were on the rise again. Still, a fierce conflict was raging between the anticlerical orientation of the Italian public schools and the private schools Catholics raised for the education of their children. The support of the private schools "lay mainly in the peasants, the working class, and the lower middle class; thus they were almost a society of their own within the larger civil society."[3]

What was the Salesian school like?[4] It was founded on freedom. For Bosco the school "was the very antithesis of a barracks or a prison. It was a place of election...."[5] A minimum of strict discipline. The boy's liberty was to be shaped gradually—by a teacher who took an interest in all that interested the boy: his family, his work, his tastes, his pleasures, his sports. Winning the youngsters' confidence, even their affection, the teacher would inculcate a knowledge of good and evil, a desire for what was best, a horror of sin, a taste for prayer. Above all, trust in God and an awareness of God's presence everywhere.

Inflexible yes, but only where his vision was concerned. "He himself talked about the way he dealt with obstacles. If they held him up too long, or if there was no way to remove them, he would go around them."[6]

Pertinent for us too is Don Bosco's plan for Salesian Cooperators. Male and female, in all parishes possible, the Cooperators were to be active collaborators with the Salesian Congregation. They fused six distinct projects. They were religious Salesians in the world. They collaborated with the Salesians in their houses (e.g., in catechesis). They supported the Salesians through prayer and contributions. They were associates for youth work and the promotion of the faith, working under bishops and parish priests. They were a confederation to combat anticlericals and Protestants, mainly through the press. They were a union to promote the moral and civil uplifting of youth.[7]

Don Bosco suffered for his vision. He found himself in conflict with his colleagues in the priestly ministry. Often misunderstood. Often sideswiped. Other Salesians in his oratory felt that their own ministries were as important as his. Parish priests resented his power to draw the young off their streets into his programs. There were painful occasions when he had to separate from coworkers. At times he felt terribly isolated. But, despite fierce pain of flesh and spirit, he refused to abandon his vision: education for the poor young, the abandoned young.[8]

II

Turn now to a courageous contemporary Salesian. I mean the Nobel laureate for peace known as Bishop Belo.[9] More formally, Carlos Filipe Ximenes, bishop of East Timor, a tiny island the size of Rhode Island. Most of us never heard of East Timor until last August, when the Timorese voted for independence from Indonesia and suffered savage reprisals from their colonizers.[10]

But the same savagery had been wreaked on East Timor for more than two decades. As many as 200,000 people, one third of the original population, have perished as a consequence of Indonesia's invasion, and many thousands have been uprooted. But much of the world has been indifferent or hostile. Including the United States. One example. Henry Kissinger, told that use of American arms for aggression was illegal under a treaty between the U.S. and Indonesia, replied: "Can't we construe [preventing] a Communist government in the middle of Indonesia as self-defense?"[11] Evidence of a Communist threat? None whatsoever.

As apostolic administrator and then bishop, Belo faced ceaseless opposition. Clergy resented his appointment without their consultation—this outsider, this lad recently out of the seminary. All the Timorese priests boycotted the ceremony that transferred episcopal power to him. Indonesian bishops kept him at a distance; military leaders turned a deaf ear to his protests against injustice. Roman bureaucracy had little patience for this troublemaker, like Romero so critical of the Salvadoran regime. The papal nuncio to Indonesia and the Roman Curia pressured him to keep quiet. When he received the Nobel prize, not a personal word from Bill Clinton.

Arguably, what propelled Belo into becoming a spokesman for his people was his special tie to young folk in the Salesian mode. Time and again young advocates of independence took refuge at his residence; some he would escort home, only to learn later that they had been arrested, tortured, killed, or were missing.

There is so much more that can be said about Bishop Belo, but it is high time I turned to Gonzaga.

III

Bosco and Belo would relate strongly to your college high school on Eye Street. Two strong reasons leap out from what I have just said: Each of these Salesians focused on the young, and each needed a God-given courage to live that focus whatever the cost.

It has been my good fortune for six and a half years to live with the Gonzaga Jesuits, to get gradually to know some of the lay faculty, and to pass perilously close to the thundering herd as I enter and leave my office. At libations and dinner with you, I have ingested more Gonzaga gossip than most patristic scholars have a right or a need to endure. And I must confess that my admiration for who you are and what you do grows—if not with each vodka and veal piccata, surely with each passing year.

Why? There is, first, your commitment to God's young. You may not always be convinced, with Jesus, that "it is to such as these that the kingdom of God belongs" (Mk 13:14). But you do believe, as Bosco and Belo believed, that each boy, however flawed, is precious in God's eyes; that your presence here is part and parcel of a vocation within a vocation; that it is a God-given privilege to open a young mind to truth and goodness and beauty, to be a channel of grace to a soul struggling with world, flesh, and devil; that though you will only rarely experience the full fruits of your efforts, small acres of God's kingdom will be fields of peace and justice and love because of you.

The second reason for my admiration? The courage it takes to keep alive your conviction, your enthusiasm, your joy. It is not quite the courage it took Bishop Belo to protest the assaults on, the murder of, his young Catholics. The threats to his life. It is rather the peril of routine; the day-after-day drudgery; the same yesterday, today, and tomorrow; the difficulty in retaining a sense of wonder, of awe, of amazement; the ability to communicate your vision to a culture that canonizes power and possessions, fame and fantasy. You may not call it courage—especially if you are still intoxicated by the vision; still entranced by the interplay between mind and mind, between heart and heart; still convinced with St. Augustine that in the last analysis one learns wisdom only from the interior teacher, God. But there it is; I have experienced it.

Good brothers in Christ: In the past two weeks I have learned much about vision and courage from Bosco and Belo. Through almost seven years I have touched vision and courage...in you and your colleagues. For that, warm thanks.

Our Lady's Chapel
Gonzaga College High School
Washington, D.C.
January 31, 1999

25
A TALE OF THREE HEARTS
Memorial of St. Claude de La Colombière

- Ephesians 3:8-9, 14-19
- Matthew 11:25-30

Today's memorial is a tale of three hearts. Three hearts linked together in a sublime symphony of love. Three hearts that combined to produce a rich Catholic devotion of long standing. A devotion that puts questions to Jesuits of today. A word on each of those three themes: (1) the three hearts, (2) the Catholic devotion, (3) Jesuits today.

I

First, the three hearts. The place: the Visitation convent at Paray-le-Monial in France. Between 1673 and 1675, our Lord appeared three times to a contemplative nun, Margaret Mary Alacoque, showed her his heart. In the first appearance, Jesus commissioned her to spread devotion to his sacred heart. In the second, he asked for Holy Communion and a Holy Hour of Reparation. In the third, during the octave of Corpus Christi in 1675, Jesus asked her to see a special feast established in reparation to his heart for the injuries done it. He added: "Go to my servant Father de La Colombière and tell him from me to do all in his power to establish this devotion and give this pleasure to my heart." And Claude did "all in his power." The young Jesuit whom Jesus identified to Margaret Mary as "my faithful servant and perfect friend" preached the devotion to the end of his short life.

For both the Visitandine and the Jesuit, the commission meant a good deal of suffering. For Margaret Mary, life in the convent was difficult. Some of the sisters did not understand, thought she was deluded. But she lived the devotion, and amid contradiction and opposition she worked to have it recognized within her order.[1]

Claude became preacher and spiritual adviser to the Duchess of York in London, with residence in the palace of St. James—at a time when English priests could not legally function in their homeland. A Frenchman he had befriended denounced him to the government for a hundred pounds sterling. He was arrested and charged with traitorous speech against the king and parliament. He was imprisoned in a damp, cold dungeon. His health deteriorated; after frequent hemorrhages he was released and sent back to France. He never really recovered. Fittingly, he lived in Paray-le-Monial, died there at forty-one.[2]

II

Move now to the Catholic devotion. A homily is not a history, the pulpit not a lecture hall. Still, it's worth knowing that here is a devotion whose roots scholars have tried to trace back to Scripture—with varying success. Did the "rivers of living water" Jesus promised (Jn 7:37) come from his belly or from his heart? Was the soldier's lance, as biblicist Marie Joseph Lagrange thought, a mortal blow at Jesus' heart (Jn 19:34)—the passage that stimulated the idea of the Church born from the pierced heart of Jesus as the new Eve from the new Adam?[3] Many of the Fathers of the Church reveled in these texts. The Middle Ages moved only gradually from the patristic theology of the wound in Jesus' side as the source of grace to preaching the heart of Jesus as the express object of a more personal devotion. For many mystics the devotion meant a more profound penetration into the mystery of Christ living in his Church through the liturgy. Still, for all the efforts of Saint Claude and Saint Margaret Mary and scores of others, the feast came about quite slowly, and it was not till 1856 that Pius IX extended the feast to the universal Church.[4]

But what is the devotion all about? In Catholicism there has always been devotion to the Word Incarnate, to the Son of God made flesh. But here we have a special form of this devotion. It focuses on Jesus' physical heart. But it doesn't rest there. The heart of Jesus is seen as a symbol. A symbol of what? Of Jesus' love on three levels. I mean the very human love that affected his sense life, the very human love that is God's gift called "charity," and the divine love that pervaded his humanity. The essence of the devotion was summed up in our response to Psalm 103, "The LORD is compassion and love" (see v. 8a).

Now in Catholic theology every part of our Lord's sacred humanity merits strict adoration. We can adore the face of Christ; we can adore the feet of Christ. Not in isolation. Not the face, the feet, separated from his humanity. No, we can adore because they are the face, the feet, of God's only Son. That is why on Good Friday one devotion has the faithful streaming to the cross, kissing the pierced feet of the Crucified. Not feet separated from Jesus' body, severed from his total humanity. The feet are sacred because they are part and parcel of Jesus' humanity, and the whole of that humanity is the humanity of God's Son.

But why the heart, usually in preference to any other part of Jesus' humanity? Because, popes and theologians have insisted, the physical heart of Christ is a *natural* symbol. Not in the sense that the heart is the physical seat of spiritual or conscious life; it's metaphor. Still, there is a real connection between our affective life and our hearts; our affective life can, often does, affect the physical heart.

Much of Western culture recognizes this, resonates to it in ever so many ways. Fidelity: "Cross my heart!" Love: "I love you with all my heart." Sympathy: "My heart goes out to you in your sorrow." Emotions as distinguished from mind play: "My head argues no, my heart feels yes."

And so Catholics now have acts that express this devotion: a feast on the Friday following the second Sunday after Pentecost; acts of reparation for sin; the monthly First Friday with Holy Hour; a Communion of Reparation; an act of consecration on the feast of Christ the King; a litany, novenas, a consecration of families, nocturnal adoration, enthronement of the Sacred Heart in the home. And there is our Apostleship of Prayer, with the Morning Offering, "I offer you my prayers and works, my joys and sufferings of this day, for all the intentions of your sacred heart."

III

And what of us? My sources, unimpeachable of course, tell me that devotion to the Sacred Heart is not dead in the pews; millions practice it in some form.[5] But my sources also tell me that the devotion "she ain't what she used to be." Like the novena in honor of St. Francis Xavier that in my early years as a priest packed St. Ignatius

Church in Baltimore with 18 services a day, devotion to the Sacred Heart of Jesus does not touch most Jesuits before or after the feast.

Why? Not because "it's only a symbol." We live on symbols: a flag, a cross, a kingdom. The "scoop" is, most Jesuits are just not interested, no longer promote the devotion in their parishes, their schools, their retreat houses; it simply doesn't appeal to them. If you need official confirmation, listen to our 31st Jesuit General Congregation back in 1965–66:

> It is no secret...that devotion to the Sacred Heart, at least in some places, is today less appealing to Jesuits and to the faithful in general. The reason for this is perhaps to be found in outmoded devotional practices. Therefore our theologians, men experienced in spirituality and pastoral theology, and promoters of the apostolate of the Sacred Heart of Jesus are urgently asked to search out ways of presenting this devotion that are better suited to various regions and persons. For, while preserving the essential nature of the devotion, it would seem imperative to set aside unnecessary accretions and adapt it to contemporary needs, making it more intelligible to the men [and women] of our time and more attuned to their sensibilities.[6]

Is it any wonder that the same Congregation declared, "Since conditions in the modern world demand firmer foundations for the spiritual life, it is necessary that from the very beginning the scholastics and brothers be educated continually and progressively to a deeper knowledge of the mystery of Christ based on Holy Scripture and the liturgy, as well as on the Society's traditional devotion to the Sacred Heart of Jesus"?[7]

I know, symbols come and symbols go. Even some symbols that stay lose their impact in this place and that. And a devotion to the humanity of Jesus that reaches his humanity through his heart can lose its impact when an individual or a culture sees no need, experiences no desire, to reach the human Jesus through heart or face or feet. Also, it's hard to sell a symbol: Either it grabs you or it doesn't. It stays and it goes. BMW gives way to Toyota, Larry Bird to Michael Jordan, Marilyn Monroe to Meryl Streep.

And yet I wonder. Yesterday, Valentine's Day, was again a great day for lovers, young and old; ceaseless sales of hearts from chocolate to gold. Hearts that say "I love you." Might it be a worthwhile experiment, say in a theology course at Gonzaga, to float the theology of devotion to the Sacred Heart and see how our students react? Or even in a Renew program at St. Aloysius? In any event, it has to begin with us, in our own hearts. We can be saved without it; but might not so rich a devotion help us and the people we serve to become more like Saint Claude, "faithful servants, perfect friends"?

Still, when all is said and done, all explanation and exhortation exhausted, I suspect that what is all-important is Paul's prayer for the Christians of Ephesus, my prayer for you: "I pray that you may have the power to comprehend, with all the saints, what is the breadth and length and height and depth,[8] and to know the love of Christ that surpasses knowledge, so that you may be filled with all the fulness of God" (Eph 3:18–19).

Our Lady's Chapel
Gonzaga College High School
Washington, D.C.
February 15, 1999

26
KOREA, KIM, AND THE CHRISTIAN CROSS
Sts. Andrew Kim, Paul Chong, and 101 Others

- Ezra 1:1–6
- Luke 8:16–18

Today our Catholic focus is Korea. The 19th century, specifically the persecutions between 1839 and 1846. Three stages to my song and dance: (1) What happened? (2) What has come of it? (3) What of us?[1]

I

What happened? First, a bit of fascinating history I cannot resist. More than 200 years ago, in 1794, a Chinese priest named James Chu entered Korea secretly. What did he find? "4,000 Catholics, none of whom had ever seen a priest."[2] The Hermit Kingdom, as Korea was known, did not admit foreigners, did not tolerate Christians. During the persecutions of the mid-19th century, over 10,000 Christians were killed: men and women, clergy and laity, married and widowed. Some were strangled, others beheaded; some died under torture, others in prison.[3]

The best-known victim of 1856? Andrew Kim,[4] the first native Korean priest.[5] His convert father, Ignatius Kim, had been martyred in 1839, age 41. As a seminarian in Macao, Andrew's efforts to steal his way back into Korea read like a melodrama, but without the conventional happy ending. Ordained near Shanghai on August 17, 1845, Andrew began his final return a week later. On a boat 25 feet long, with his bishop and another priest. Fighting storms, winds, and rapids, running onto rocks and sandbanks, they finally cast anchor in an obscure place; Kim and his bishop moved north to Seoul.

We have no details of his priestly life that final year.[6] We know he had gone northwest of Seoul to explore how to smuggle missionaries into Korea despite the border patrol. He had finished his mission happily when he was arrested. From a letter of his we know he was ordered to apostatize, refused, was brutally tortured. And we have his death sentence in the *Annals of the Great Council* in Seoul: "His Majesty, having come to the room called Heui-tjyeng-tang, summoned there the Prime Minister and the high dignitaries of the administration for guarding the frontiers. He has ordered that the criminal Kim-tai-ken be executed in military fashion and his head suspended."

And so it happened at a river south of Seoul. The death sentence was read. Andrew cried out to the people: "I am in my last hour. Listen carefully to me. If I have associated with foreigners, it is for my religion, for my God. It is for Him that I die...." Made to kneel before his executioners, he asked calmly, "Am I in the right position? Can you strike easily?" Asked to turn a little, he did, then said, "Strike. I am ready." With the eighth stroke his head was severed.

Dead at 25. Father and son beatified in 1925, raised to sainthood in 1984, with layman Paul Chong and a hundred others,[7] when John Paul II made his pastoral visit to South Korea.

II

What has come of it? Has the blood of Korea's martyrs become the seed of Korea's Catholic Christians? For the most part, a resounding yes. Religious freedom was granted in 1883; steady growth followed. The cathedral in Seoul was begun in 1888; a seminary opened in 1891; by 1911 Korea had 77,000 Catholics. True, the Korean War (1950–53) meant invasion by Communists, persecutions, bishops and priests imprisoned and put to death. Still, by 1953 there were 166,000 Catholics in the country; in 1964 South Korea counted 628,000 Catholics. The Church has seminaries and convents, schools from elementary to college, hospitals and orphanages, 12 leprosaria, a Catholic press.[8]

The 1990s? Two dioceses in North Korea, three archdioceses and 11 dioceses in South Korea. As of 1995, Catholics in South Korea "comprise[d] a little more than 6 percent of the total population of some 43 million."[9] About 2.6 million Catholics. North Korea? Since the Korean War, says one authority, "there have been no reports of Catholic life in Communist North Korea."[10]

III

How might all this touch us? First, a fairly obvious realization: Holiness is not a question of age. In the early Church, Agnes of Rome was martyred at 13, Polycarp of Smyrna at 86. More recently, among our Korean martyrs, a boy of 13, a woman of 79. Andrew Kim was beheaded at 25; Cardinal Bernardin died of cancer at 68. Paradoxically, all of them, and many more, remind me of a pertinent prayer in our breviary—a psalm prayer that struck me during the Office of Readings on Thursday of Week III. It is a prayer I prayed aloud this past July when the Justice Jubilee celebrated my 85th in Los Angeles:

> Eternal Father, you give us life despite our guilt and even add days and years to our lives in order to bring us wisdom. Make us love and obey you, so that the works of our hands may always display what your hands have done, until the day we gaze upon the beauty of your face.

To bring us wisdom....

Second, what is this wisdom Andrew Kim had at 25 and I am still struggling to grasp at 85? St. Paul preached it succinctly to the Christians of Corinth: "We proclaim Christ crucified...Christ the power of God and the wisdom of God" (1 Cor 1:23–24). Our wisdom is not earthly success, important as this may be. Our wisdom is the cross—Christ's cross and our own. Not slavish imitation of the Crucified; as disciples, our wisdom is to "follow" wherever he leads us. Andrew Kim's cross was a constant frustration: his ceaseless yearning to return to Korea, to serve his people. He did return, for a year—a year that now no one in Korea or elsewhere can recall. As poet Paul Claudel said of St. Francis Xavier, who died alone six miles from the China of his dreams, "He did what he was told to do—not everything, but all he was able to do."[11]

For most of us, the cross is not some sort of swift beheading. It is increasingly a four-letter word...loss. It is God stripping us gradually of so much we have valued: hair and health, energy and enterprise, approbation and applause, mind and memory, parents and relatives and friends and companions of Jesus leaving us in death, leaving us a little or a lot more lonely. Our prayer has to be the wisdom of Christ in Gethsemane's garden: "Father, if you are willing, remove this cup from me; yet, not my will but yours be done" (Lk 22:42). The first half of the prayer slips trippingly from my tongue;

the second half does not come easily. And still, the cross is not loss, unless we say no to it.

Third, Kim speaks to us from another culture. Let the 103 Korean martyrs expand our horizons, broaden our Catholic outlook. Korean Catholics are part of us. Paul's cry is poignantly pertinent here: "In the one Spirit we were all baptized into one body...were all made to drink of one Spirit" (1 Cor 12:13). If North Korean "members are suffering, all [of us] suffer together with [them]"; if South Korean "members are honored, all [of us] rejoice together with [them]" (v. 26). Or do we?

Martyrs of Korea, open our hearts!

Our Lady's Chapel
Gonzaga College High School
Washington, D.C.
September 20, 1999

27

EXPERIENCE CHRIST, BEAR WITNESS TO CHRIST
Feast of Sts. Simon and Jude, Apostles

- Ephesians 2:19–22
- Luke 6:12–16

Distressing for a homilist on this feast is a simple fact: About Simon and Jude we know practically nothing. Oh yes, they are listed in all three Synoptic Gospels and in Acts as apostles, the Twelve specially chosen by Jesus. But no details, no stories, no pictures, no faces. And in Christian tradition we have only legends not historically verifiable. So then, let's simply talk about apostles: apostles then, apostles through the centuries, and the apostles you and I are expected to be.[1]

I

Apostles then. What made Simon and Jude, what made the Twelve, special? For Luke, these extraordinary disciples were not simply to "be with him," as Mark puts it (Mk 3:14); "they were to be his 'emissaries' (*apostoloi*, persons sent out), indeed, even witnesses to him."[2]

If you look elsewhere in the New Testament, the criteria for an apostle seem to be primarily two: The apostle is a witness to the risen Christ and has a commission from Jesus to proclaim the Christ-event.[3] On these criteria Luke builds in Acts, when the question arises, who will take the place of the Judas who betrayed Jesus? Whoever succeeds to his place must carry three characteristics. He must be a male; he must have "accompanied" the Eleven "during the whole time that the Lord Jesus moved in and out among us"; and he must be "a witness to [Jesus'] resurrection"—not witnessed it with his own eyes, simply one who can testify that Jesus is risen, is alive (Acts 1:21–22).

Men who lived and moved about with Jesus, men who could and did testify to a Jesus triumphant over death, could guarantee what Oscar Cullmann called "the continuity between the risen and historical Jesus"—such were Simon and Jude.

Given these basic facts, Simon and Jude have no face. We don't know where they went when the apostles dispersed; we don't know what they did. Iconography represents Simon with a saw, for supposedly he was martyred by being sawn in two; Jude gets a halberd, a kind of long-handled axe that supposedly accounted for his demise. It is somewhat ironic that Jude may always be best remembered for interrupting Jesus' last discourse—a single sentence in John: "Judas (not Judas Iscariot) said to him, 'What can have happened that you are going to reveal yourself to us and not to the world?'" (Jn 14:22). Apart from that, nothing in the New Testament, and nothing reliable in the tradition.

II

Move on now to apostles through the centuries. Not the technical "successors to the apostles"; rather, men and women who in a genuine sense have been "sent," have walked with Jesus, and have testified by word and work that this Jesus of Nazareth is gloriously alive.

I mean Mary Magdalene, featured down the ages as "apostle to the apostles." Why? Because she was the first to be commanded by Jesus to proclaim him risen, alive. "Go to my brothers and say to them, 'I am ascending to my Father and your Father, to my God and your God.'" And John tells us, "Mary went and announced to the disciples, 'I have seen the Lord'" (Jn 20:17–18).

I mean Francis of Assisi. Not only the poor and penitential Francis, but the apostle to all of God's creation, the Francis with a profoundly Christian love of creation, of nature. The Francis who loved all of God's creatures, not only the poor but animals and plants, natural forces, even Brother Sun and Sister Moon. The Francis whom John Paul II commended to our imitation when he called on the world to address exhaustion of the soil and uncontrolled deforestation; when he asked us to contemplate nature's beauty, recognize its restorative power for the human heart; when he made bold to assert that Christians "must realize that their responsibility within creation and their duty toward nature and the Creator are *an essential part of their faith.*"[4]

I mean Francis Xavier, apostle to Portugal's new empire in India. The Xavier who wrote to King John of Portugal:

> It is a sort of martyrdom to have patience and watch being destroyed what one has built up with so much labor.... Experience has taught me that Your Highness has no power in India to spread the faith of Christ, while you have power to take away and enjoy all the country's temporal riches.... It will be a novel thing...to see yourself at the hour of death dispossessed of your kingdoms and seignories, and entering into others where you may have the new experience, which God avert, of being ordered out of paradise.[5]

The Xavier who died on a lonely island, six miles from the China of his dreams, waiting for a boat, a brown sail that never came.

I mean the seventeenth-century French Jesuit apostles to your own Hurons, martyrs who seeded the Huron missions, seeded your land, with their blood: Antoine Daniel, the first martyr of Huronia; Jean de Brébeuf and Gabriel Lalement, their hearts torn out before they died, their warm blood drunk by savages, pieces of their flesh roasted and eaten while they looked on; Charles Garnier, struck down by two bullets, dead of two axe strokes that penetrated his brain; the unforgettable Noel Chabanel, brilliant professor of rhetoric in France, utterly out of place in Huronia, binding himself by vow to remain with the Hurons, yearning to die a "martyr in obscurity."

I mean Dorothy Day, apostle to the poorest of the poor. She found it difficult to enjoy Communion when other images of God were hungry, could not enjoy the warmth of eucharistic consolation aware that she had a blanket and others did not. Convinced that the gospel had *not* been preached to the poor, she lived with them, amid rats and roaches, filth and squalor.

III

Why these examples? Two reasons. (1) These are concrete examples of the biblical justice you have been exploring this week: fidelity to relationships that stem from our covenant cut in the blood of Christ. They show us how graced men and women have loved God above all else; have loved their sisters and brothers, especially the less fortunate, like other selves; have touched the earth, creation, with reverence, as a gift of God not to be feverishly clutched but to be generously shared. (2) For my third point: the apostles you and I are expected to be. You see, these men and women and untold thousands of others down the ages lived in new ways the characteristics of an apostle. They had experienced a living Christ and they bore witness to him in their lives.

I have little if any difficulty with our manner of witnessing, though like all things human it can always stand improvement. This evening I am even more interested in, challenged by, another characteristic of the original apostles: They lived and moved with Jesus, walked with him. My thesis? Unless you and I experience a living Jesus, do our own walking with him, we risk failing as apostles.

One example of such experience. Back in 1978, theologian Karl Rahner wrote a striking essay titled "Ignatius of Loyola Speaks to a Modern Jesuit."[6] Rahner put on the lips of Ignatius, with remarkable insight, some account of the saint himself and the task that faces Jesuits today. One of the most striking sections has apostolic relevance not only for sons of Ignatius but for all who are "sent" by Christ as the original apostles were sent. Relevant because here Ignatius focuses on his experience of God.

> As you know, my great desire was to "help souls," as I put it in my day; to tell people about God.... I was convinced that first, tentatively, during my illness in Loyola and then, decisively, during my time as a hermit in Manresa I had a direct encounter with God. This was the experience I longed to communicate to others.... I am not going to talk of forms and visions, symbols, voices, not of the gift of tears and such things. All I say is I knew God, nameless and unfathomable, silent and yet near, bestowing Himself upon me in His Trinity. I knew God beyond all concrete imaginings. I knew Him clearly in such nearness and grace as is impossible to confound or mistake....
>
> God Himself. I experienced God Himself, not human words describing Him.... This experience is grace indeed, and basically there is no one to whom it is refused. Of precisely this was I convinced.[7]

This is not the knowledge we shall have in heaven; it is still imperfect. But it is genuine knowledge, true experience. It reminds me of philosopher Jacques Maritain's insistence that the culmination of knowledge is not the concept; it is experience. I feel God!

This, good brothers in Christ, this is the kind of relationship with God that makes for an effective Christian apostle. Not simply knowing *about* God; knowing God. Not only touched *by* God; touching God. For me personally, in the twilight of my existence, it raises ever more insistently a question I dare not avoid: Do I actually know God? Not a concept, an idea of God: God is One and Three, God is all-knowing and all-loving. Rather the kind of knowledge that in John's Gospel is never an abstraction; it is not even simply linked with love; it is love. Not knowledge first, then love; no, loving knowledge. The knowledge where I am one with what I know, one with whom I know.

Pray, my fellow apostles, pray agonizingly to know God that way, to touch God, to feel God. Not only will it produce a more effective apostle. It's a splendid preparation for the way you and I will know God as God is, love the God who is Love. And by all means remember Ignatius' conviction about this experience, this grace: "basically there is no one to whom it is refused."

Happy hunting.

The Nottawasaga Inn
Alliston, Ontario, Canada
October 28, 1999

28

FROM BONIFACE TO BERNARDIN TO...?
Memorial of St. Boniface, Apostle of Germany

- Acts 19:1–8
- John 16:29–33

It isn't easy to preach on Boniface; he was a man of many parts. Since this is a homily and not a lecture, let me (1) highlight his most important parts, (2) indicate their significance for the Church, and (3) suggest how his way of proceeding might touch our own lives.

I

First, Boniface was a man of many parts. At the risk of boring you, a small selection of facts. For much of my life I thought this apostle of Germany was a German. Actually, he was born in England, in Wessex, and his name was Winfrid. His name would be changed later by Pope Gregory II, in honor of a martyr of that name. He was educated by Benedictines, first at Exeter, then at Nursling (between Winchester and Southampton). Nursling was significant, because there he imbibed three Anglo-Saxon monastic ideals, three loves that were to characterize his life: love for learning, love for Rome, and love for missionary activity.

It was the third love that led him to Germany. Consecrated a bishop, he did not want a diocese. Gregory II had given him broad missionary jurisdiction among unbelievers. It was what he wanted: an independent sphere of activity. This independence was linked with a genuine attachment to the papacy: reports to Gregory II and Gregory III, three visits to Rome, one for a whole year.

His travels are the stuff from which legends are born: Thuringia and Friesland, Hesse and Bavaria. He established bishoprics and abbeys, founded the most celebrated of his monasteries at Fulda, a place of spiritual renewal for Boniface and the center of Germany's religious and intellectual life. Gregory III urged him to evangelize the Old Saxons, commissioned him to organize the German Church. This organization he effected in closest union with Rome, looking to the pope for authorization, protection, and guidance.

Trials on the way, of course; obstacles too complex for a homily to detail. His first missionary journey, to Friesland, to join the famous missionary Willibrord, was a disaster. The ruler of Friesland, Duke Radbod, had declared war on Christians, destroyed churches and monasteries, drove Willibrord into exile, sent what was left of the Church into hiding. Unable to preach, Boniface had no choice but to return to England in a few short months, defeated. Ten years in Thuringia, where he tried to reform a clergy that was incontinent, heretical, unreceptive. Three years under the masterful tutelage of Willibrord, then on to Hesse, which had never been evangelized, people unwilling to surrender their old religion and superstitions. It was there that he felt the tribes needed a display of power. With an axe he approached the sacred oak at Geismar, the oak dedicated to the god Thor, split the tree in four parts that we are told fell to the ground in the shape of a cross. And there stood Boniface, axe in hand, unharmed by tribal gods, strong in the power of the one God.

Back once again in Thuringia. No help there from the clergy; but he had learned in Friesland that he could not spread God's word alone; so he appealed to England for help. Nuns and monks responded enthusiastically for many years. Then on to the Frankish Church, also sadly in need of reform. He set up councils and synods, instituted reforms that revitalized the Church there.

For all the opposition, Boniface's work of reorganization was largely completed before his influence declined after the coronation of Pepin. Importantly, his methods of evangelization became a model for missionaries who followed. Apostle of Germany, yes; but he brought to Germany not only a Christian faith; he brought a Christian civilization.

His final mission took him once more to Friesland. Highly successful, but it lasted only a year. In 754, as he was preparing a group of neophytes for confirmation, an enemy band attacked his camp. He and 53 companions were massacred. Apparently he would not permit them to resist, told them to trust in God and to welcome death for the faith. An aged lady declared on oath that she saw him protect himself with a Gospel book. The same book, tradition claims, is now at Fulda; the same tradition claims that the cuts you can see in the pages were made by the swords of his assassins.[1]

II

The significance of Boniface for the Church? I return to his three loves. Take the first: love of learning. That tradition traces back to Basil the Great and Benedict of Nursia. It is summarized in the title of a minor classic by Dom Jean Leclercq, *The Love of Learning and the Desire for God.*[2] For the Schools, for Scholasticism, theology's aim was knowledge; and the way to knowledge was through the question. In the monasteries the aim was not so much knowledge as experience; and the way to experience was not so much the question as desire. The significant difference was the importance the monastery accorded to the experience of union with God.

Experience? It simply means that in study and reflection the Benedictine tradition highlights an inner illumination, what Benedict called an *affectus,* a way of savoring and relishing divine realities. It means that if you want to "know" God, you need a lived faith. This personal experience is closely linked with a whole environment, promoted by the experience of a fervent community. It is a biblical experience inseparable from liturgical experience. It is experiencing the Church, an experience undergone in the very midst of the Church. It presupposes the pursuit of the spiritual life in a community whose essential aim is the search for God. It promotes the presence in the Church of spiritual men and women rather than intellectual masters.[3]

Second, his love for Rome, for the chair of Peter. I find it a refreshing relationship. On the one hand, Boniface regularly sought advice from Rome, regularly requested authorization for his reforming activities. On the other hand, for all his recourse to Rome, Boniface

> depended on his monasteries to give permanence to his work in rural areas. The *ingens multitudo* of Anglo-Saxon monks and nuns who followed him to the Continent peopled his houses and established new ones. Boniface introduced Benedictine nuns into the active apostolate of education, anticipating by many centuries the work of religious women in that field.[4]

His third love is perhaps the most obvious: missionary activity. Here the Benedictine influence on Boniface is almost palpable; for

Anglo-Saxon Benedictinism was characterized by a powerful attraction to missionary work.[5] It was an attraction that cast its spell on young Winfrid and never left him.

III

Finally, what of you and me? To be practical, let me focus on the Archdiocese of Cincinnati, while recognizing that not all of you are ministering here. I suggest that the Benedictine influence on Boniface's love of learning might speak eloquently to you as well. By lauding "love of learning" I do not intend to make scholars out of parish priests. I simply commend to you the kind of learning Boniface inherited. I mean what I sketched above. In your study and your reflection, what should animate you, energize you, inspire you is...desire. Desire for God. A deep desire. Not simply to know *about* God, but to *know God, know Jesus, know the Holy Spirit.* To experience God. Not a vision, not an apparition. Simply a personal relationship that thrills through each day. A grace indeed, but my own Ignatius Loyola insisted it is a grace that is refused to no one who yearns for it. But this experience of God, says the Benedictine tradition, is best fostered, promoted, sustained if it is closely linked with a whole environment. In your situation, a spiritual life within a fervent community of priests, a community for whom an essential aim is the search for God. Too abstract? Let me concretize this with an example close to home, dear to Cincinnati.

I suspect you know that Cardinal Joseph Bernardin referred to his decade as archbishop of Cincinnati as "the greatest blessing in my priesthood." Of this he wrote this revealing paragraph:

> The priests of Cincinnati were especially helpful for my spiritual growth. Several years ago I sensed that administrative responsibilities were eating away at my interior life. I told several young priests that I felt they were praying more and better than I. I told them I wanted and needed their help. They generously took me into their lives of prayer and helped me come closer to the Lord. Theirs was a wonderful and permanent gift.[6]

His priest friend John Hotchkin recalls that "After this Cincinnati prayer experience, the skilled and gifted ecclesiastical administrator became someone indefinably different, a person of hope, not just a person of plans and expectations, but a true person of hope, hope that because it clings to the person of Jesus cannot be derailed."[7]

A clear example of what priests of prayer can accomplish not as isolated individuals but as a community of desire. What some of you did for Bernardin, all of you can do for one another. Must do for one another. For as you shrink in numbers, all the more must you grow in community. Distance may discourage, demands on your time deter; but the effectiveness of your preaching, especially your effort to make biblical justice a staple of your diocese, will depend largely on the spirituality, the communal conversion, you bring to it. When your people, more than half a million believers, are challenged not by an occasional, infrequent activist, but by a presbyterate that has caught the justice fire, is terribly in love with God, God's people, and God's earth, I promise you a response unprecedented in your parishes.

Yes, what some of you did for Bernardin, all of you can do for one another. Help one another to become priests of prayer. For it is only priests of prayer who can "sell" God's justice; because God's justice is love, and it is only priests of prayer who can "sell" God's love.

What some of you did for Bernardin, won't all of you do for one another?[8]

Mt. St. Mary's Seminary of the West
Cincinnati, Ohio
June 5, 2000

29
OF PREACHING, PASTORING,
AND PRAYING
Memorial of St. Charles Borromeo

- Romans 14:7–12
- Luke 15:1–10

At first glance, Charles Borromeo does not strike us as an ideal subject for priestly imitation. Not because there are peccadillos or scandals in his résumé. The problem is his ecclesiastical career. With an uncle as pope, Pius IV, Charles was destined for high service in the Church. Pius called him to Rome, advanced him rapidly through a brilliant ecclesiastical career. He held several posts in the Roman Curia, was created a cardinal at 21 or 22, as well as perpetual administrator of the Archdiocese of Milan, titular archbishop there for the rest of his life. His gifts for administration were extraordinary: summoning six provincial councils and 11 diocesan synods, implementing the Council of Trent, reforming the Church. Astonishingly pastoral, and effective as well. The credits are mind-blowing.[1] Remarkable life for a man who was only 46 when he died. But what is there in his life for you and me?[2]

Quite discouraged, sleepless late one night, I felt impelled to look at the breviary for Borromeo's memorial. From a sermon at the last synod he attended three pertinent instructions for priests leapt forth. Instructions on preaching, on pastoring, on praying.

I

First, preaching. "If preaching is your job, first preach by the way you live." The advice recalls a critical center of this retreat/workshop. I mean biblical justice. I mean the justice of God that includes but rises above the ethical justice that gives to every man, woman,

158

and child what each deserves, what each can claim as a right, not because they are powerful or prosperous, simply because they are human, as human as you and I. The justice of God that includes but rises above the legal justice that is utterly impartial, symbolized by a blindfolded lady with scales and a sword. The justice of God that lays three demands on the people of God: Love the Lord your God with all your heart and soul, all your mind and strength, above every human idol. Love every human person like another self, another I, especially the less fortunate, the downtrodden. Touch "things," God's material creation, all that is not God or the human person, with reverence, as gifts of God to be shared generously, not clutched possessively.

Now it is biblical justice that must hold the highest priority in our preaching; this has to be the heart of our homilies. For this is the justice Jesus inherited from his tradition, the justice he suggested when he unveiled his program of salvation in the synagogue of his native Nazareth: "The Spirit of the Lord is upon me, for [the Lord] has anointed me; He has sent me to preach good news to the poor, to proclaim release for prisoners and sight for the blind, to send the downtrodden away relieved" (Lk 4:18). This is the justice that leaps forth from the Last Judgment, when Jesus will welcome the just to God's kingdom with an astonishing reason: "I was hungry and you gave me food, I was thirsty and you gave me something to drink, I was a stranger and you welcomed me, I was naked and you gave me clothing, I was sick and you took care of me, I was in prison and you visited me. [For] just as you did it to one of the least of my brothers and sisters, you did it to me" (Mt 25:35–36, 40).

My point (and it is Borromeo's as well) has a jarring focus. This is not something we simply preach to our people. No, "first preach by the way you live." It is not enough for our ministry, not enough for our salvation, that we *preach* good news to the poor; we too must "send the downtrodden away relieved." We too must take seriously to ourselves the tough language of the Letter of James: "Can faith [alone] save you? If a brother [or sister] is naked and lacks daily food, and one of you says to them, 'Go in peace, keep warm and eat your fill,' and yet you do not supply their bodily needs, what is the good of that?" (Jas 2:14–16).

I too must ask if I should apply to myself the sharp challenge of John Paul II to what he called "the civilization of 'consumption' or 'consumerism'": the "excessive availability of every kind of material goods [that] makes people slaves of 'possession' and of immediate gratification, with no other horizon than multiplying or continually replacing what we already own with others still better."³

Like Dorothy Day, who insisted that the gospel has *not* been preached to the poor, am I somewhat uncomfortable with the food of the Eucharist when not far from me another human person does not have enough to eat?

II

Second, pastoring. "If you are in charge of a parish, don't neglect the parish of your own soul." What might this sentence mean for a priest today, particularly in a parish? Permit me three swift suggestions.

Suggestion number one: a serious retreat each year. Preferably eight days, under skilled direction. Away from home: a lakeside, a mountain top, perhaps a desert atmosphere. A leisurely look at yourself, your world, your people, your God. Especially a genuine *experience* of Christ. Not simply more knowledge; rather, the kind of knowing that is a kind of loving. A chance to recapture a sense of wonder over so much we now take for granted: a leaf turning red, the water of a stream trickling through your fingers, a child licking a chocolate ice cream cone, a ruddy glass of Burgundy, a cross outside Jerusalem. Borromeo would agree.

Suggestion number two: continuing education. I mean a ceaseless yearning to grow in wisdom as well as grace. To open your mind and heart beyond the parochial. To make your own the insights of a Bernard Lonergan or the spirituality of a Carlo Martini. To grow in appreciation of the rainbow of cultures that surround you: Portuguese and Italian, English and Irish and Scottish, French and German, Polish and Ukrainian, Vietnamese and Philippine, Slovenian and so many others. To sense how God may be gracing your new millennium with a new Pentecost—many tongues, but not erecting a contemporary Tower of Babel, only readying imperceptibly a kingdom of justice, of peace, of love. Borromeo would approve.

Suggestion number three: time for yourself. A priest friend of mine in the States—in Virginia Beach—is available to his people 20 hours a day. But, not available from three in the afternoon to seven. That is *his* time. For whatever he may need or like: to breathe, to fill the cup, to grow in mind and spirit, to prepare a homily, to read a book, to cook an Italian dinner for friends. I commend it to you. For whatever you need or want: a nap or a run, a spiritual classic or a contemporary novel, continuing education or daily contemplation, Mozart or Celine

Dion—whatever returns you to your neglected self or to your people energized, eager, enthusiastic. You owe it to yourself, owe it to your people. Something like this you simply must create—literally for Christ's sake, literally for your life in Christ. Borromeo would applaud.

III

Third, praying. Listen to this same 16th-century bishop:

> My brothers, you must realize that for us churchmen nothing is more necessary than meditation. We must meditate before, during, and after everything we do. The prophet says: "I will pray, and then I will understand." When you administer the sacraments, meditate on what you are doing. When you celebrate Mass, reflect on the sacrifice you are offering. When you pray the office, think about the words you are saying and the Lord to whom you are speaking. When you take care of your people, meditate on the Lord's blood that has washed them clean. In this way, "all that you do becomes a work of love."
>
> This is the way we can easily overcome the countless difficulties we have to face day after day, which, after all, are part of our work: In meditation we find the strength to bring Christ to birth in ourselves and in other men [and women].[4]

I agree, heartily. I would only add that your "meditation" ought not be always, or usually, a matter of words, of reasoning, fashioning concepts, ideas. More frequently it should embrace contemplation. I mean the contemplation that is not for mystics merely but for everyday living, the contemplation Carmelite William McNamara defined as "a long loving look at the real."

Here the "real" is not some distant, far-removed God in the heavens. The real is all that is. The real is fire and water, earth and air. The real is this man, this woman, this child. The real is Auschwitz and Dachau, East Timor and Kosovo. The real is Poland's Solidarity and New York's Covenant House. The real is the Royal Ontario Museum and the Toronto Maple Leafs. Above all, the real is God One and Three within you; it's Jesus alive. Paradoxically, alone excluded from contemplation is what we commonly associate with it: abstraction, where a leaf is no longer green, water no longer ripples, and God no longer smiles.

This "real" you must "look" at. Not only with your eyes. In contemplation your whole being—mind and imagination, senses and passions—thrills to the real. Not study, not feverish activity; simply your graced self inexpressibly one with God, with God's human images, with the earth that carries deep within it a trace of divinity. In contemplation I simply "see."

Some enchanted evening sit by a gently flowing stream, your hand in its current. Two possible reactions. (1) Why, that's H_2O. (2) No word, no concept, only the experience, the feel of water laughing its way through your fingers. At its best, contemplation is oneness; contemplation is love.

Good brothers in Christ: We Westerners have in large measure betrayed our ageless tradition. It goes back to Jesus, alone with his Father on the mountain, in the desert, in the garden. There is a degree of truth in the adage *Laborare est orare,* "To work is to pray." But it can be dangerously seductive. Unless we cherish a personal relationship with God, unless we can consistently look upon things and persons and God with a long loving look, our activity is likely to end in frustration and failure.

Contemplation, my friends, is not a luxury; it is the mark of a lover, of a Christian, of a priest.

In swift summary: (1) First preach by the way you live. (2) Don't neglect the parish of your own soul: a serious retreat, continuing education, time for yourself. (3) Look long and lovingly at the real.

The Nottawasaga Inn
Alliston, Ontario, Canada
November 4, 1999

WEDDING HOMILIES

30
BLEST, HAPPY, FORTUNATE
ARE YOU BECAUSE....
Wedding Homily 1

- Song of Songs 8:6–7
- 1 Corinthians 12:31–13:8
- Matthew 5:1–12

Today is clearly a day of blessings, a day of gifts. But I wonder if you are fully aware how beneficent a blessing, how gracious a gift, has been given to all of you in the last 15 minutes. What blessing, what gift? Christ our Lord has just spoken to you! Not in a vision, an apparition. Simply what the Second Vatican Council declared so clearly and so profoundly in 1963: Christ "is present in his word, since it is he himself who speaks when the holy Scriptures are read in the church."[1] Believe it: Jesus has just spoken to you. And what our good Lord said to you was not casually plucked from some 1800 pages of the Bible because a nuptial Mass has to have something read from Scripture. The three readings—from the Song of Songs, from St. Paul, and from the Gospel of Matthew—were carefully culled by Ken and Ping from God's own Book for a very good reason: These texts spoke to them; these are words from God that spoke to their love, touched intimately their life as man and wife.

That being so, let me suggest to you what our gracious Lord has said to Ping and Ken, what he has just said to all of us. Three passages, three ideas.

I

The Song of Songs, or the Song of Solomon, is a collection of love poems. A woman speaks to her beloved, and he to her. They speak so openly, so ardently, so sexually that you may wonder how such language can be repeated in church; there was a time it might have been "banned in Boston." How on earth did it ever become part of Scripture?

However it happened, one verse you heard explains a great deal: "Love is a flame of the LORD" (Cant 8:6). As one Scripture scholar has intepreted it, "the fire of love is a fire of Yahweh, a participation in the Lord's white-hot love."[2] Human sexual love is good, is a gift, can even be a symbol of divine love. Human indeed, but sacred as well, especially when it is consecrated in a sacrament, the sacrament of marriage, within Christ's own Eucharist.

It is God surprising us once more, God's way of spelling out for us the full humanness, the rich earthiness, of human loving. We need not be embarrassed. We have God's own guarantee that the love of man and woman, sexual love included, is a good thing. Not indeed everything our culture dignifies by the word "love." Not what Hollywood and TV too often offer as love: the one-night stand, the instant gratification, "you like it, you do it." Rather the kind of love for which a God of love shaped man and woman similar but not the same. The kind of love that engages Ken and Ping in their wholeness; where to love is to share, not so much what they have as who they are. All they are, till death do them part.

Wonder of wonders, in their kind of love Ping and Ken reveal something of what God's love must be like—the Son of God who took our flesh as his very own, the Christ who commanded, "Love one another as I have loved you" (Jn 15:12). For his was a total love; nothing was held back; there was no "mine and thine," those ice-cold, destructive words. A passionate love, for it was not a head trip; it was intense, it consumed his whole self. Such was Christ's love; such is the love we celebrate today.

Little wonder that Ken and Ping can say with the woman in the Song, "Love is strong as death" (Cant 8:6). Such is their love: the love that began as mistaken identity in a school library five years ago, the love that has grown through struggle and sensitivity, has endured exotic foods and limped after marathons, the love that reaches a high point this afternoon.

II

The love that is so lyrical, so musical, in the Song of Songs, St. Paul brings down to earth. He makes one thing lucidly clear. You can talk like the angel Gabriel, you can be as smart as Einstein, your faith can move the Rockies, you can give your millions to the United Way, you can even donate your body to science, but if you don't have love, you are nothing; and nothing you do has any value whatsoever (1 Cor 13:1–4).

But what kind of love is St. Paul demanding of Ken and Ping? A very practical love (1 Cor 13:4–7).[3] They have to be "patient." Easy enough if you're a hermit; difficult wherever two occupy the same space, if they don't care for each other's friends, if one enjoys "Jerry Springer" and the other loves "Touched by an Angel."[4] So far, no problem here; but our chaotic, changing, fast-paced culture can play havoc with the best of intentions.

St. Paul doesn't want Ping and Ken to be "envious." Each of them has special gifts, and at one time or another a world in search of healing may celebrate the medicine man and not the management technology consultant; at another a Bill Gates world may lock into the technologist and forget the healer. Here my hopes for them are high, for as Ken wrote to me, "We are sensitive to each other's needs, endorse each other's goals. We are ready to face the challenges of everyday life united as one." I like the pride each takes in what the other achieves.

St. Paul doesn't want Ken and Ping to "insist on [their] own way." I don't see either of them doing that; but in our unpredictable future, situations may arise where truth is at stake and neither Ken nor Ping sees compromise as possible. It is then that tempers have been known to flair among the most devoted of lovers. It is then that crises are born. It is then that they shall need the skills that attend good communication. Not a stony silence; not steel-angry eyes; not thin lips closed in stubbornness. What they shall need then is to be aware of the God who lives in each of them; aware that the Holy Spirit is the counselor the Lord has given them just for such tensions; aware especially of the gifts Paul says the Spirit gives to those who believe. Listen to these gifts: "love, joy, peace, patience, kindness, generosity, faithfulness, gentleness, and self-control" (Gal 5:22–23). With such gifts in each of you, how can you simply insist on your way?

III

From the Gospels Ken and Ping have borrowed the Beatitudes. A Beatitude is, an exclamation, a cry of congratulations. It recognizes reasons for rejoicing: Blessed are you, happy are you, fortunate are you because.... Without ignoring the Beatitudes in Matthew's

Gospel, I shall suggest a set of beatitudes I believe say something specific to Ping and Ken as they begin their life together.

The stimulus for my beatitudes? In St. Louis in late January,
Pope John Paul II sounded a provocative theme. It was suggested by
the infamous Dred Scott decision of the Supreme Court in 1857, a
decision that placed African Americans outside the scope of consti-
tutional protection.

> American culture faces a similar time of trial today. Today the
> conflict is between a culture that affirms and celebrates the gift
> of life, and a culture that seeks to declare entire groups of
> human beings—the unborn, the terminally ill, the handicapped,
> and others considered unuseful—to be outside the boundaries
> of legal protection.[5]

My beatitudes for Ken and Ping center on...life.

Blest, happy, fortunate are you because you have parents who
brought you into life, have given you *their* life, have nourished you to
human living without thought of themselves, even when you were at
your most unreasonable, parents whose life-giving love has made this
day possible. Blest in siblings who have shared their lives with you
because for some strange reason they think "you're the greatest." Blest
in friends who in varied ways have played a part, featured or support-
ing, in the ways your lives have been shaping for three decades.

Blest, happy, fortunate are you because each day you bring life
to each other. When you, Ken, can write, "I feel truly *blessed* to have
found my other half, my richest treasure filled with endless compassion, love, and devotion"; when you, Ping, can write, "I love Ken
more and more each day, and I look forward to spending the rest of
my life with him as his wife and best friend"—then each of your lives
has been enriched twice over.

Blest, happy, fortunate are you because your life together is not
built on two sets of brown eyes, high IQs, a bright smile; it is a gift
from above, a gift of incredibly new life. Etch in your hearts St. Paul's
exclamation, "If you are in Christ, you are a new creation. See, everything has become new!" (2 Cor 5:17). How can it not be new? A
Trinity dwells in you as in a temple: a Father who calls you son and
daughter; a Christ who feeds your life with his body and blood, soul
and divinity; a Holy Spirit who is light for your minds, strength for
your wills.

Blest, happy, fortunate will you be if the love you share with
each other is not hugged to yourselves, if it is flung out lavishly to the
acre of God's earth you inhabit. A whole little world, but especially

the still unknown men and women who are less fortunate than you, who will look to you for some meaning to life, look to you for healing. Especially the children, in a rich country where one of every five children is growing up in poverty—so unfree in "the land of the free."

Blest, happy, fortunate will you be if wherever you find a culture of death you try to insert life—from the beginning of existence to its exit, from the unborn child to the trembling elderly. Here I rejoice because both of you care so deeply for others. Because early on, Ken served as a crisis-intervention counselor at a mental-health center; because he sees the sick as persons rather than patients. Because Ping seems fashioned from a wondrous wedding of sensitivity and compassion.

Blest, happy, fortunate will you be if you remember that without God you cannot lift a finger—literally; blest if you can continue to find in the Eucharist the most powerful source of your effectiveness with others.

In summary, Ken and Ping: Blest, happy, fortunate will you be if this day's recessional, your gladsome exit, your waltzing down the aisle is not a swift stroll to the Country Club before the rest of us get there. The recessional is symbolic. I mean, it represents your movement from church to world, from altar to people, from Christ crucified on Calvary to Christ crucified at the crossroads of our country.

With all that in mind, Ken and Ping, you approach the moment not so much of truth as of love. God within you and all around you—your families and friends as joyous witnesses—give yourselves to each other freely and without reservation. And in that giving, give yourselves to the little worlds that hunger for your kind of loving, thirst for your Christlike living.

Sacred Heart Cathedral
Raleigh, North Carolina
April 10, 1999

31
SOMETHING BEAUTIFUL:
FOR GOD, FOR TWO, FOR A WORLD
Wedding Homily 2

- Song of Songs 2:10–14
- 1 Corinthians 12:31–13:8

Back in 1971, a British journalist, Malcolm Muggeridge, authored an admiring appreciation of Mother Teresa of Calcutta. He titled his book *Something Beautiful for God.*[1] Something similar, something beautiful, is happening here today. But I want to expand on Muggeridge's title; I shall sketch my scenario under three headings. For this afternoon we are privileged to experience (1) something beautiful for God, (2) something beautiful for a young couple, and (3) something beautiful for a whole little world. A word on each.

I

First, the marriage of Jennifer and Lee is something beautiful for God. But, you say, how can this be? A Jew and a Catholic marrying? With backgrounds and histories so different: 20 centuries of hostility; cries of "Christkillers"; forced baptisms and gruesome ghettos; the Holocaust in a country boasting its ancient Christian culture? They differ in so much that has to do with religion, with God, with an agonizing question: Has the promised Messiah come in Jesus, or "are we to wait for another?" (Lk 7:20). How can today's celebration be beautiful for God?

Beautiful for God because this wedding is a splendid symbol. It calls to mind a dream God had and still has: to create on earth a single family, a people of God linked in love. Not that one marriage can produce that family; at times it increases the problems. Still, the love of Jennifer and Lee recalls the dream in Eden, when God shaped man and woman in God's own image and likeness, shaped them to fashion other images of God who through the centuries might help break down what St. Paul called "the dividing wall, the hostility between us" (Eph 2:14).

Concretely, there is so much Jennifer and Lee can share. The God of Abraham, Isaac, and Jacob is the God of Jesus. The God before whom Jennifer genuflects is the God in whom Lee believes. Lee can in good conscience pray with Jennifer, "Our Father, who art in heaven, hallowed be thy name, thy kingdom come, thy will be done on earth as it is in heaven." And Jennifer need not hesitate to take to herself what Moses proclaimed to Israel:

> Hear, O Israel: The LORD is our God, the LORD alone. You shall love the LORD your God with all your heart, and with all your soul, and with all your might. Keep these words that I am commanding you today in your heart. Recite them to your children and talk about them when you are at home and when you are away, when you lie down and when you rise.
>
> (Deut 6:4–7)

Still echoing in my memory after 33 years is a plea from revered Rabbi Abraham Joshua Heschel for dialogue in language and love:

> What unites us? Our being accountable to God, our being objects of God's concern, precious in his eyes.... What unites us? A commitment to the Hebrew Bible as Holy Scripture, faith in the creator, the God of Abraham, commitment to many of his commandments, [to] justice and mercy, a sense of contrition, sensitivity to the sanctity of life, to the involvement of God in history, to the conviction that without the holy the good will be defeated....[2]

In that context, I see our one God looking down at this lovely scene and saying: "To me, true love is always something beautiful. Especially when two images of my love, different in so many ways, link their lives in my presence. Your love, Lee and Jennifer, is something beautiful *for me*."

This was touchingly expressed by Jennifer when she wrote to me, "Being in love with Lee is a gift—like God smiling on us."

II

Second, today's marriage is something beautiful not only for God but for Jennifer and Lee. You see, if any single word has lost any meaning, has been prostituted in our culture, it is "love." With a gigantic assist from TV, love is used to describe a one-night stand, a chemical attraction, a romp in the hay. If you like it, do it. If it pleasures you, have at it.

But genuine love takes on substance when we recall the first reading from Scripture carefully chosen by Lee and Jennifer for their wedding. I am glad they so chose; for the Song of Songs is unique in the Bible. It is, from beginning to end, a love song—more accurately, a collection of poems about human love and courtship that would be appropriately sung at weddings. It is sensuous, it is sexual, it is erotic. Not explicitly religious, it is still a book of the Bible. Happily so; for it is God's passionate assurance that the profound love of man and woman is something beautiful in God's eyes, something beautiful for a man and a woman. In fact, as the book draws to a close, we are told that "Love is a flame of the LORD" (Cant 8:6). The fire of love is man and woman sharing in "the Lord's white-hot love."[3]

In Scripture married love is a favorite image for the love that links God and God's people. God betroths Israel to Himself, at times must reproach Israel for her infidelity. Jesus has the Church for his bride: Husbands are to "love your wives, just as Christ loved the Church and gave himself up for her, to make her holy" (Eph 5:25–26). Why such imagery? Two strong reasons. (1) Because the love of husband and wife has an intimacy that in Jewish and Christian tradition has no parallel. (2) Because married love demands a lasting fidelity. As Yahweh covenanted with Israel, as Jesus covenanted with the Christian community, so today Lee and Jennifer covenant with each other, a solemn compact where each freely promises to be faithful to the other until death does them part. A breath-taking commitment, such that Yahweh and Jesus both take marriage as a superb symbol for the love they have for their people.

Jennifer and Lee, your covenant with each other is indeed something beautiful not only for God but for you. It is your privilege to see to it that your love for each other—your intimacy with each other, your fidelity each to the other, the friendship you claim "is one of the cornerstones of [your] relationship"—actually does resemble the kind of faithful love that marked and marks the God of Abraham, the Father of Jesus. For such is the love you discovered in Paul's letter to the Christians of Corinth, the love you had us proclaim to this assembly: patient and kind, not jealous or arrogant, never rude or self-seeking, not prone to anger or brooding over injuries, finding joy only in what is true. Such is God's love; such must be your love. Daily challenges to fidelity, to be scotch-taped to your refrigerator—and your TV.

III

Third, not only is today's marriage something beautiful for God, something beautiful for Jennifer and Lee. It is something beautiful for others. Obviously for all here gathered. Parents and grand-parents without whose very own love this day would never have dawned. Siblings and cousins who think "you're the greatest" since strawberry daiquiris. All manner of relatives and friends whose contribution to this day is recorded only by angels.

Still, the "others" I have in mind are a little world not gathered here. They are summed up in a passage from the prophet Isaiah, a challenge from the God of us all:

> Is not this the fast that I choose:
>   to loose the bonds of injustice,
>   to undo the thongs of the yoke,
> to let the oppressed go free,
>   and to break every yoke?
> Is it not to share your bread with the hungry,
>   and bring the homeless poor into your house;
> when you see the naked, to cover them,
>   and not to hide yourself from your own flesh?
> Then your light shall break forth like the dawn,
>   and your healing shall spring up quickly....
> Then you shall call, and the LORD will answer;
>   you shall cry for help, and He will say, Here I am.
>   (Isa 58:6–9)

My point is this: The recessional that will close this celebration, Mendelssohn's "Wedding March," is not primarily a prelude to a party. It is a movement to a whole little world somewhat hidden from Jennifer and Lee. I mean the world registered in *The State of America's Children Yearbook 1999*.[4] It is the world of forgotten children. In America the younger you are the poorer you are. In the next half hour "200 children will drop out of school; 45 children will be born into poverty; 16 children will be born at low birthweight; five children will be arrested for violent crime; and one child will be wounded by gunfire."[5] In the next half hour.

The most endangered species in America is not an owl in Arizona; it is our children. Among industrialized countries the

United States ranks first in the number of millionaires and billionaires, first in health technology, first in defense expenditures, but 18th in the gap between rich and poor children, 17th in efforts to lift children out of poverty, 18th in infant mortality, and last in protecting our children against gun violence.[6]

I have a dream. Something beautiful for America's children. I dream of a day when every newly married couple gifted with the good things of God's earth will see to it, in a personal way, that *one child* born into degrading poverty is able to rise from such squalor; or that *one child* with AIDS or a disability has the care he or she needs to lead a decent human life; or that *one child* with a learning problem finds a teacher to correct it; or that *one child* has prenatal care, is immunized, has enough to eat, lives in rat-free housing, gets health insurance. The needs are legion; but so are America's gifted newlyweds.

Lee and Jennifer, this is not to end on a negative note, not to cast a shadow over your celebration. Quite the contrary. You will rarely know a joy comparable to the joy you experience when the eyes of a child light up with hope because of you. I am aware of you as impressively compassionate. I know that this unique union you are about to fashion will prove to be something beautiful for God, for yourselves, and for those you know and love. I simply pray that the same love will prove to be something beautiful for an imperiled child of God not yet known to you—waiting for such as you to answer his or her unspoken cry for help, for love. It will not tear you away from your work, will not narrow the *National Geographic* or deenergize Energy Star. It will simply be your response to Yahweh's call to you through Isaiah "to let the oppressed go free" (Isa 58:6), your response to Jesus' plea, "Let the little children come to me" (Mt 19:14). Something beautiful for one child.

Jennifer and Lee, the hour has come. The moment for something beautiful: for God, for yourselves, for others. Something beautiful.

Pasadena, Maryland
June 5, 1999

32

EVERYONE WHO LOVES IS BORN OF GOD
Wedding Homily 3

- Song of Songs 2:8–10, 14, 16; 8:6–7
- 1 John 4:7–12
- John 15:9–12

If you were listening carefully to the three readings from Scripture, one word could not have escaped you. It was repeated so often, in such powerful contexts. A word so common in our culture, so often misused or mangled, that it has lost much of its meaning. The word is...*love*.

Then why have Kim and Mike chosen these readings for their wedding day? Because God's Book has given a fresh dimension to the word *love* and to the rich reality within it. The readings you heard tell us three crucial truths about love—truths that touch intimately the oneness that binds this dear couple, truths that should speak to all of us, but especially to the wedded among you. (1) The love that links Kim and Mike comes from God. (2) This love from God is seasoned by sadness and laughter. (3) This link of love should move them together to a still wider love for the less fortunate.

So then, sit back, but not too comfortably, and let a confirmed bachelor reveal what married love is about.

I

First, the love that links Mike and Kim comes from God. You heard the Song of Songs proclaim it: Not only is love "strong as death"; love is "a flame of the LORD" (Cant 8:6).[1] The fire of love is man and woman sharing in "the Lord's white-hot love."[2] You heard the First Letter of John proclaim it: "Love is from God; everyone who loves is born of God and knows God. Whoever does not love does not know God, for God is love" (1 Jn 4:7–8).

What does this mean? To love genuinely—the loving that is a gift of self, of one person to another—is to share in God's own love. In fact, the breathless way Kim and Mike love each other is possible only because God is Love. Not simply God loves; God *is* Love. Capital *L*. Love is God's very nature. God is the model without beginning for every love that has ever begun. For in the Trinity, in God One and Three, there is indeed I-and-Thou, distinct persons, Father, Son, and Holy Spirit; but never "mine-and-thine," those ice-cold words. But not a stagnant, motionless, inert nature. God's love is God in action. Listen again to John's letter: "God's love was revealed among us in this way: God sent His only Son into the world so that we might live through him. In this is love, not that we loved God but that He loved us and sent His Son to be the atoning sacrifice for our sins" (1 Jn 4:9–10).

Never has God's love been more powerfully revealed than on Calvary. God the Father gave His only Son to a cruel crucifixion. Because He loved us. And God's Son? "Greater love than this," Jesus declared, "no one has: to lay down life" itself for those you love (Jn 15:13). God's Son not only said it; he did it.

Mike and Kim know this; they want to love somewhat as God loves. But to love as God loves is not possible without God. Mike's wit and Kim's grit, his sharpness of mind and her unyielding courage, will not do it—unless God is part of it. Happily, the God who gave them their love as precious gift did not retire behind a cloud once they had discovered it. They know that the God who gave His own Son to a criminal's cross for love of them will not leave them to their own devices in the years ahead.

The proof? Today's ceremony. This is not merely a memorable Mass. Today's vows, a mutual self-giving for ever, shape what Catholics call a sacrament: a visible, audible sign of God present in two-made-one. Present today and present tomorrow. It is God's pledge that wherever Kim and Mike go, whatever they do, whenever their marriage poses problems, God will be there! Not always obvious; sometimes, to their dismay, a hidden God; but always there. There with His all-powerful grace, with His Holy Spirit, as light for their minds, strength for their wills. There with Jesus' flesh for their food, his blood for their drink, the Eucharist without which, Jesus declared, "you have no life in you" (Jn 6:53). There with his church— not some cold institution, but what St. Paul called the Body of Christ, a tightly-knit community wherein "If one member suffers, all suffer together with it; if one member is honored, all rejoice together with it" (1 Cor 12:26).

It takes more than two to make a marriage, to make it work, to make it last. The good news? The Second Letter of Paul to Timothy says it succinctly: "If we are faithless, [Christ] remains faithful—for he cannot deny himself" (2 Tim 2:13).

Yes indeed, true love is from God: Kim's love for Mike, Mike's love for Kim. From God yesterday, from God today, from God tomorrow.

II

Second, this love that is from God, this love that links Mike and Kim for ever, is seasoned, will be seasoned, by sadness and laughter. If their love was made in heaven, they must still live their love on this earth, with its satisfactions and its sorrows, its delights and its disappointments, its triumphs and its tragedies. They have already experienced this. I saw it with my own eyes one day in 1984. I was standing at a bedside in the Georgetown University Hospital. Kim, then a student at Mount Vernon College, lay there absorbing a bitter frustration. Dialysis had been her constant companion for weeks. A kidney for transplant had been found, joy unconfined. But then...further examination revealed a mismatch. The transplant had been canceled.

What amazed me was not Kim's inner strength, her power to endure. What amazed me, delighted me, was this young lady cheering up the downcast doctors, the downhearted nurses, consoling *them*, encouraging *them*, making *them* laugh. Laughter with her life in the balance.

Nor is Mike a stranger to all this. He first met Kim, almost a decade later, at a discussion on organ donation. At that time her health was again in peril; her kidney transplant was failing.

Mike's own sister was waiting for a transplant, and he was terribly concerned. Mike was with Kim when she underwent a last dialysis before her third kidney transplant. All this time, she confesses, "his incredible sense of humor kept me laughing a lot and constantly. His presence in my life at that time kept my mind off dialysis treatments and the wait for [still another] kidney." And both of them admit that Mike's struggle to discover where he was meant to serve God—in a lifelong, celibate union with Jesuits as unpredictable as I, or in a lifelong, total union with a lady as challenging as Kim—tested each of them, separated them, reunited them.

Yes, their lives have already been seasoned by sadness and laughter. For all its agonies, the experience is a promising prelude for the years to come. Kim's words are not only an inspiration to Mike; they should give new life to all of us:

> I know that my own future will be filled with many challenges related to my health, my work, and my family, but it strengthens me to know also that Michael will be there to love me, support me, and guide me. He challenges me to reach higher, demand better of others and myself, and to believe in myself. I expect that God has great plans for both of us. My hope is that we will always be there for each other, to listen and encourage. My prayer is for my own continued good health, a loving relationship with God throughout our life together, children if we are so blessed, and for an outlet or work for both of us where we can use our unique experiences to help others.

III

"Use our unique experiences to help others." These words suggest my third point: how the love that links Mike and Kim might touch a still wider world, the world of the less fortunate. The challenge comes from Christ himself; you heard it; Kim and Mike chose it: "This is my commandment: Love one another as I have loved you" (Jn 15:12). As Jesus loved: loved the leper banished from civilized society; loved the man possessed "howling and bruising himself with stones" (Mk 5:5); loved blind Bartimaeus begging to see again; loved the lady bleeding for 12 years; loved the people, his own people, who shouted "Crucify him!" Yes, loved the soldiers who nailed him to a bloody cross.

Here I focus on a singular segment of Jesus' love. I mean his stern admonition to his disciples, "Let the little children come to me, for it is to such as these that the kingdom of heaven belongs" (Mt 19:14). That sentence synthesizes a conviction of mine, a context, and a dream.

The conviction? The recessional at a wedding is not primarily the signal for a rapid rush to the reception. So here: Today's recessional, Beethoven's "Ode to Joy," should be more than a happy hike from Holy Trinity to the Halcyon House. It is symbolic. It represents a movement from church to world, from altar to people, from Christ crucified outside Jerusalem to Christ crucified at the crossroads of our cities.

The context? Children—our country's most endangered species. Statistics? Every day in America two of our young die from HIV infection; six commit suicide; 11 are homicide victims; 13 die from firearms; 36 die from accidents; 78 babies die; 237 children are arrested for violent crimes; 420 children are arrested for drug abuse; 1,353 babies are born without health insurance; 2,162 babies are born into poverty; 2,789 high school students drop out; 3,453 babies are born to unmarried mothers; 5,388 children are arrested.[3] Each day. In a nation that among industrialized countries ranks first in the number of millionaires and billionaires, first in health technology, first in defense expenditures, but 18th in the gap between rich and poor children, 17th in efforts to lift children out of poverty, 18th in infant mortality, and last in protecting our children against gun violence.[4]

The dream? I dream that every newly-married couple gifted with the good things of God's earth will see to it that one child born into abasing poverty can rise to human growing; or that *one child* has enough to eat, lives in rat-free housing, gets health insurance; or that *one child* will not die from very low birthweight or lack of prenatal care; or that *one child* does not drop out of school; or that *one child* crippled will get a wheel chair; or that *one child* with AIDS has the care needed to lead a decent human life; or that *one child* will not be punished because his parents are illegal immigrants; or that *one child* in desperate poverty will receive a kidney transplant. Yes, the needs are legion; but so are America's gifted newlyweds.

Here Kim and Mike enter the picture. Their backgrounds give uncommon promise: Mike with migrants and refugees, with international relief and development in Russia, Africa, and Asia; Kim with two decades of intimacy with dialysis and transplants, even her seven years keeping the U.S. Senate house in reasonably good working order.

Kim and Mike, this is not to put a damper on your own ode to joy. Quite the contrary. There is no emotion to compare with the joy of seeing your love light hope in the eyes of a child without a future. And the joy will be deepened, multiplied, if thousands upon thousands of couples like you focus each on one child. It can change the faces of America's children, change the face of America—from the home of the brave to the land of the truly free.

A love that comes from God; a love that has been seasoned by sadness and laughter; a love that promises hope to the hopeless. Dear Kim and Mike, the moment has come to seal that love in a sacrament—a sacred promise to God, to each other, and to a whole little world, a promise that guarantees God's own fidelity to all you are and all you do...for ever. For ever.

Holy Trinity Church
Washington, D.C.
June 19, 1999

33
WEDDED LOVE: SALT AND LIGHT
Wedding Homily 4

- Genesis 1:26–28, 31
- Romans 12:1–2, 9–13
- Matthew 5:13–16

A verse from the Hebrew Testament, from the Psalms, expresses what we all feel today:

> This is the day the LORD has made;
> let us be glad and rejoice therein.
> (Ps 118:24)

And we do rejoice. We are enraptured. We are still amazed at the miracle of it all: that Rumson should encounter Perth in Micronesia, that a man and a woman from two ends of the earth should meet somewhere in the middle and fall in love, that two minds, from D.C.'s Georgetown and the University of Western Australia, should run along similar paths.

Still, the very intensity of your joy may have kept you from realizing another reason for rapture. You see, the same God who has brought Andrew and Courtney together has just spoken to you. Not in a dream; not in a vision. In three passages from the only book God ever wrote. For as the Second Vatican Council declared so simply and so profoundly, "Jesus Christ is present in his word, since it is Christ himself who speaks when the holy Scriptures are read in the church."[1]

Three passages were proclaimed to you that not only reveal God's mind. They were chosen by Andrew and Courtney. Not at random, not thoughtlessly, but because they say something of supreme importance to this dear couple for their life together, for their lifelong love. And so, let's see what God has said to them, and what God might

181

be saying through them to you and me. God's word in a garden; God's word from an apostle; God's word from the lips of God's Son.

I

First, God's word in a garden. "And God said: 'Let us make humankind in our image, to our likeness'" (Gen 1:26). It blows the human mind. Think on it: Every single one of you is like God. Not God; like God. Not because you have Courtney's hazel eyes or Andrew's brown, a sparkling personality. Rather because you share two of God's own prerogatives: You have the power to know and the freedom to love.[2] The power to know, which in John's Gospel is never divorced from love; the power to love, a love that John's First Letter tells us "is from God" (1 Jn 4:7).

But, wonder of wonders, this imaginative God fashioned not one image of Himself, but two. "Male and female God created them" (v. 27). Similar yes, but not the same. Created Andrew not to shape Courtney in his own image, another Andrew; created Courtney not to shape Andrew in her own image, another Courtney. No. Each is to help shape the other more like God.

It's a breathtaking vocation, isn't it? It doesn't belittle your love for each other. On the contrary, it raises your love to a higher level, intensifies the power of your love, reveals what human love can do, what love is capable of doing. You see, no one of us can reflect all of God's wondrous beauty, all of God's incomparable love; for God *is* Love. What you are called to do is to reflect God's love each in your own way—as man, as woman. And, marvel of marvels, Courtney and Andrew, the more completely, the more selflessly, the more genuinely you love each other, the more deeply will you resemble God, and the more likely you are to help shape each other like God, help the other to love like God. I mean like the God who loved us so much that He gave His own Son to a crucifying cross for us.

I sense that Andrew and Courtney already know this. I sensed it from a short paragraph Courtney wrote me. She emphasized their oneness on important issues, but added with delightful humor:

> On a superficial level Andrew and I are quite different and play off each other nicely. In many respects he is the voice of reason while I am the more flighty one. He is a numbers guy, while I tend to be the one with general knowledge and the keeper of random fast facts. He's the tidy one, while my messy tendencies have reached legendary status (this is a fact my mother would be

all too happy to verify). I enjoy cooking and look forward to bettering my skills—the day Andrew learns to make toast will be one for the history books. He considers himself the more independent type and has no problems venturing out on his own; I thrive in more social situations. We do have very different interests and because of this we help to expand each other's world little by little each day. All these things manage to spice up our day-to-day life together....

"We help to expand each other's world little by little each day." I find this appraisal fascinating, and not superficial at all. It suggests vividly that Courtney and Andrew will let each other, even help each other, mirror the same God in different ways.

II

Now God's word in Genesis, thrillingly true, is somewhat abstract. To bring their imaging of God from the Garden of Eden to the Garden State, from the apple in Eden to the Big Apple, from outer space to "down under," Courtney and Andrew have borrowed from the apostle to the nations. You heard St. Paul urging you, "Let [your] love be genuine," without hypocrisy. He tells you to "hate what is evil, hold fast to what is good" (Rom 12:9). But he doesn't leave it vague. He has told you not to model yourselves on the behavior of the world around you. Not that all of American and Australian culture is evil; only that some of it is. Americans among you might remember Lee Atwater, who almost singlehandedly turned the Bush campaign around in '88. Dying of a brain tumor at 40, he confessed:

> The 80's were about acquiring—acquiring wealth, power, prestige. I know. I acquired more wealth, power and prestige than most. But you can acquire all you want and still feel empty. What power wouldn't I trade for a little more time with my family! What price wouldn't I pay for an evening with friends!
>
> It took a deadly illness to put me eye to eye with that truth, but it is a truth that the country, caught up in its ruthless ambitions and moral decay, can learn on my dime. I don't know who will lead us through the 90's, but they must be made to speak to this spiritual vacuum at the heart of American society, this tumor of the soul.[3]

I dare not speak as an expert on Australia. I have experienced the macho male; the racism that confronts the Asian and the Aboriginal; discrimination in housing and employment among ethnic populations; a fair dose of the materialism and consumerism John Paul II has assailed; spousal abuse, drug addiction, teenage suicides.

Who will lead us, if not through the 90s, then into the next millennium? Our dear couple has answered that, has told us through the Gospel they selected, the Gospel that was just now proclaimed to you.

III

To cap St. Paul, Andrew and Courtney chose a breathtaking Gospel: "You are the salt of the earth. You are the light of the world" (Mt 5:13–14). Now Jesus was not pulling two lovely images, salt and light, out of the air. In his Palestine, before refrigerators, salt was a must—to keep meat and fish from corrupting, from rotting, even to improve their taste. And in the one-room cottage of the Oriental peasant, only the common clay oil lamp allowed Jesus to read the Torah once the sun had set, see his mother and his disciples, walk with sure foot and light heart.

You, Andrew and Courtney, are to be salt to your little earth. What Jesus is telling you is that on such as you this world depends for its moral well-being. I dare not predict where the Christ who links you today will lead you, precisely where and how you are to spread your salt. I do hope and pray that, through your influence on the business world that engages you, the economy will serve people, not people the economy. Perhaps even more importantly, I hope and pray that you will be graced to further a fond dream of mine. It is a dream for America's children.

It is one aspect of inhuman living where disciples of Jesus have a frightening task, where you can make a difference. In this "land of the free," where one of every five children grows up in a poverty that mangles minds and brutalizes bodies; where federal officials delight to tell us that in 1998 *only one of every ten* teenagers used cocaine, marijuana, or other illegal drugs;[4] where guns have turned schools into death camps; where each night a million runaway youngsters sleep on our streets; where each year 12,000 boys and girls flee to a New York Covenant House from pimps and prostitution; where children suffer from a 50-percent divorce rate—such as you must be the salt that slows or stops the corruption.

I look forward to a day when each Christian family blessed with a fair portion of this world's goods, stimulated by the blood of Christ coursing through their veins, will take care of just a single one of Jesus' troubled little ones. A wheelchair or an operation, a drug problem or an education, release from abuse or freedom from hunger, a shoulder to rest on or a story to sleep on. The needs are endless.

You know, it would change our country, miracle the millennium. Each of these children is an image of God. Each is a living plea to us from the Jesus who urged us, "Let the little children come to me, and do not stop them; for it is to such as these that the kingdom of heaven belongs" (Mt 19:14).

When you waltz from this church to the strains of Handel's *Water Music,* your graceful movement will be taking you beyond a loving, laughing, liquid reception. A Catholic recessional, you see, is a movement from church to world, from altar to people, from Christ crucified on Calvary to Christ crucified at the crossroads of your two countries.

And you, Courtney and Andrew, can indeed be light to this shadowland of children that surrounds you. God has gifted you beyond your deserving: parents without whose love and sacrifice this day would never have dawned; siblings who for some reason think you're the greatest since sliced bread; keen minds that have been opened to deep ideas and far places; hearts made aware of the poor and suffering here and abroad; a living faith energized by the body and blood of the risen Christ. These gifts of knowledge and love are given not to be clutched possessively but to be shared profusely. This much I can promise you: Your love for each other will touch new heights each time you see your love bringing heartening hope into the empty eyes of a little image of Jesus.

Come then, Andrew and Courtney, and in this graced moment proclaim your lasting yes to each other, to your God, and to a small world of God's images yearning for new life from your love.

Holy Cross Church
Rumson, New Jersey
August 28, 1999

34
A LOVE THAT REACHES OUT
Wedding Homily 5

- Song of Songs 2:8–10, 14, 16a; 8:6–7a
- 1 Corinthians 12:31–13:8a
- John 15:9–12

During the last quarter hour something startling happened here. In your excitement over a lovely bride and a reasonably handsome groom, you may not have heard it. What happened? God spoke to us. Yes, God spoke to all of us. How? Through the only book God ever wrote; we call it "the Word of the Lord." God spoke to us through three messages: (1) from a man and a woman in love, (2) from an apostle who brought love down to earth; (3) from God's own Son commanding us to love as he loved.

I

First, God's message from a man and a woman in love. From the Song of Songs only a small selection was proclaimed to you. A romantic selection: "My beloved says to me, 'Arise, my love, my fair one, and come away'" (Cant 2:10); "Many waters cannot quench love, neither can floods drown it" (8:7a). But you heard none of the startlingly sexual passages, which a generation ago would have been "banned in Boston." How did such an explicitly sexual set of love poems ever get into Scripture, into the Bible?

The last verse read to you says it all. You may have missed it: "Love is a flame of the Lord" (8:6b). God is telling us a profound truth that many a Christian has missed across the centuries: Human sexual love is not something to be ashamed of. The intimate love between husband and wife is a sharing in God's love: "The fire of love is a fire of Yahweh, a participation in the Lord's white-hot love."[1]

186

Not the one-night stand; not the sheerly physical attraction and casual coupling that get high Nielsen ratings on TV. No. The genuine love that links a man and a woman such as Cynthia and Matt—the kind of love that reaches to the depths of their being, that links hearts as well as bodies, spirits as well as flesh, the whole person seen and unseen.

A sharing in God's own love. What can that mean? God loves with God's whole self. So much so that the First Letter of John can declare, "God *is* Love" (1 Jn 4:8). Love is God's name. Love is what God is. Not has; is. Not only today or tomorrow; always. Loves us even when we forget God, sin against God, even deny God.

Such is the love in which we share. We cannot love with the fulness of God; only God can love that much. But our own love can be like God's—more and more like God's the more selfless, the more total, the more passionate our love.

Cynthia and Matt: Scotch-tape to your refrigerator that swift sentence from the Song of Songs: "Love is a flame of the LORD." Your love for each other. A flame from God's own love.

II

But the love that is so sensual in the Song of Songs is not all there is to love. The passage from Paul lifts love to our minds and hearts. He begins by waxing rhapsodic over love. Put what you heard into today's language. If I can preach with the passion of Martin Luther King, sing with the power of Pavarotti, but do not love, I am making nothing but noise. If I can predict what will happen in 2000, understand what the Trinity is all about, have the kind of faith that moves the Rocky Mountains, but do not love, I am a cipher, zero, nothing; I don't exist. If I give away all I possess to feed the hungry, if after all this I give my body to be burned (in Paul's time "the most horrible of deaths"[2]), but do not love, I gain nothing.

Then Paul gets very practical. "Love is patient, kind; love is not envious or boastful, arrogant or rude; love does not insist on its own way, is not irritable or resentful; love rejoices in the truth; love endures everything" (1 Cor 13:4–7). That's love. But what about lovers? What happens when you live in the same house for five to fifty years, eat together, talk together, sleep together, watch TV together, have different sets of friends, disagree on politics, cannot agree on Monday Night Football or National Public Radio? Not easy, especially in the close quarters of marriage, when the little things become major crises, as can happen, I assure you, even in Jesuit communities.

The solution? Not primarily from the psychiatrist's couch, much as I esteem it. The kind of love St. Paul commends can only endure if God is an intimate part of your life together. I say this not because it's a line you expect of a priest. God's own Son made this clear:

> Remain in me as I remain in you. Just as a branch cannot bear fruit by itself without remaining on the vine, so neither can you bear fruit without remaining in me. I am the vine; you are the branches. He who remains in me and I in him is the one who bears much fruit, for apart from me you can do nothing.
>
> (Jn 15:4-5)

Oh yes, there is much you can do apart from Jesus. Without Jesus you can gorge on a pizza, broker a business deal, have a stimulating sex life, sin to your heart's content. What is impossible apart from Jesus is the kind of love that "bears all things, believes all things, hopes all things, endures all things" (1 Cor 13:7). The kind of love that makes for golden anniversaries.

That is why Matt and Cynthia vow their love in the context of a Eucharist. This is not simply a lovely setting for a wedding. They promise lifelong love here because the Eucharist is the most powerful source of God's grace we have: Jesus present as you gather in his name, Jesus present in his word proclaimed to you, Jesus present within you in what looks like bread, feels like bread, tastes like bread, but is not bread—is Jesus himself within you, body and blood, soul and divinity.

Here is the food for your journey together, what Jesus called "the bread of life" (Jn 6:35, 48), the bread of which he said, "Let me firmly assure you, if you do not eat [my] flesh and drink [my] blood, you have no life in you" (v. 53)—you are not alive with God's own life. Here is your strength when the clouds gather, when the going gets tough, when sickness sets in or boredom, when human frailty threatens to destroy love. The one same Christ within both of you, now and for ever.

III

What brings love to its most sublime heights? The words of Jesus, "This is my commandment: Love one another as I have loved you" (Jn 15:12). Jesus went on to indicate what this might mean in the concrete: "Greater love than this no one has, to lay down his life for those he loves" (v. 13). Precisely what Jesus did: It was the supreme sacrifice of his life, his death on a cross. Not only for those who loved him. St. Paul expressed it powerfully: "...perhaps for a good person someone might actually dare to die. But God proves His love for us in that while we still were sinners Christ died for us" (Rom 5:7-8). For all of us.

Such, Cynthia and Matt, is the ultimate in love God sets before you. It is not likely that either of you will be called to die for the other. The paradox in marriage is this: The more difficult command may well be to *live* for the one you love. Dying can come swiftly; living for the other is a lifelong task.

In that context, Jesus' first command to you is: Live for each other. It does not mean that Matt forgets himself, doesn't develop his own talents for business, his own likeness to God. It does not mean that Cynthia fades into the background, walks a step behind Matt wherever he goes, fuses her personality with his. Each of you has as an ideal to help the other become more like God—Matt in his way, Cynthia in her way.

Cynthia and Matt, one splendid way of doing this is for you to live together *for others*. As Jesus did. You see, unless your love for each other expands beyond your two selves, unless your love for each other moves out to, touches, the earth you walk and the people who surround you, it risks its own death.

You two are richly gifted: parents without whose love this day would never have dawned; siblings who for some reason think you're "the greatest" since strawberry daiquiris; education at Georgetown and Richmond beyond the reach of millions; work that pleasures you; a faith that strengthens you, a hope that extends beyond the grave, a love that reaches out beyond your love for each other.

A love that reaches out—there's the key verb. For these gifts, of nature and of grace, are given you not to be clutched possessively; they are given to be shared generously. Let me share with you a dream of mine.

Never far from you will be a whole little world most of us read about but never actually touch. I mean the world that is America's children. I mean specifically the children at risk. In the richest nation on earth, one of every five children grows up below the poverty line. Not the genteel poverty of the child Jesus in Nazareth. No. The kind of poverty that mangles minds and bruises bodies; the kind of poverty that kills.

In America the younger you are the more vulnerable you are. Every 40 seconds a child is born into poverty. Every minute a child is born without health insurance. Every two minutes a baby is born less than five pounds, eight ounces. Every three minutes a child is arrested for drug abuse. Every six minutes a child is arrested for a violent crime. Every 18 minutes a baby dies. Every two hours a child or youth under 20 is killed by a firearm. Every four hours a child or youth under 20 commits suicide. Every 11 hours a child or youth under 25 dies from HIV infection.

Among industrialized countries, America is first in military technology, in military exports, in defense expenditures, in millionaires and billionaires, in health technology, but 17th in efforts to lift children out of poverty, 18th in infant mortality, last in protecting our children against gun violence.[3] As our country has grown richer, its children have grown poorer.[4]

My dream? I dream of the day when every married couple gifted by God with a fair share of this world's goods will reach out to one child at risk—one child. It might be a wheel chair or the cost of child care; it might be teaching a child to read or offering a shoulder for rest. It might even be participation in World Share: $15 a month for poor families, and two hours a month of community service.[5] It could change the face of America. And in the process, through your love for these children, your love for each other and for your own children would be immeasurably intensified. For this is to love as Jesus loved.

Come then, Cynthia and Matt, join your hands and your hearts in a wondrous promise of love: love for each other, love for the one Christ within you, love for the bruised little images of God that will surround you.

Our Lady of Mount Carmel Church
Asbury Park, New Jersey
September 18, 1999

35

A LOVE THAT HUNGERS FOR JUSTICE
Wedding Homily 6

- Song of Songs 2:8–10, 14, 16a; 8:6–7a
- 1 Corinthians 12:31–13:8a
- Matthew 5:1–12a

For sheer joy, it's hard to outshine a wedding. Joy over a man and a woman in love, a man and a woman we love. But in our joy we might have overlooked someone else in this gathering. In focusing, as we should, on the way Kim and Joe speak to us in their love, we might not have listened carefully to another voice: I mean Christ our Lord speaking to us when the Scriptures were read to us. You see, the three selections from Scripture proclaimed to you are not just another regulation from Rome. They were chosen by Joe and Kim because each of these passages from the only book God ever wrote is meaningful to their marriage. So then, let me talk a bit about the significance of God's Word for the precious love we celebrate today. Three realities about love, especially the love that links a man and woman together for life.

I

First, a basic reality. You heard the Apostle Paul; listen to him once more, even more intently. "If I speak in the tongues of mortals and of angels, but do not have love, I am a noisy gong or a clanging cymbal. And if I have prophetic powers, and understand all mysteries and all knowledge, and if I have all faith, so as to remove mountains, but do not have love, I am nothing. If I give away all my possessions, and if I hand over my body to be burned, but do not have love, I gain nothing" (1 Cor 13:1–3).

Not just a pretty piece of poetry. Put that paragraph in today's language, and let it sink in. If I have the extraordinary eloquence, the silken syllables, the rolling thunder of Martin Luther King ("I Have a Dream"), but do not have love, I am nothing more than a pair of brass plates clanging together to make a noise. If I can see what America will be like in 2500, if I can unveil the mysteries of the human brain, if my faith is strong enough to move the Rocky Mountains to Chicago, but do not have love, I am nothing, a nonentity, a cipher, zero; I don't exist. If I give away more billions than Bill Gates ever dreamed of having, if I give away my very body for whatever science wants to do with it, but do not have love, it profits me nothing; it is of no use to me, it does me no good whatsoever.

Today we celebrate love, love incarnate in Kim and Joe. The kind of love the Hebrew Song of Songs extols. Yes, the Song of Songs is sensuous, is even erotic, because it's the whole person, spirit in flesh, that gives itself. It's what the prophet Jeremiah called "the voice of mirth and the voice of gladness, the voice of the bridegroom and the voice of the bride, the voices of those who sing, as they bring thank offerings to the house of the Lord" (Jer 33:11). All-important here is God's word near the end of the Song, "Love is a flame of the Lord" (Cant 8:6b); genuine love between lover and beloved is a sharing in God's own white-hot love.[1]

Such, Joe and Kim, such is the wondrous love that flames between you. It stems from God. Some call it chance, but I prefer to see God's grace guiding your steps from Milwaukee and Michigan, from Menomonee Falls and Southfield, into Chicago. It was God's grace that brought brown eyes and blue together in an elevator, in a laundry room, at the breaking of the bread in St. Clement's, in the marathon brunches at Max's Deli. It was God's grace that pervaded your lengthy conversations and (a Whelan miracle) the occasional silences. It was God's grace that struck the proverbial Irish bachelor in the Grotto at Notre Dame, finally extracted from him that long-overdue proposal, "Will you?" Joe may very well be right when he writes: "The way I figure it now is that a loving and persistent God saw that Kim was in my presence—and I in hers—on a number of occasions and that, eventually, she would appear on my radar screen. Thanks to the grace and good work of the Holy Spirit, along came one of those epiphanies and I saw the light where Kim was concerned."

II

Yes, the love of Kim and Joe is indeed a flame of the Lord, a sharing in God's own love. Still, a problem remains. Strangely enough, the problem is love itself. It isn't easy for one man and one woman to live together "until death do [them] part." When St. Paul wrote, "Love is patient, is kind, is not envious or boastful, not arrogant or rude, not irritable or resentful, does not insist on its own way, endures all things" (1 Cor 13:4–7), he wasn't writing in a vacuum, empty space. Genuine love is a tough love; romance clashes with reality, courtship with routine. Is it any wonder that half the marriages in America do not endure till death?

If you want to see why, cast a critical eye on TV's early-afternoon "soaps." If "The Bold and the Beautiful," "The Young and the Restless," "One Life to Live" reflect marriage, family life, in America, we are in deep trouble. Communication? No one listens. Voices are raised together to the boiling point; shoulders are shrugged and backs are turned; with a stinging retort he or she bursts from the room in angry triumph.

For a love that lasts, let me focus on one phrase from Paul, "Love does not insist on its own way." An important phrase for a reason little known, a reason we theologians cherish. You see, though God fashioned the first man and the first woman in the image of God, shaped each like God, He made man and woman similar but not the same; like each other but not identical. Each was to mirror God, reveal something of God, but each in his and her own way, man in his way, woman in hers.

Let me turn concrete. Listen to Kim: "One of Joe's personality traits that I deeply respect is his commitment to things in which he believes. His defense of things he holds dear is sometimes mind-boggling. From the Democratic Party to the proper way to shake a martini, his perseverance is always evident. I tend to avoid conflict and sometimes may acquiesce to preserve peace."

All well and good. But If Joe were to insist on his way only, his way always, he would be shaping Kim in *his* image, not in God's. Joe's God-given task is to help Kim mirror God in her own way: the way she thinks, the way she feels, the way she loves. And Kim's God-given task is to help Joe mirror God in his own way: the way he thinks, the way he feels, the way he loves. Not always to agree; but by calm disagreement, by respectful sharing, often they will learn from each other, improve through the other. Not anxious to win, only that both may grow, develop, as persons: in their own right, their own way. Similar but not the same. Through love each of you is to become more like God. Not more and more like each other; more and more like God. Such is the profound meaning of marriage. Two become one so that the more dearly you love each other, the more deeply will each of you resemble God.

For that to happen, you have to listen. To listen, to really listen, is a difficult art. Most conversations are not conversations at all. I keep silent (because civility demands it) till you have finished; then I say exactly what I would have said if you had not spoken at all. No. For that moment or hour I give to you not only my ears but my whole self, eager to understand, hoping to learn. Here is respect at its highest; here is genuine love. Here is a love that promises to last.

III

A third reality. The love of Joe and Kim has to be lived not in paradise, not in outer space, not on some desert island, but on planet Earth. A planet where unceasingly love struggles with hate, abundance with hunger, power with weakness, sanctity with sin, peace with war, gentleness with violence—where death never takes a holiday. Concretely, right now their love plays in Chicago. And much as I admire Chicago, I cannot forget a sentence from a sermon by a Lutheran theologian from this city: "Absolutely according to man's decision the city can become a theatre of grace in which humanity can be richly realized, or it can become a humanly intolerable hell, a stifling intersection of procedures for industrial convenience and, in Chicago's instance, conventioneers' frivolity."[2]

What has all this to do with your love? Listen to an experienced woman psychologist:

> A love that is not for more than itself will die—the wisdom of Christian tradition and the best we know from psychology both assure us of this truth. It is often very appropriate at the early stages of a relationship that the energy of romance and infatuation exclude the larger world from our vision. But over the long haul an intimate relationship...which doesn't reach outward will stagnate.[3]

I am not concerned today with romance or infatuation. I do rejoice that the love of Kim and Joe is actually reaching outward. I am delighted that they chose for their Gospel the Beatitudes in Matthew from the lips of Jesus. Especially one Beatitude: "Blessed are those who hunger and thirst for justice" (Mt 5:6). Not the justice that is vengeance, but the biblical justice that includes loving every human person, every child, as an image of God, like another self. Let me tell you why I rejoice.

Last week Senator Bill Bradley told the Democratic convention that if all the 13.5 million poor children in America were gathered in one place, they would form a city bigger than New York—and "we would then see child poverty as the slow-motion national disaster that it is." Editorialized the *New York Times:* "It was a reminder to affluent Americans of their moral obligation to do something about America's 'ill-fed, ill-used and ill-educated' children. 'If we don't end child poverty in our lifetime,' Mr. Bradley said, 'shame on me, shame on you, shame on all of us.'"[4]

I am aware that your governor has highlighted a study that shows Illinois' child-poverty rates to be among the five lowest in the nation.[5] And yet, figures from the U.S. Census Bureau for 1998 (the latest figures available) reveal that in Illinois 13.5 percent of the children were living in poverty: 472,287 children.[6]

In that context, I am impressed by Kim the pediatrician, who begins her day at Northwestern's Prentice Hospital examining newborn babies, then spends a full day seeing patients, is on call several nights a week listening to parents of sick children, advising them on earaches and fevers, on broken limbs and concussions, on gastrointestinal maladies and whatever. A poor child is as precious to her as the prosperous.

And Joe? This eloquent son of St. Patrick has written powerfully for others—ghost writer extraordinary; clients will testify to that, from the New York Stock Exchange to a scoundrel or two. I resonate to his deeper yearning: to write something on his own—as he expresses it, "something that actually matters." Given his hunger and thirst for justice, I would love to see him focus on human-interest stories from his vast experience and Kim's, stories that might awaken Chicagoans to the plight of their poor, the injustices to their immigrant children, physical and sexual abuse of God's little ones, perhaps even a personal in-depth series on politics in the city that the original Mayor Daley declared "must rise to higher and higher platitudes."

Much of your future is hidden from your eyes. *Not* hidden is a thrilling newness that should overshadow whatever you do: From this day forward, neither of you will act in isolation from the other. Each of you still your own person, but Joe in every child Kim touches with love, Kim in every word Joe crafts from a computer. And always there, binding your hands and hearts together, will be the Christ who is ceaselessly shaping you in his own likeness.

Kim and Joe, you have been generously gifted: loving parents without whom this day would never have dawned; siblings, relatives, and friends who think you're "the greatest" since sliced bread; exciting education in Rockne land; a shared faith within a church you treasure; the body and blood of God's own Son to seal your love today and nourish it through the years ahead. Rich reasons for gratitude—gratitude you express beyond comparison in this Eucharist which literally means "thanksgiving."

Come then, Joe and Kim, and in the presence of God and God's community, in a sacrament crafted by Christ for such love as yours, murmur those sacred syllables that will link your lives for life.

St. Clement's Church
Chicago, Illinois
August 26, 2000

MEDLEY

36
NOT TO BE SERVED BUT TO SERVE
Thirty-fifth Anniversary of an Ordination

- Acts 2:1–11
- 1 Corinthians 12:3b–7,12–13
- John 20:19–23

Pentecost Sunday. A splendid day to talk about priesthood.[1] For our first Pentecost was the day on which the Holy Spirit promised by Jesus descended upon the first Christian community, touched not only their tongues but their whole being, transformed them from fearful folk into such confident, enthusiastic, charismatic Christians that some of the "devout Jews from every nation under heaven living in Jerusalem" were convinced that at nine in the morning these strange people were drunk.

Priesthood. Father Concannon has forbidden me to focus on him. A splendid restraining order, for it allows me to stress three priesthoods intimately related: the priesthood of Jesus, the priesthood of all the faithful, and the priesthood of the ordained. Still, no promise of mine can prevent you from touching what I say about priesthood to a particular priest, trying to grasp what has kept him so priestly a priest for 35 years.

I

First, the priesthood of Jesus. Why? Because it is the priesthood of Jesus Father Concannon is privileged to share, is vowed to continue. Here let me concentrate on the New Testament Letter to the Hebrews.[2] The central idea? Jesus is the high priest of the New Covenant, *the* priest we priests must resemble but can never reproduce. His priesthood began when the Son of God came to earth wearing our flesh. Then it was, we read, "The LORD has sworn and

199

will not change His mind, 'You are a priest for ever'" (Heb 7:21). For ever, "because he continues for ever. Consequently he is able for all time to save those who approach God through him, since he always lives to make intercession for them" (vv. 24–25). He lives to intercede with his Father for us.

Not only that: "it was fitting that we should have such a high priest, holy, blameless, undefiled, separated from sinners, and exalted above the heavens. Unlike the other high priests, he has no need to offer sacrifices day after day, first for his own sins, and then for those of the people; this he did once for all when he offered himself" (vv. 26–27). One sacrifice: Calvary.

Sinless yes, but marvelous to relate, "we do not have a high priest who is unable to sympathize with our weaknesses, but we have one who in every respect has been tested as we are.... Although he was a Son, he learned obedience through what he suffered, and having been made perfect, he became the source of eternal salvation for all who obey him" (Heb 4:15; 5:8–9).

And the mission of Jesus the priest? He summed it up in the synagogue of his native Nazareth: "The Spirit of the Lord is upon me; for [the Lord] has anointed me, has sent me to preach good news to the poor, to proclaim release for prisoners and sight for the blind, to send the downtrodden away relieved" (Lk 4:18). The all-important words? "The Spirit of the Lord is upon me." The Holy Spirit.

Think of *this* Jesus! A priest then, right now, and for ever; a priest who was born for others, for us; a priest who learned from experience on earth what it means to wear our weakness; a priest who offered himself on a criminal's cross for every human being from Adam to the last antichrist; a priest whose very presence at this moment with his Father is a living, ceaseless prayer for you and me, for our salvation; a priest who is our one and only *Savior,* our unique way to God. Such was, such is, the priesthood of Jesus Christ.

II

Turn now to the priesthood of all the faithful. I much fear, good friends, that too few of our laity have taken to heart the remarkable sentence in the First Letter of Peter: "You are a chosen race, a royal priesthood, a holy nation, God's own people, in order that you may proclaim the mighty acts of Him who called you out of darkness into His marvelous light" (1 Pet 2:9).

Twenty-eight years ago, an unpublished report on a theology of priesthood included this pithy paragraph highly important for all of you:

> The Church, as a people, witnesses to the Word by proclaiming faith in the Lordship of Jesus *(kerygma)*, manifests itself to the world as a community of unity and charity *(koinonia)*, positively relates to the world in terms of service *(diakonia)*, and worships God by offering the sacrifice of praise and thanks *(eucharistia)*.[3]

Offering the sacrifice of praise and thanks. Never forget what the ordained priest says at the Offertory: "Blessed are you, Lord, God of all creation. Through your goodness we have this bread to offer...we have this wine to offer." As the bishops declared at Vatican II, "the faithful join in the offering of the Eucharist by virtue of their royal priesthood."[4] As early Fathers of the Church put it, "The Church is the 'we' of Christians."

The whole Church does this; the whole Church is a priestly people. We are one common enterprise, with a common mission and many ministries. Such is the universal priesthood of all the faithful. All of us are called to continue the saving work of Christ, each with his or her calling, his or her charism, his or her competence. Christian ministry is a shared responsibility. There is no one of you who is not, in a genuine sense, a minister of the gospel.[5] Vatican II itself, in its Constitution on the Church, tells us that "the Church as a whole, including the laity, has a total task which may suitably be summarized under the three captions of witness, ministry, and fellowship."[6]

By what power are you enabled to exercise this priesthood? By the Power that is the Holy Spirit, "because God's love has been poured into [your] hearts through the Holy Spirit that has been given to [you]" (Rom 5:5).

III

Turn now to the ordained priest. A natural turn, for ordination should not separate us from the rest of the faithful, is not a God-given Oscar for brilliance in theology. Ordination is a summons to service; and under God, it is you we are ordained to serve. Not easy, if only because you are who you are and we are who we are. You may be "a chosen race, God's holy people," but you are not a monolith, a single rigid entity. You have your likes and dislikes, your passions and prejudices, from the position of the altar and the greeting of peace to divorce and the ordination of women.

And we? We priests were not prefabricated in a factory. We are all the colors of the rainbow, speak different languages. We represent all types of personality: extroverts and introverts, thinkers and doers, spontaneous and deliberate. We share the faults of sinful humans, can be as small as the next man. We get discouraged when we do not live up to our ideals and your expectations. We get frustrated when our plans for you do not materialize. We are saddened when our homilies leave you cold, light up like a Christmas tree when we delight you. We get lonely for friendship, for love, find aging hard to enjoy alone.

And yet, despite the downside, surmounting all that discourages, we are in love. We love the Church. I don't mean the building, lovely as it is. I mean God's people; I mean the men, women, and children God has entrusted to our care; I mean you. I mean the devout among you and the lukewarm; those who love us and those who couldn't care less; the haves and the have-nots; the strict and the not-so-strict; the young, the middle-aged, and the elderly. We have given up experiences that are wonderfully attractive: marital intimacy, children and grandchildren, a career—only because the sacrifice can open us up to a larger world, to ever so many more of you.

Where do we find our joy? In celebrating, in sharing with you the Word of life and the Bread of life, in pouring saving waters on the heads of your little ones, in conveying to you God's own forgiveness, in witnessing to the love you share in marriage, in praying with you as you prepare to meet your Lord and Savior. Like Jesus, we try to "deal gently" with you, because, like Jesus, we too are "subject to weakness" (Heb 5:2).

To us, each of you is precious, a child of God, an image of Jesus. We love especially those of you who are struggling, so many discouraged, so many who have experienced tragedy. We try to love you as Jesus does. We fail at times, but we never stop trying. For our trust is not in ourselves, in our naked humanness; our trust is in the Holy Spirit who orchestrated our ordination, the Spirit whose gifts, St. Paul assures us, are "love, joy, peace, patience, kindness, generosity, faithfulness, gentleness, and self-control" (Gal 5:22–23).

We love you because "all of us were baptized into one body...and we were all made to drink of one Spirit" (1 Cor 12:13). All of us together make up the Body of Christ, wherein no one can say to any other, "I have no need of you" (v. 21). We love you most dearly in the center and focus of our worship, the Eucharist. For, as a remarkable priest marveled back in 1981,

> Where else in our society are we all addressed and sprinkled and bowed to and incensed and touched and kissed and treated like *somebody*—all in the very same way? Where else do economic czars and beggars get the same treatment? Where else are food and drink blessed in a common prayer of thanksgiving, broken and poured out, so that everybody, *everybody* shares and shares alike?[7]

Fifty-eight years a priest, I still stand in awe at the altar, in astonishment before such as you. And I still weep when I read that only 30 percent of Catholics in our country share this experience Sunday after Sunday.

Fifty-eight years a priest, I presume to play a bit loose with my promise to Father Concannon. I suggest that at this moment, as the Holy Spirit once again fills the entire house in which we are gathered, we stand together for one brief moment. Why? To give thanks. In the silence of our hearts, express our gratitude to the gracious God who for 35 years has gifted our church, your diocese, all of you and more, with a priest who, like Jesus, "came not to be served but to serve, and to give his life" so that others might "have life," God's life, and "have it in overflowing fulness" (Mt 20:28; Jn 10:10).

Father Concannon, may the Holy Spirit who filled the original Christian community with such infectious enthusiasm continue to intoxicate you and the people so dear to you for rich years to come.

St. Charles Borromeo Church
Brunswick, Maine
May 23, 1999

37
WORKERS OF THE WORLD, UNITE!
Labor Day Homily

- Genesis 1:26–2:3
- 1 Thessalonians 3:6–12
- Matthew 6:31–34

Labor Day has a humorous aspect: Labor Day is a day on which most of us do not labor. Still, each Labor Day raises a problem about labor, about work. A problem in a special way for Christians, because work touches us to God's creation, to our sinfulness, to our redemption in Christ, to the development of God's kingdom.[1] A homily is not a lecture, not a theological treatise, not a history. A homily should touch God's Word to your life. So then, let me suggest three aspects of work that might stimulate your thinking, perhaps enrich your living. Very simply, (1) the Catholic ideal; (2) the harsh reality; (3) the challenge to us.

I

First, the Catholic ideal. How does the best of Catholic tradition, of Catholic reflection, look on labor, on work? It goes back to the Creator we will shortly confess in our Creed, "Maker of heaven and earth, of things visible and invisible." The Creator who on the sixth day of creation "looked on everything He had made, and indeed it was very good" (Gen 1:31). And then "God rested from all the work that He had done" (Gen 2:2).

But that was not the end of creation. God had something thrilling in mind for us. It harks back to the sixth day of creation: "God said, 'Let us make humankind in our image, according to our likeness'" (v. 26). Ever since then, each human person comes into this world like God. Not God; like God. Sharing at least two of God's precious prerogatives: We have the power to know, and we have the freedom to love.[2]

It is in this context that our faith unfolds God's ideal for us in our work. Work is not just a way to make a living. It is that, but it is more. In God's plan, by our work we who have been fashioned like God are to continue what God has begun, become cocreators with God in shaping this world the way God wants it shaped. A fine theologian summed it up shrewdly: "We are not merely stewards working for an absent landlord. Our God is working...and inviting us to join in that work."[3] Technology is not God's rival. At its best, technology images God's own creative power. We humans, by God's gifts to us, make the things of God build up God's world, help men and women become more human, more like God.[4] Not the slaves of the machine; its master, under God.

Wonder of wonders, our role as cocreators goes profoundly deeper than the six days of creation. It goes back to God's own Son in our flesh, the Jesus whose own work was living and dying for us. Everything he did had one purpose: to destroy the hostility sin had created between us and God, between us and our sisters and brothers, between us and the earth that sustains us. And the work his Father had given him to do, that work he said "is finished"—finished on a cross (Jn 20:30). But not our work. It is now our task, our burden, our privilege, with God's grace, to make Christ's redeeming work, his will for the world, a reality in our time. It is ours to move God's reign over the world closer to the moment when Christ will return to present his kingdom to his Father. It is our task, as Vatican II phrased it, "to penetrate and perfect the temporal sphere with the spirit of the gospel."[5]

God's images on earth, cocreators with God, disciples of Jesus in transforming our earth—such is the dignity of work, the worth of our work, in God's eyes. And our dignity as workers as well. Hence the right of each worker to be treated with respect, as a person and not a cog in an impersonal economy. The right to a fair wage, a living wage, a family wage. The right to safe, healthy working conditions. The right to freely form and freely join labor unions, the right to participate in decisions that affect your life and your livelihood.

II

Such, in brief, is a Catholic vision of work and the worker. Beautiful, isn't it? But there's a problem. The problem is not the vision but the reality—the harsh reality that so often clashes with the vision. What am I thinking of?

I am thinking of child labor. Across the world, in countries poor and countries rich, more than 250 million children work, many of them at risk from hazardous conditions, labor that abuses them for shameful profit.[6] Their most basic rights, their health, even their lives are in jeopardy.[7]

I am thinking of the millions of men and women in our flourishing economy who cannot find work, the millions whose jobs are boring, at times dehumanizing, jobs that are too small for the human spirit or even drain it beyond endurance. I ask you: Who hands out Big Macs and French fries on an assembly line and sees this as serving God or the common good? Who of us says "thank you" to the men who scrub the toilets at an airport? How many employers know the names of the women who clean their offices at night?

I am thinking of the women in our country who consistently are paid less than men for the same type and amount of labor. Of women who complain that their gifts and competences are not recognized by state or church. Of Catholics who charge that the Church all too often does not pay its workers a just wage.[8]

I am thinking of labor unions. In the last half of the 19th century and earlier in this century the labor movement was a significant force in enabling an immigrant church to raise families, to become a thriving middle class, to take part in America's growth. Unions divided the Catholic Church a hundred years ago,[9] but, as AFL-CIO president John Sweeney told us, "Without the family, there would have been no love. Without the Church, there would have been no redemption. But without the union, there would have been no food on the table."[10] And unions divide us now. In fact, "the labor movement is currently very much on the defensive and numerically is weaker than it has been at any time since the twenties."[11] There are Catholic institutions that oppose unionizing in their ranks, or make it perilous for employees to form or join unions.

I am thinking of businesses that resort to part-time hiring to avoid paying employee benefits.

I am thinking of a chilling change in our climate, where an America that earlier welcomed immigrants with open arms now sees them as a threat to the economy, to native jobs, to our way of life.

I am thinking of single mothers trying to balance a minimum wage and an impossibly expensive child care.

III

The Catholic ideal, the harsh reality; they clash. The clash leads directly to my third point: What in the concrete is the challenge to us? What does the clash demand of you and me? A handful of suggestions.

First suggestion: Recognize a quality called "dignity." In yourself, in your work. Recognize that work, in God's eyes, has a special worth, an intrinsic worth, a value, even a kind of nobility. Whatever you do—send a skyscraper soaring, invent Internet, scour a restroom, shine someone's shoes—you are giving praise to God, and your work helps to bring God's dream for His world to reality...*if.* If you do your work out of love for God, love for your sisters and brothers. Here you cooperate with your Creator and your Redeemer, with God and His Christ. But the dignity does not stem in the first instance from the type of work we do. God does not judge our worth by the kind of work that engages us, does not rank our worth by our title, our salary, our prestige. The worth of our work God judges by how we do it and why.

A difficult idea to grasp, but terribly important. Not all works are equal in making the world a better place. A U.S. President or a Congressman, a CEO or a union official, a bishop or a banker—these wield powers for good or evil not equaled by a garbage collector or a cleaning woman. And still, in God's eyes a garbage collector who does his work faithfully, a cleaning woman who makes her little world more attractive and usable, obscure men and women who bring a measure of happiness to the people they serve, are moving God's dream in creation, Christ's work of redemption, nearer to realization—at times more effectively than an executive working only for private interest, personal gain.

Jesus' command to all of us is crystal clear: "Let your light shine before men and women, that they may see your good works and give glory to your Father in heaven" (Mt 5:16). Whatever our job, it has a primary purpose: to make our world a more human place for ourselves and our sisters and brothers. Not to grow proud or take the credit to ourselves, but that those we touch by our work may turn to God, give praise to the God who alone has the power to change hearts, to transform the world through us.

Good friends and workers, recognize your dignity!

Second suggestion: Recognize the dignity in your sisters and brothers, those who command and those who obey, the worth of their work in God's eyes. Not envy; that way God's kingdom is not advanced. Rather, praise God, thank God, for the multicolored ways God uses all of us to renew the earth, to serve humankind.

Third suggestion: Look for ways to serve the less fortunate. This, said Jesus, is how we shall be judged: "I was hungry and you fed me, I was thirsty and you gave me something to drink, I was a stranger and you welcomed me, I was naked and you clothed me, I was sick and you took care of me, I was in prison and you visited me" (Mt 25:35–36). This too is work, "works of mercy."

Fourth suggestion: Work for justice. We Americans are profiting from child labor in other countries: in some of the clothes we wear, some of the shoes we run in, some of the vegetables we eat. It will not do to say, "It's not my problem." It is my problem, America's problem. You know, Nike was forced by a *New York Times* column to reexamine its low-wage policies in Indonesia, where more than a third of its products were manufactured.[12] A problem becomes my problem if I profit from it.

Fifth suggestion: Let not unions and management turn into enemies. The slogan "Workers of the world, unite" is no longer the communist cry for class struggle; it is the Christian call for collaboration. Collective bargaining is tough. We may differ, but after harsh words, reconciliation; after reconciliation, a fresh purpose together.

A final word; it touches today's Gospel. If you enter the main parking lot at Georgetown University between 2:30 and 10:00 p.m., you will be greeted at the booth by an African-American lady. She drives a sports utility vehicle (SUV). The hood of her car has a bug screen on which you can read in bright letters "Matthew 6:33." What is Matthew 6:33? Today's Gospel: "Strive first for the kingdom of God and His justice, and all these things will be given to you as well." Ask her how she is and you will receive, with a brilliant smile, always the same answer: "I'm blest by the Best."

Good friends: Whatever you do, whatever your work, do it literally "for Christ's sake," to build his kind of world, to transform your small acre of God's earth into a place of peace, of love, of justice, and you will be "blest by the Best."

Basilica of the Shrine
of the Immaculate Conception
Washington, D.C.
September 5, 1999

38

WALK IN LOVE
A Jesuit for Fifty Years

- 1 Kings 19:4–8
- Ephesians 4:30–5:2
- John 6:41–51

How do you measure 50 years? Especially when those 50 years move from the sidewalks of New York to Osorno in Chile, from Santiago to Samoa, from D.C. to Richmond and Charlotte and back again. When those 50 years embrace classroom and parish, shelter and soup kitchen, counseling and Cursillo, word processor and pulpit, Epiphany and Nova and Pax. Yes, a nine iron, a racquet, and a ski.

Fortunately for me, our jubilarian has summed up his Jesuit half century in two words: *walking together*. With apologies to him, let me put my own spin on that expression. For I see him walking together in three ways: (1) walking with God, (2) walking with Jesuits, and (3) walking with you.

I

For these 50 years Joseph Michael McCloskey has been walking with God. I am not about to paint a rose garden. Joe will be among the first to testify that walking with God is not one wondrous waltz; it's more like a Polish polka. It's an awesome experience, if only because he experiences God's presence and God's absence, God's face open and God's face hidden.

God's presence. I have long sensed that our dear friend can say with the Jesuits' founder, Ignatius Loyola,

> I had a direct encounter with God. I am not going to talk of visions, symbols, voices, the gift of tears. All I say is I knew God, nameless and unfathomable, silent and yet near, bestowing

209

Himself upon me in His Trinity. I knew God beyond all concrete
imaginings. I knew Him clearly in such nearness and grace as is
impossible to confound or mistake. I experienced God Himself,
not human words describing Him. This experience is grace
indeed, and basically there is no one to whom it is refused.[1]

It is what Ignatius expected of each of his sons, then and now
and always. On the other hand, there is what has been called "the
dark night of the soul," when God allows even Jesuits to experience
God's absence. Or, if not His absence, the cross of Christ. It
reminds me of St. Teresa of Avila addressing God during a particularly crucifying time: "Why do you treat me like this?" God's
answer: "I treat all my friends like that." Teresa's retort: "No wonder you have so few."

Walking with God is rarely, if ever, a ceaseless Eden, "the Lord
God walking in the garden at the time of the evening breeze" (Gen
3:8). That is why St. Ignatius in his *Spiritual Exercises* speaks of spiritual desolation, "such as darkness of soul, turmoil of spirit, attraction to what is base and worldly, and restlessness caused by many
disturbances and temptations, all of which can lead to lack of faith,
hope, and love. [You] may find [yourself] completely apathetic, lukewarm, and unhappy, as if separated from God."[2]

To borrow Joe's rhetoric, Jesus "dogs" his life, hounds him
day and night. Hounded him through two heart attacks and a pace-
maker. Hounded him until in what he humorously calls his "retire-
ment" he discovered that work and fun, labor and pleasure, Christ
and people, altar and putting green are not in competition, are not
two separate lives, are linked splendidly together in his basic Jesuit
commitment: "Take, O Lord, and receive all my liberty, my memory, my understanding, my whole will, all I have and all I possess.
You gave them to me; to you, Lord, I return it all." The birdie and
the bogey.

Joe's walk with God reminds me of Francis Thompson's poem
"The Hound of Heaven," a God who pursues us relentlessly, hears us
confess:

> ...though I knew His love who followèd,
> Yet was I sore adread
> Lest, having Him, I must have naught beside.[3]

Yes, until Joe heard from God, heard from Jesus:

> All which I took from thee I did but take,
> Not for thy harms,

But just that thou might'st seek it in My arms.
   All which thy child's mistake
Fancies as lost, I have stored for thee at home:
   Rise, clasp My hand, and come![4]

II

A second walk: Joe walks together with fellow Jesuits. It's not a minor part of these 50 years, like joining a club, with dues and periodic "blasts." This Society of Jesus is precisely that: a society, a community, a fellowship. Individuals indeed; for we are not fashioned in a factory, on an assembly line. But for all our differences, for all our multicolored ministries, for all our eccentricities and idiosyncrasies, we are a family, one big, sprawling, arguing and loving, bewildering and caring, manic and depressive, obnoxious and lovable family.

Strangely, Joe came to appreciate his Jesuit family by being distanced from it. Distanced for years at a time. Picture him in Western Samoa, with the nearest Jesuit 2000 sea miles away. Picture him driving a truck in Santiago, as lonely for family as an immigrant cab driver in Washington. Picture him in a Virginia retreat house, living pretty much alone with God for ten years. You who are his family by blood or love can appreciate the loneliness of this distance runner.

In our Gonzaga family Joe has recaptured community. With us who share his commitment and respect it, Joe is free to be himself, doesn't have to prove anything, is accepted for what he is and who he is, is assured that his ministries are worthwhile. He can spar with us, give as well as take, let his flaws hang out, charm us with a McCloskey smile. He can literally read our lips, respond slyly to what he has not actually heard. His joy is our joy; we delight in his gifts, his compassion, his love for people, his care for the McKenna downtrodden, even his desperate efforts to outdrive Tiger Woods.

This younger brother I envy. Why? He pleasures as much in his nonalcoholic beer as I do in my vodka gimlet. More importantly, he is not afraid to die, because loving Jesus as he does, he is looking forward to a multimillion-man reunion with the Society of Jesus in heaven.

III

A third walk: Joe walks together with you. Here is where I see his three vows coming into daily play—vows that a profound Jesuit theologian, John Courtney Murray, saw as a radical risk: the risk of not becoming a man.[5] By the vow of poverty, Father Murray argued, a religious risks declining responsibility for his livelihood, risks "an inert, parasitic life—living off the collectivity," risks remaining irresponsible. By the vow of chastity, he risks refusing to enter the world of Eve, risks a premature senility (sex is dead), thinking himself whole when he is not. He risks remaining the proverbial bachelor, "crotchety, emotionally unstable, petulant, and self-enclosed." By the vow of obedience, he risks declining "the most bruising encounter of all," the encounter with his own spirit and its power of choice. He risks being other-directed, with his choices made for him, refusing ultimate responsibility for them. He risks "an end both to aspiration and conflict"; he can spare himself "the lonely agony of the desert struggle."[6]

Your presence here suggests your answer to a question: Have the vows freed our jubilarian or enslaved him? Specifically, has the vow of poverty actually liberated him from a slavish attachment to things, to possessions, to what is "his" to clutch and to keep? Has the vow of chastity released him for warm human relations that draw you not only to him but to Christ, freed him from a confining absorption in any one person and from a "play the field" mentality? Has the vow of obedience delivered him from a damnable preoccupation with his own wants, his own good pleasure, his own satisfaction, rather than the will of God and the needs of God's people—your needs? Your presence here suggests strongly your enthusiastic answer.

You may have noticed that the word "priest" has not entered this homily. Only because all his ministry is priestly, as long as he is responding to what the Church is asking of him at this moment in her history. Not knowing—as young Mary of Nazareth did not know—all that God might ask; knowing only that it is God asking. All his ministry is a living-out of his call to follow one only Master. His call, like Jesus' call, not only to "offer gifts and sacrifices for sin" (Heb 5:1) but to "deal gently" with all of us "since he himself is subject to weakness" (v. 2). This very Eucharist, "the living bread that came down from heaven" (Jn 6:51), is the heart and soul of Joe's ministry. For very shortly he will utter the words of Jesus that sum up magnificently these precious 50 years, tell us why he walks together with God in the company of his Jesuit brothers: "This is my body [and it is] given for you." For you.

A final word in summary. In the second reading that was pro-claimed to you, a passage from the Pauline Letter to the Christians of Ephesus, there is a concise command that fits beautifully with all I have struggled to express. The command? "Walk in love" (Eph 5:2).[7] To remember Joseph McCloskey is to remember that command. For this has been his life. He has walked in love with God, has walked in love with his companions in Christ, has walked in love with you. What then? Another command, a command of Jesus to each and all of us: "Go and do likewise" (Lk 10:37).

Church of St. Aloysius Gonzaga
Washington, D.C.
August 13, 2000

39
YOU ARE GOD'S BUILDING
Dedication of Buildings,
Gonzaga College High School

- Wisdom 2:12, 17–20
- 1 Corinthians 3:9–11, 16–17
- Mark 9:30–37

Good friends of God and Gonzaga: How, in the name of all that is holy, how do you preach about a building? Lovely to look at, delightful to see. A product of the generosity of thousands; a tribute to a long-time Jesuit teacher, two grateful lay graduates, a husband and wife quietly bountiful to a school they treasure. But what is it that calls for so brilliant a blessing, with a cardinal presiding, a packed church, graduates by the hundreds forsaking golf's fairways on a Sunday afternoon? I know, we bless everything under creation save sin. On Labor Day Cardinal Mahony of Los Angeles blessed the hands of workers. I myself have blessed a boat; it sank instantly. What is so special about today?

The answer struck me suddenly two Sundays ago. It was then I roamed for the first time through Ruesch and Cantwell born anew. The insight began at one of the corridor cabinets, a quotation from an American Indian, Crazy Horse: "A very great vision is needed, and the man who has it must follow it as the eagle seeks the deepest blue of the sky." As the eagle seeks. With that as introduction, I walked through spacious halls, looked into capacious classrooms, each a marvel of studied practicality in a modern mode. An adventure in awe. And what is the vision? It came to light in three stages: (1) in a single word important for intelligent Christian living; (2) in a swift sentence proclaimed to you in today's reading from St. Paul; (3) in a picture from a sleepless night. A word, a sentence, a picture. A word on each.

I

First, the word, so important for intelligent Christian living. To have "a very great vision," you need a *symbol*. Bear with me, think along with me. For these buildings make sense not simply as architectural wonders, masterpieces of brick and stone and wood. To make sense, you have to see them as symbols. What is a symbol? A symbol is a reality that works mysteriously on your consciousness, on your imagination, so as to suggest a meaning not easily compressed into a sentence. You encounter symbols day after day: a cross atop a church, a flag fluttering in the breeze, a swastika worn by a superpatriot, Star Wars, a stretch limo, Georgetown's Hoya, the Purple G. Yes, the Purple G.

But symbols are caught, not taught. I don't tell you what incense wafted over a coffin means; you tell me what it says to you. I don't tell you what baptismal water means when an infant is submerged; you tell me. I don't tell you what a Lincoln Continental, the Marlboro Man, Tiger Woods, McKenna's Wagon symbolize; you tell me what they say to you. I don't tell you what the Purple G means; you tell me. A sobering example: the cross of Christ. The cross says one thing to a Christian, quite another to a Jew. And these are not just objects out there, objects to be known. A symbol is an environment I inhabit. You and I live off symbols, live in symbols, the way we live in our bodies. To Hell's Angels a Harley-Davidson is not just a motorcycle, a machine; it represents a whole way of life, a life those "angels" live.

These buildings, what do they say to you—all of you, but especially those of you who occupy them? I know what they say to *me*. I walked slowly though your math and science section, stepped into the chemistry lab, with all its potential for discovering created reality, and I remembered when God looked over everything He had made and declared, "It is very good" (Gen 1:31). Every substance in chemistry's vocabulary is a gift of God, precious, to be treasured, touched with reverence. I recalled the Jesuit tradition in the sciences: astronomers like Clavius and Secchi, mathematicians like Kircher and Boscovich, Matteo Ricci introducing science and Christ to China. Little wonder that in one science classroom Jesuit poet Gerard Manley Hopkins proclaims, "The world is charged with the grandeur of God."

I wandered into the extensive language area. It seemed to breathe ancient Latin lyrics, today's sibilant Spanish, fluid French, heavy German.... And I remembered the insight of Presbyterian

preacher and novelist Frederick Buechner, "Words are our godly
sharing in the work of creation, and the speaking and writing of
words is at once the most human and the most holy of all the businesses we engage in. The ultimate purpose of language, I suspect, is
so that humanity may speak to God."

I walked through the capacious music center; I could almost
hear your symphonic wind ensemble rendering your favorite
"Fantasia on an Irish Hymn." Even more profoundly, for me music,
Gonzaga music, is power. Not only love and economics make the
world go round; music runs them a close third. For me music,
Gonzaga music, creates community—around a piano, on a street cor-
ner, in your theatre, in church. If African Americans are born
singing, whether "I danced in the morning" or "Were you there
when they crucified my Lord?" the rest of us had better catch up.

I walked into a religion classroom where the seats were
arranged in a rectangle. It was made for a Lucien Longtin class, for
intense discussion on everything from Deuteronomy's "great God
mighty and awesome, who...executes justice for the orphan and the
widow, and who loves the strangers" (Deut 10:17–18) to the dialecti-
cal materialism of Karl Marx. For a religion classroom is not just
another space with a cross. The room speaks not only of a God who
gave His only Son to a crucifying death; it speaks of the agonies and
the doubts that torture the human mind as it searches for the true,
the beautiful, and the good.

I walked into a history classroom and I marveled once again
how our minds can cross oceans faster than light, touch Kosovo and
Crete, Sicily and the Sudan, reach back to primitive man and
dinosaurs, to a God-man bleeding out his life on a cross outside
Jerusalem.

Yes, this and so much more is what the new Gonzaga says to
me...to me. The million-dollar question? What does this new Gonzaga
say to *you*? What does it symbolize to *you*? No more than an architectural gem? A teacher you love to hate? Four years of drudgery? Fun
and games? Or does it shape something akin to Crazy Horse's "great
vision"? If a vision, would you please struggle to put it into words?

II

Second, a swift sentence from St. Paul. To grasp it, go back in
time, back 2600 years, back to an Old Testament prophet...Jeremiah.
He is addressing God's people, his people: "Hear the word of the

LORD, all you people of Judah, you that enter these gates to worship the Lord. Thus says the LORD of hosts, the God of Israel: Amend your ways and your doings, and let me dwell with you in this place. Do not trust in these deceptive words, 'This is the temple of the LORD, the temple of the LORD, the temple of the LORD'" (Jer 7:2b–4). Jeremiah's point? The temple was indeed a sacred place. Sacred because the temple sheltered the Ark of the Covenant, where Moses had placed the two tablets of stone containing the ten commandments. The temple was Yahweh's throne. But, Jeremiah thundered, this splendid structure will not "save" the people, will not automatically protect them from the enemy. It will save only if the people act justly. Only if they cease oppressing the widow, the orphan, and the alien, cease shedding innocent blood, cease going after other gods.

Return to today. For years to come, Bellwoar and Ruesch, Cantwell and Collins will proclaim, with St. Paul, "*You* are God's building; *you* are God's temple." You see, these buildings, built so splendidly on the sacrifices of Gonzaga friends, are not automatons, robots; they will not work miracles of the mind and the soul. Somewhat as the Lord's temple could not of itself protect the Jewish people, so these splendid buildings will not of themselves create intelligence, learning, scholarship; will not of themselves fill your minds with knowledge, your hearts with goodness, your lives with morality; will not create, make out of nothing, men for others.

Each Gonzaga student, each Eye Street eagle, has to realize that this impressive structure will be empty, empty of meaning, unless those of you who occupy the space live, like Crazy Horse, "a very great vision, follow it as the eagle seeks the deepest blue of the sky." You yourselves must be Gonzaga's symbol to the little world that sees you, to the men and women who come into contact with you. *You* are the living building; *you* make the building of brick come alive.

How do you catch the vision, how become symbols yourselves of what the Purple G means? Happily, it doesn't have to happen through an off-the-wall IQ, a Brad Pitt personality. Remember what St. Paul declared: "Don't you know that you are God's temple and that God's [Holy] Spirit dwells in you? God's temple is holy, and you are that temple" (1 Cor 3:16, 17b). This is not pretty poetry; it is Christian realism. "The Spirit of God," Paul says, "has made His home in you" (Rom 8:9). And two characteristics of this Holy Spirit within you are light and power (for you Greek students, *dynamis,* dynamite). In the power of the Spirit you can understand what escapes normal comprehension, see beneath the surface of things, see beyond the obvious, grasp what the Purple G means. And the

Spirit is fire. That is why we pray, "Come, Holy Spirit, fill the hearts of your faithful, and kindle in us the fire of your love"—the fire that can change you and the acres of God you walk each day. Feel the fire, my young friends; for it is there, inside of you.

III

Third, a picture. Ten nights ago I was sleepless, tossing restlessly, concerned over this day, this homily. From the deep recesses of my memory a picture emerged. The scene: old Ireland, some centuries ago—Ireland poor, Ireland persecuted. In a forest glen a fallen tree. Straddling the log, two persons: an aging man, white hair, intense features; facing him, a youngster the age of a Gonzaga freshman, eyes aglow. The picture? The legendary Irish schoolmaster, handing down the faith of the Irish and the wisdom of the ages, transmitting to another generation what I once found in the title of a Benedictine's book, *The Love of Learning and the Desire for God.*

In that Irish schoolmaster I glimpsed Gonzaga's teachers. Forty-three men and 18 women who have caught a vision. Not the vision of Crazy Horse; the vision of Ignatius Loyola. Contemplatives in action. Contemplatives: men and women who have learned to look long and lovingly at the real. In action: linking your lives to what you have seen. Men and women who touch your students to God's greater glory and to the promotion of justice that is the special Jesuit mission today; men and women who, in the spirit of today's Gospel, welcome each child in the name of Christ. Largely because of you, "words are [Gonzaga's] godly sharing in the work of creation"; largely because of you, McKenna's Wagon is not a hayride; it is a mission of mercy, a carriage of compassion. It actualizes what Mother Teresa described in a commencement address here in 1988:

> One day I was walking down the street and I saw a man sitting there looking most terrible, so I went to him and shook his hand (and my hand is always very warm), and he looked up and said, "Oh, what a long, long time since I felt the warmth of a human hand." He brightened up, he was so full of joy that there was somebody that loved him, there was somebody who cared.

What delights me in Gonzaga's teachers is your unceasing enthusiasm, your love for these eaglets. For seven years I have sensed it, seen it in your eyes. The problem? Time tends to dull the gloss, the luster, on all of us. Routine takes over, one day becomes much like every other, students all begin to look alike. If that enthusiasm needs rekindling, the new buildings might well inspire a renewal. We might adapt to our situation what Paul said to Corinth's Christians: "If anyone is in Christ, there is a new creation; everything old has passed away; see, everything has become new!" (2 Cor 5:17). Let the rebirth in Ruesch, the incandescence in Cantwell, inflame you each day.

Good friends of God and Gonzaga: Indeed we have good reason to have our cardinal bless our buildings. For a blessing is an expression of praise, of thanks, of petition. Praise to our gracious God, from whom all our blessings flow—even new buildings. Thanks to you, whose generosity has made this day possible, made this truly a day the Lord has made. Petition: prayer for a fruitful future, ever rich in fidelity: fidelity to God, loving God above all idols; fidelity to God's human images, loving every man, woman, and child like another self; fidelity to God's earth, touching with reverence, with awe, all that God has created.

Church of St. Aloysius Gonzaga
Washington, D.C.
September 24, 2000

40
JUSTIFIED BY GOD'S GRACE
Homily for Reformation Sunday

- Jeremiah 31:31–34
- Romans 3:19–28
- John 8:31–36

What is it you can expect of a homily on Reformation Sunday, especially if you are a child of the Reform? Expect of a visiting Jesuit, with all our heavy involvement in the Counter Reform? Happily, I have spent 11 years in the Lutheran-Catholic Dialogue in this country, have experienced Lutheran churches as communities of grace and salvation, even came swiftly to the embarrassing conclusion that there are Lutheran theologians smarter than I am! Happily, too, the liturgical readings for Reformation Sunday—God's Word to you and me—are remarkably relevant to each and every reformation. In harmony with these three readings, three stages to my homily, three persons speaking to us: Yahweh, Paul, and Jesus; three awesome messages: covenant, grace, and freedom.

I

First, Yahweh, Jehovah. The short oracle proclaimed to you has been called "one of the profoundest and most moving passages in the entire Bible."[1] Hear it, in part, again:

> The days are surely coming, says the LORD, when I will make a new covenant with the house of Israel and the house of Judah....This is the covenant: I will put my law within them, and I will write it on their hearts....They shall all know me, from the least of them to the greatest; for I will forgive their iniquity and remember their sin no more.
>
> (Jer 31:31–34)

Within the Book of Consolation, a consoling promise: The exodus from Babylon will be greater than the exodus from Egypt. This time no need for intermediaries such as Moses, priests, prophets; Yahweh will intervene directly. The result? God's people will recognize "God in every action and situation." This time everyone will be faithful; man and woman will be re-created with the human intelligence and willpower to fulfil God's plan for them.[2] It is Ezekiel's "new heart and new spirit."[3]

Now this covenant, its meaning, has been reinterpreted in the New Testament. Reinterpreted by Luke's Jesus and by St. Paul: "This cup that is poured out for you is the new covenant in my blood" (Lk 22:20; 1 Cor 11:25). Reinterpreted especially in the Letter to the Hebrews, the longest Old Testament quotation in the New Testament (Heb 8:8–12). The author reproduces the whole text from Jeremiah and applies it to Jesus, "the mediator of a better covenant, which has been enacted through better promises" (v. 6).

A homily is not the place to argue how the Old Testament has been fulfilled in the New. For our purposes this morning, the new covenant cut in the blood of Christ promised a new humanity, a redeemed humanity, a reformed humanity. Essentially established on Calvary, but never quite realized on earth. A community ever in need of reformation. What Vatican II declared so frankly and humbly in its Decree on Ecumenism: "Christ summons the Church, as she goes her pilgrim way, to that continual reformation of which she always has need, insofar as she is an institution of men [and women] here on earth."[4] I submit that in all honesty all of us, whether children of the Reformation or children of the Counter Reformation, must subscribe to an insightful affirmation by Jesuit historian John W. O'Malley:

> Imagination and creativity must enter every reform if it is not to be utterly irrelevant and dreary beyond human endurance. As a matter of fact, creativity has been at the heart of every success-ful reform and renaissance, even when men seriously believed that they were doing nothing else than transposing the past into the present. Creativity, which is radically opposed to slavish imi-tation, implies both utilization of the past and rejection of the past. The outcome of creativity, in any case, is something *new*.[5]

Always some measure of reform, always something new, in the institution and in the individual—through every prayer mur-mured, through each act of repentance for the past, through the

Eucharist which Catholics claim is the summit and source of all the Church's dynamism.

II

All of which leads into the second reading from God's only Book, the passage from Paul's Letter to the Christians of Rome. Perhaps the most striking sentence is this: "All have sinned and fall short of the glory of God; yet all are justified by His grace as a gift, through the redemption that comes in Christ Jesus. Through his blood God has presented him as a means of expiating sin for all who have faith" (Rom 3:23–25).

Justified by God's grace. This day, my sisters and brothers in Christ, is an extraordinary day. Not only for Lutherans, because you celebrate a Reformation that changed the face of Christianity. An extraordinary day for Lutherans and Catholics alike; for this very day, in the historic city of Augsburg in Germany, a Joint Declaration on the Doctrine of Justification is being signed by the Lutheran World Federation representing the vast majority of the world's Lutherans, and the Catholic Church with the blessing of Pope John Paul II.[6] A lengthy document, but what does it assert in brief?

> 40. The understanding of the doctrine of justification set forth in this declaration shows that a consensus in basic truths of the doctrine of justification exists between Lutherans and Catholics....
> 41. Thus the doctrinal condemnations of the 16th century, insofar as they relate to the doctrine of justification, appear in a new light. The teaching of the Lutheran churches presented in this declaration does not fall under the condemnations from the Council of Trent. The condemnations in the Lutheran confessions do not apply to the teaching of the Roman Catholic Church presented in this declaration.[7]

What in the concrete do both churches affirm?

> 15. Together we confess: By grace alone, in faith in Christ's saving work and not because of any merit on our part, we are accepted by God and receive the Holy Spirit, who renews our hearts while equipping and calling us to good works.[8]
> 20. When Catholics say that persons "cooperate" in preparing for and accepting justification by consenting to God's justifying action, they see such personal consent as itself

an effect of grace, not as an action arising from innate human abilities.[9]

There is still much to be done, "continued and deepened study of the biblical foundations of the doctrine of justification," "further common understanding" of the doctrine beyond what has already been dealt with.[10] But on the "basic truths" there is clear agreement.

What does it mean for you and me, for Lutherans and Catholics today? I submit that each of our communities, each parish, must set itself to understand this historic agreement. Justification by God's grace is fundamental to all genuinely Christian teaching and living. It dare not remain the preserve, the private possession, of officials and theologians. The agreement must make its way to the pews if the struggle for the unity of the churches is to survive.

III

Finally, a fitting conclusion to all I have said: our third reading, from John. "If you abide in my word, you are truly my disciples; and you will know the truth, and the truth will make you free" (Jn 8:31–32). Now "The truth will make you free" has become a trite phrase in political oratory. But there is nothing political here; truth and freedom here are religious values. The "truth" here, what is it? God's revelation in Jesus; for as Jesus states quickly, "If the Son makes you free, you will really be free" (v. 36). And the freedom is freedom from sin.[11]

It is another way of saying what St. Paul cried out to the Christians of Galatia, "Christ has set us free. Do not submit again to a yoke of slavery" (Gal 5:1). And to the Christians of Rome, "The law of the Spirit of life in Christ Jesus has set us free from the law of sin and of death" (Rom 8:2). The freedom that concerns Jesus here is freedom from sin.

How free are we? Here Lutherans and Catholics are not perfectly at peace. Lutherans understand the Christian as "at the same time righteous and sinner." Righteous in that in Christ we have been made just before God. Sinners in that sin still lives in us; we "repeatedly turn to false gods and do not love God with that undivided love which God requires as [our] Creator."[12] Still, this sin does not separate us from God. Catholics claim that "the grace of Jesus Christ imparted in baptism takes away all that is sin 'in the proper sense.'" What remains is "an inclination (concupiscence) which comes from sin and presses toward sin" but "is not sin in an authentic sense."[13]

Happily, both Lutherans and Catholics agree that "the enslaving power of sin is broken on the basis of the merit of Christ. It no longer is a sin that 'rules' the Christian, for [sin] is itself 'ruled' by Christ, with whom the justified are bound in faith."[14]

We can live with this; for both agree that through Christ sin no longer has dominion over us, no longer tyrannizes us, no longer is our master. Weak as we are of ourselves, we are perennially in peril of sinning; strong as we are in Christ, we no longer have to sin. In that sense we can adapt to our Christian experience what Martin Luther King Jr. cried aloud about the black experience: "Free at last! Free at last! Thank God, we are free at last!"

Free indeed—but free for what? Not a Luther scholar, I still dare to suggest that the Luther of 1999 might smile on both our houses if we were to shout from the housetops and live in the streets a thesis of his that surely commands our combined assent: The freedom a Christian has through faith is freedom to render the service of love. "Lo, that is how love and joy in God flow out of faith, and how love gives rise to a free, eager, and glad life of serving one's neighbor without reward."[15]

Here, my friends, is freedom for the Christian: the freedom to serve. And here is hope for humankind in a new millennium.

Central Lutheran Church
and
St. Thomas More University Parish
Eugene, Oregon
October 31, 1999

NOTES

Homily 1

1. This homily was preached during the third annual conference of the Southern Maryland Jubilee Year, "Returning to the Father: The Brink of the 3rd Christian Millennium," in Solomons, Maryland.
2. See John R. Donahue, S.J., *What Does the Lord Require? A Bibliographical Essay on the Bible and Social Justice* (Studies in the Spirituality of Jesuits 25/2: March 1993; St. Louis, Mo.: Seminar on Jesuit Spirituality, 1993) esp. 19–27.
3. Origen, *Homily on the Book of Judges* 2.3.
4. So Benedict T. Viviano, O.P., "The Gospel according to Matthew," *The New Jerome Biblical Commentary*, ed. Raymond E. Brown, S.S., Joseph A. Fitzmyer, S.J., and Roland E. Murphy, O.Carm. (Englewood Cliffs, N.J.: Prentice-Hall, 1990) 42:133, p. 666.
5. Vatican II, Constitution on the Sacred Liturgy, no. 10.
6. John Paul II, encyclical "On Social Concern," Dec. 30, 1987 (Washington, D.C.: United States Catholic Conference [1987]) 48–49; italics in text.
7. Quoted by Sean McDonagh in a short "Viewpoint" article in the (London) *Tablet* 248, no. 8021 (April 30, 1994) 514.
8. John Paul II, message for the World Day of Peace, Jan. 1, 1990, English text, "Peace with All Creation," no. 15, *Origins* 19, no. 28 (Dec. 14, 1989) 465–68, at 468.

Homily 2

1. 10:30 p.m., December 31, 1999.
2. Constitution on the Sacred Liturgy, no. 7.
3. Ibid., no. 10.

Homily 4

1. See Raymond E. Brown, S.S., *The Gospel according to John (I-XII)* (Garden City, N.Y.: Doubleday, 1966) 170–71.
2. Vatican II, Constitution on the Sacred Liturgy, no. 7.
3. A contemporary film that has entranced millions.
4. See Brown, *John* (n. 1 above) 377.
5. Quoted by Brown, ibid. 434, from the second of the so-called "Eighteen Benedictions."
6. Raymond E. Brown, S.S., *The Gospel according to John (XIII-XXI)* (Garden City, N.Y.: Doubleday, 1970) 752.

Homily 5

1. In John Bartlett, *Familiar Quotations* (11th ed.; Boston: Little, Brown, 1950) 1064.

Homily 6

1. John R. Donahue, S.J., "Biblical Perspectives on Justice," in *The Faith That Does Justice: Examining the Christian Sources for Social Change*, ed. John C. Haughey, S.J. (Woodstock Studies 2; New York: Paulist, 1977) 68–112, at 69; should be supplemented by J. P. M. Walsh, S.J., *The Mighty from Their Thrones* (Philadelphia: Fortress, 1987).
2. Mario DiCicco, O.F.M., "What Can One Give in Exchange for One's Life? A Narrative-Critical Study of the Widow and Her Offering, Mark 12:41–44," *Currents in Theology and Mission* 25, no. 6 (December 1998) 441–49, at 446.
3. Joseph A. Fitzmyer, S.J., *The Gospel according to Luke (X-XXIV)* (Garden City, N.Y.: Doubleday, 1985) 1321.
4. Mark Searle, "Serving the Lord with Justice," in Mark Searle, ed., *Liturgy and Social Justice* (Collegeville, Minn.: Liturgical, 1980) 13–35, at 25.
5. Ibid.
6. See ibid. 28.

Homily 7

1. This homily was preached on the Monday of Holy Week to the seminarians and faculty at Theological College of the Catholic University of America, Washington, D.C.
2. Marian Wright Edelman, "Foreword: Is America Fair to Its Children?" in *The State of America's Children Yearbook 1999* (Washington, D.C.: Children's Defense Fund, 1999) XI.

3. Rev. Michael Bryant, 20-year Roman Catholic chaplain at the District of Columbia Detention Center, during a Woodstock Theological Center Forum discussion on "The U.S. Penal System: Restorative and/or Retributive Justice?" *Woodstock Report*, no. 61 (March 2000) 4–10, at 4.
4. Ibid.
5. Ibid.
6. Ibid. 5.
7. See Robert M. Morgenthau, "What Prosecutors Won't Tell You," *New York Times,* Op-Ed, Feb. 7, 1995.
8. See Margaret Carlson, "Death, Be Not Proud," *Time* 155, no. 7 (Feb. 21, 2000) 38.
9. Quoted by Msgr. George G. Higgins in *Why I Am a Priest,* ed. Lawrence Boadt, C.S.P., and Michael J. Hunt, C.S.P. (New York/Mahwah, N.J.: Paulist, 1999) 16.

Homily 8

1. Gerard Manley Hopkins, "God's Grandeur," in *The Poems of Gerard Manley Hopkins*, ed. W. H. Gardner and N. H. MacKenzie (New York: Oxford University, 1970) 66.
2. Bill Wagner, "Still Working for Understanding: Christians and Jews," *St. Anthony Messenger* 100, no. 3 (August 1992) 36–41, at 40.
3. See the review by Pheme Perkins of Elisabeth Schüssler Fiorenza's *Jesus, Miriam's Child, Sophia's Prophet: Critical Issues in Feminist Christology* (New York: Continuum, 1995) in *America* 172, no. 17 (May 13, 1995) 26–27, at 26.
4. The meaning of this verse is disputed; thus, it has been suggested that "the afflictions are Paul's, not Christ's," and that therefore "This verse reflects the belief that those who proclaim the gospel would have to endure hardships and afflictions" (Maurya P. Horgan, "The Letter to the Colossians," *The New Jerome Biblical Commentary*, ed. Raymond E. Brown, S.S., Joseph A. Fitzmyer, S.J., and Roland E. Murphy, O.Carm. [Englewood Cliffs, N.J.: Prentice-Hall, 1990] 54:16, p. 880).
5. Frederick Buechner, *The Hungering Dark* (New York: Seabury, 1969) 45–46.
6. A reference to a very moving film entitled *Life Is Beautiful.*
7. An expression I change slightly from Karl Rahner's "dying in installments"; see his "Following the Crucified," *Theological Investigations* 18: *God and Revelation* (New York: Crossroad, 1983) 169–70.

Homily 9

1. In this first section I have profited from the learning and insights of Joseph A. Fitzmyer, S.J., *The Acts of the Apostles* (Anchor Bible 31; New York: Doubleday, 1998) esp. 268–73, 312–14.

2. Second Vatican Council, Dogmatic Constitution on Divine Revelation, no. 8 (tr. *The Documents of Vatican II,* ed. Walter M. Abbott, S.J. [New York: Herder and Herder, 1966] 116).
3. Robert W. Hovda (1920–92), priest of the Diocese of Fargo; text taken from his memorial card.
4. Gerard Manley Hopkins, "The Wreck of the Deutschland," in *The Poems of Gerard Manley Hopkins,* ed. W. H. Gardner and N. H. MacKenzie (London: Oxford University, 1970) 63.

Homily 10

1. On this whole pericope I have profited from Joseph A. Fitzmyer, S.J., *The Gospel according to Luke (X-XXIV)* (Garden City, N.Y.: Doubleday, 1985) 1572–85.
2. From an essay "Ignatius of Loyola Speaks to a Modern Jesuit," in Karl Rahner, S.J., *Ignatius of Loyola,* with an Historical Introduction by Paul Imhof, S.J. (London and New York: Collins, 1979) 9–38, at 11–13.
3. John Paul II, encyclical *On Social Concern,* Dec. 30, 1987 (Washington, D.C.: United States Catholic Conference, n.d.) 48–49.
4. "Peace with All Creation," no. 15 in English text, *Origins* 19, no. 28 (Dec. 14, 1989) 468.

Homily 11

1. This homily was preached to priests of the Dioceses of Saskatoon and Prince Albert, Canada, during the Woodstock Theological Center project Preaching the Just Word.
2. Lawrence Boadt, C.S.P., "Ezekiel," *The New Jerome Biblical Commentary,* ed. Raymond E. Brown, S.S., Joseph A. Fitzmyer, S.J., Roland E. Murphy, O.Carm. (Englewood Cliffs, N.J.: Prentice-Hall, 1990) 20:83, p. 324.
3. Pheme Perkins, "The Gospel according to John," ibid. 61:135, p. 969.
4. Perkins, ibid. 61:138, p. 968. For a brief discussion of "model" or "noble" as preferable translation of the Greek *kalos* in this chapter, see Raymond E. Brown, S.S., *The Gospel according to John (I-XII)* (Garden City, N.Y.: Doubleday, 1966) 386, n. 11.
5. Perkins, ibid. 61:141, p. 969.
6. I have not yet discovered the precise source of this quotation.

Homily 12

1. This homily was given immediately preceding the 2000 National Memorial Day Concert, during a Mass for the producer, Jerry Colbert, and some of his associates, relatives, and friends, together with a few of the actual performers.

2. William Sloane Coffin, *The Heart Is a Little to the Left: Essays on Public Morality* (Hanover, N.H.: University Press of New England, 1999) 8.

Homily 13

1. This homily was delivered to priests of the Diocese of Yakima in Washington State during a Preaching the Just Word retreat/workshop. Ordinarily that Thursday, within the sixth week of Easter, would find Catholics celebrating the feast of the Ascension. But Washington is one of the states where the solemnity of the Ascension has been transferred to the following Sunday, and so Thursday, May 13, was observed as an Easter weekday, with the readings continuing on from Acts and John.
2. Raymond E. Brown, S.S., *The Gospel according to John (XIII-XXI)* (Garden City, N.Y.: Doubleday, 1970) 729. Brown does not share this interpretation.
3. The 40 days are probably a round number, with an Old Testament background.
4. *On the Sunday of the Pasch* 52–54 (Corpus christianorum, ser. lat. 78, 550).
5. Joseph A, Fitzmyer, S.J., "The Ascension of Christ and Pentecost," *Theological Studies* 45 (1984) 409–40, at 424.
6. Brown, *John* (n. 2 above) 730.
7. Melanie McDonagh, "Face to Face with Catastrophe," (London) *Tablet*, April 17, 1999, 512–14, at 514.
8. In v. 22 Jesus says "I shall see you again," whereas in v. 16 he has said "you will see me." As Brown sees it, "one may suspect that [these] are simply the two sides of a coin, much as the 'you in me and I in you' indwelling of which we have several examples" (*John* [n. 2 above] 722).

Homily 14

1. Here I am dependent on Raymond E. Brown, S.S., *The Gospel according to John (I-XII)* (Garden City, N.Y.: Doubleday, 1966) 497–501. Brown capitalizes "Truth" in this passage.
2. M. Basil Pennington, O.C.S.O., "Wisdom," *The New Dictionary of Catholic Spirituality,* ed. Michael Downey (Collegeville, Minn.: Liturgical, 1993) 1042–43, at 1043. I have profited from this article in fashioning the present section.
3. Ibid. 1043.
4. New York: New American Library, 1961.

Homily 15

1. This homily was preached to fathers and mothers of *former* Gonzaga College High School students during an evening intended to inform them of extensive plans for the renovation of the school.

230 TO BE JUST IS TO LOVE

2. For the purposes of this homily, I am focusing on the Father, not on the Son.

3. I am aware that this section of "Isaiah" may well have been written by a different author than chapters 1–39, an author "who lived some 150 years later during the Babylonian exile" (Carroll Stuhlmueller, "Deutero-Isaiah and Trito-Isaiah," *The New Jerome Biblical Commentary*, ed. Raymond E. Brown, S.S., Joseph A. Fitzmyer, S.J., and Roland E. Murphy, O.Carm. [Englewood Cliffs, N.J.: Prentice-Hall, 1990] 21:2, p. 329).

4. Letters to the Editor, *Washington Post*, May 19, 1998, A20.

5. Leo the Great, *Sermon 1 on the Birth of the Lord* 3.

Homily 16

1. Statistics for 1998; see Children's Defense Fund, *The State of America's Children Yearbook 2000* (Washington, D.C.: Children's Defense Fund, 2000) 4.

2. See the article, primarily concerned with Latin America, by John F. Talbot, S.J., "Who Evangelizes Whom? The Poor Evangelizers," *Review for Religious*, November-December 1993, 893–97. On p. 896 Talbot quotes this passage from Sobrino's *Resurrección de la verdadera Iglesia* 137–38.

3. Cardinal Joseph Bernardin, "The Church's Response to the AIDS Crisis," *Origins* 16, no. 22 (Nov. 13, 1986) 383–85, at 384.

4. I am borrowing from the text in *Sister Thea Bowman, Shooting Star: Selected Writings and Speeches,* ed. Celestine Cepress, FSPA (Winona, Minn.: Saint Mary's Press, 1993) 31, itself taken from *Origins* 6 (1989) 114–18.

5. John Paul II, "Peace with All Creation," no. 15, *Origins* 19, no. 28 (Dec. 14, 1998) 468.

6. Quoted by Sean McDonagh in a short "Viewpoint" article in the (London) *Tablet* 248, no. 8021 (April 30, 1994) 514.

7. Jackie A. Giuliano, "Healing Our World: Weekly Comment," June 21, 1999, www.healingourworld.com.

8. David Van Biema, "The Killing Fields," *Time* 144, no. 8 (Aug. 22, 1994) 36–37, at 36.

9. Second Vatican Council, Decree on Ecumenism, no. 12, tr. *The Documents of Vatican II,* ed. Walter M. Abbott, S.J. (New York: Herder and Herder/Association Press, 1966) 354–55.

10. Decree on Ecumenism, no. 3 (tr. *Documents* 345).

Homily 17

1. For this paragraph see Roland J. Faley, T.O.R., "Leviticus," *NJBC* 4:28, p. 69.

2. A reference to the professional basketball team in Washington, D.C., and its recently acquired inspiration in the front office.
3. See editorial in *America* 182, no. 3 (Jan. 29–Feb. 5, 2000) 3.
4. From an e-mail of Dec. 29, 1999, sent me by Thomas L. Sheridan, S.J.
5. See George M. Anderson, S.J., "Immigrants in Detention," *America* 182, no. 2 (Jan. 15–22, 2000) 13–15, at 15. I have profited much from this informative article.

Homily 18

1. This homily was preached to priests of the Diocese of Spokane, Washington, during a Preaching the Just Word retreat/workshop.
2. From notes taken during one of Fr. William's conferences. For details on the institute, see my article "Without Contemplation the People Perish," *America* 127, no. 2 (July 22, 1972) 29–32.
3. Gerard Manley Hopkins, Poem 57, "As kingfishers catch fire" (ed. W. H. Gardner and N. H. MacKenzie, *The Poems of Gerard Manley Hopkins* [4th ed.; London: Oxford University, 1970] 90).
4. John M. Buchanan, "Essentials of Preaching," privately produced for a *The Living Pulpit* conference on April 27, 1994, at the Chicago Temple-First United Methodist Church, Chicago.
5. Washington, D.C.: Children's Defense Fund, 1999.
6. Ibid. ix-x.
7. Ibid. xi; I have selected 11 out of 25 of the "key facts about American children."
8. See ibid. xv.

Homily 19

1. This homily was preached to clergy and laity of the Diocese of Helena, Montana, during a Preaching the Just Word retreat/workshop held at Carroll College in Helena.
2. See Joseph Sittler, "Ecological Commitment as Theological Responsibility," *Idoc*, Sept. 12, 1970, 75–85; also his remarks in *Vatican II: An Interfaith Appraisal*, ed. John H. Miller, C.S.C. (Notre Dame, Ind.: University of Notre Dame, 1966) 426–27.
3. Message for the World Day of Peace, Jan. 1, 1990, "Peace with God the Creator, Peace with All of Creation"; English text, "Peace with All Creation," *Origins* 19, no. 28 (Dec. 14, 1989) 465–68.
4. Here I am deeply indebted to information provided by Tim Stevens of the Greater Yellowstone Coalition, Bozeman, Montana. I am aware that my three examples present only the environmentalists' position. I have been made aware of the complexity of the issues (e.g., the arguments of loggers respectful of the land but baffled by the intransigence

of environmentalists). Unhappily, time did not allow an objective presentation of all sides in one homily.
5. Tim Stevens and Meredith Taylor, "The Great Bear Is Not Out of the Woods Yet," *Livingston Enterprise*, Dec. 4, 1998.
6. See Bernard J. F. Lonergan, S.J., *Method in Theology* (New York: Herder and Herder, 1972).

Homily 20

1. So Benedict T. Viviano, O.P., "The Gospel according to Matthew," *The New Jerome Biblical Commentary* (Englewood Cliffs, N.J.: Prentice-Hall, 1990) 42:96, p. 658.
2. Theodore Ross, "The Personal Synthesis of Liturgy and Justice," in K. Hughes and M. Francis, eds., *Living No Longer for Ourselves: Liturgy and Justice in the Nineties* (Collegeville, Minn.: Liturgical, 1990) 27.
3. This homily was preached on the first full day of a Preaching the Just Word retreat/workshop for members of the Maryland Province of the Jesuits; this day put the emphasis on biblical justice in the context of God's creative call to community.
4. *New York Times,* July 29, 2000, A27.
5. Marian Wright Edelman, "Foreword" to *The State of America's Children Yearbook 2000* (Washington, D.C.: Children's Defense Fund, 2000) xv.
6. Quoted by Edelman, ibid. xxiii.
7. Edelman, "There's No Trademark" (n. 4 above).
8. Pedro Arrupe, Letter of Nov. 14, 1980, to the whole Society, *Acta romana* 18 (1980) 319–21.
9. So M. Robert Mulholland Jr., *Invitation to a Journey: A Road Map to Spiritual Formation* (Downers Grove, Ill.: InterVarsity, 1994), quoted by Lawrence S. Cunningham in a brief review, *Commonweal* 121, no. 1 (Jan. 14, 1994) 41.

Homily 21

1. The parable is indeed a literary masterpiece; e.g., "The final half verse plays on [Hebrew] words that sound alike but have radically different meanings" (Joseph Jensen, O.S.B., "Isaiah 1–39," *The New Jerome Biblical Commentary* 15:14, p. 233).
2. I have changed the third person ("he") to the second person ("you") to avoid gender language that might irritate and to make the words of Jesus more personal in the context of the homily.
3. Raymond E. Brown, S.S., *The Gospel according to John (XIII-XXI)* (Garden City, N.Y.: Doubleday, 1970) 660.

Homily 22

1. My Preaching the Just Word retreat/workshop, conducted with Father Raymond Kemp for priests of the Diocese of Lafayette-in-Indiana, Indianapolis. This homily closed the activities.
2. So Elias D. Mallon, "Joel, Obadiah," *NJBC* 24:3, p. 400.
3. Ibid. 24:18, p. 403.
4. Additional wonders of Yahweh are then listed: judgment of the nations in the Valley of Jehoshaphat; additional oracles against Tyre, Sidon, and Philistia; war against the nations. But these would needlessly complicate the role of Joel within the purposes of my homily.
5. Useful here is William J. Bausch's recent *Catholics in Crisis? The Church Confronts Contemporary Challenges* (Mystic, Conn.: Twenty-Third, 1999).
6. See ibid. 2.
7. See ibid. 158.
8. Ibid. 54.
9. Ibid. 158.
10. Quoted, without exact reference, in Bausch, ibid. 154.

Homily 23

1. *New York Times,* Jan. 26, 1999, A1.
2. This homily was written for the Catholic version of the 1999 Children's Sabbath manual of the Children's Defense Fund, a sample homily for the 29th Sunday in Ordinary Time, cycle A, to galvanize thousands of Catholic congregations into greater service and advocacy on behalf of children. Unfortunately, the Gospel for that Sunday (Mt 22:15–21: "Give to the emperor what belongs to the emperor") could not be fitted without violence into the CDF theme, "Ready to Learn, Ready to Succeed." The small segment from St. Paul's First Letter to the Thessalonians does have genuine relevance, as suggested in my final two paragraphs.
3. See, for details, Arloc Sherman, *Wasting America's Future* (Children's Defense Fund; Boston: Beacon, 1994) 12, 15, 19, 20, 22, 25, 27. I have translated Sherman's factual data to a more personal rhetoric.
4. See *The State of America's Children: Yearbook 1998* (Washington, D.C.: Children's Defense Fund, 1998); see 48–51, "Spotlight on Education."
5. See Raymond F. Collins, "The First Letter to the Thessalonians," *The New Jerome Biblical Commentary*, ed. Raymond E. Brown, S.S., Joseph A. Fitzmyer, S.J., and Roland E. Murphy, O.Carm. (Englewood Cliffs, N.J.: Prentice-Hall, 1990) 46:14, p. 774.

Homily 24

1. I have profited much from Pietro Stella, *Don Bosco: Life and Work* (2nd rev. ed., tr. John Drury; New Rochelle, N.Y.: Don Bosco Publications, 1985).
2. Ibid. 125.
3. Ibid. 126.
4. Here I depend on an older biography, Henri Ghéon's *The Secret of Saint John Bosco*, tr. F. J. Sheed (London: Sheed & Ward, 1935) esp. 194 ff.
5. Ibid. 195.
6. Ibid. 174.
7. See ibid. 245. Stella details the problems associated with the idea; ibid. 245 ff.
8. See ibid. 118.
9. Belo was the name of his godfather; it was added to his parents' names as a sign of respect for his baptismal sponsor.
10. For the data on East Timor I am indebted to Arnold S. Kohen, *From the Place of the Dead: The Epic Struggles of Bishop Belo of East Timor* (New York: St. Martin's Press, 1999). For a fine summary and evaluation of Kohen's biography, see the review by Drew Christiansen, S.J., in *America*, Dec. 18–25, 1999, pp. 22–23.
11. See Kohen, ibid. 13.

Homily 25

1. See M. L. Lynn, "Alacoque, Margaret Mary, St.," *New Catholic Encyclopedia* 1 (1967) 217.
2. See Joseph N. Tylenda, S.J., *Jesuit Saints & Martyrs: Short Biographies of the Saints, Blessed, Venerables, and Servants of God of the Society of Jesus* (Chicago: Loyola University, 1984) 46–49.
3. See, e.g., the discussion of Jn 7:37 ("from his belly [heart?] shall flow rivers of living water") in Raymond E. Brown, S.S., *The Gospel according to John (I-XII)* (Garden City, N.Y.: Doubleday, 1966) 320–24; and Jn 19:34 (on Calvary "blood and water flowed out" from Jesus' side) in Brown, *The Gospel according to John XIII-XXI* (1970) 935–36.
4. For a succinct summary of this devotion and its history, see C. J. Moell, "Sacred Heart, Devotion to," *New Catholic Encyclopedia* 12 (1967) 818–20.
5. Exact figures are impossible to come by, mainly because formal enrollment has largely ceased.
6. Decree 15, no. 4, *Documents of the 31st and 32nd General Congregations of the Society of Jesus* (St. Louis: Institute of Jesuit Sources, 1977) 147, no. 241. Confirmed by the 32nd General Congregation, 1974–75, Decree 11, no. 43, ibid. 482, no. 244.
7. Decree 8, no. 9, *Documents* 99, no. 86.

8. It is not clear to what these dimensions refer. They have sometimes been taken to refer to the dimensions of the Jerusalem Temple or of Jerusalem (Ezek 42, 47, 48; Rev 21:9–27). In this context, however, they may describe God's plan of salvation or, *"more likely, the love of Christ,* which is mentioned in the preceding and following verses" (Paul J. Kobelski, "The Letter to the Ephesians," *The New Jerome Biblical Commentary,* ed. Raymond E. Brown, S.S., Joseph A. Fitzmyer, S.J., and Roland E. Murphy, O.Carm. [Englewood Cliffs, N.J.: Prentice-Hall, 1990] 55:23, p. 888); emphasis mine.

Homily 26

1. This homily was preached during one of the weekly liturgies of the St. Aloysius Gonzaga Jesuit community in Washington, D.C.
2. C. A. Herbst, S.J., "Korea," *New Catholic Encyclopedia* 8 (1967) 254–56, at 255. The original impulse apparently goes back to Christian literature obtained from Jesuit missionaries in Peking and studied by a group of educated Koreans.
3. See C. A. Herbst, S.J., "Korea, Martyrs of," ibid. 256–57.
4. For convenience's sake, I shall use Kim rather than the fuller Kim-tai-ken or Taegon, as did Herbst, n. 5 below.; similarly, Chong rather than Chong Hasang.
5. See C. A. Herbst, S.J., "Korea's Martyr-Patron," *American Ecclesiastical Review* 137 (1957) 330–41; also his shorter article, "Kim, Andrew, Bl.," *New Catholic Encyclopedia* 8 (1967) 181. Herbst wrote from Seoul, where he was professor of history at Sogang Jesuit College.
6. The details in this and the following paragraph are summarized from Herbst, "Korea's Martyr-Patron" (n. 5 above) 337–40.
7. I presume that Andrew's father was one of the 103 Korean martyrs raised to sainthood in 1984.
8. See Herbst, "Korea" (n. 2 above) 255.
9. *The HarperCollins Encyclopedia of Catholicism,* ed. Richard P. McBrien (Harper San Francisco, 1995) 741.
10. Ibid.
11. Paul Claudel, "Saint Francis Xavier," in *Coronal* (New York: Pantheon, 1943) 190.

Homily 27

1. This homily was delivered during a Preaching the Just Word retreat/workshop for priests of the Archdiocese of Toronto, Canada. It was the first of three five-day retreats, to accommodate all the priests of the archdiocese.
2. Joseph A. Fitzmyer, S.J., *The Gospel according to Luke (I-IX)* (Garden City, N.Y.: Doubleday, 1981) 615.

3. See ibid.
4. See John Paul II's message for the World Day of Peace, Jan. 1, 1990, "Peace with God the Creator, Peace with All of Creation"; English text, "Peace with All Creation," *Origins* 19, no. 28 (Dec. 14, 1989) 465–68; quotation at 468, emphasis mine.
5. *Monumenta Xaveriana* 1, 509–12; translation in James Brodrick, S.J., *The Origin of the Jesuits* (New York: Longmans, Green, 1940) 133–34.
6. It is the first section (pp. 9–15) of Karl Rahner, S.J., *Ignatius of Loyola*, with an Historical Introduction by Paul Imhof, S.J. (London/New York: Collins, 1979). The translation, by Rosaleen Ockenden, was made on the German original, *Ignatius von Loyola* (Freiburg i. B: Herder, 1978). I have reproduced this translation in my text, with several minor changes.
7. Ibid. 11–13. Rahner's theology of religious experience has been challenged, but there is a solid basis for it in the Christian mystical tradition; see my *Long Have I Loved You: A Theologian Reflects on His Church* (Maryknoll, N.Y.: Orbis, 2000) 188–90.

Homily 28

1. For the factual information in this homily, I have profited from S. Hilpisch and C. M. Aherne, "Boniface, St.," *New Catholic Encyclopedia* 2 (1967) 665–68. Also helpful was an article by Terry Matz, "St. Boniface of Mainz," which is available under *Catholic Online Saints and Angels* at http://www. saints.catholic.org/index.shtml. For data on the legend of Boniface as the one who introduced Christmas practices (carols, Advent wreath, Christmas tree) into Germany, see http://www.suite101.com/ article.cfm/natural_health/26826. See too "Boniface, St.," *The Oxford Dictionary of the Christian Church*, ed. F. L. Cross (3rd ed., E. A. Livingstone; New York: Oxford University, 1997) 223–24.
2. New York: New American Library, 1961.
3. See ibid. 213–14.
4. Hilpisch and Aherne, "Boniface, St." (n. 1 above) 668.
5. See A. G. Biggs, "Benedictines," *New Catholic Encyclopedia* 2 (1967) 288–95, at 290.
6. Joseph Bernardin, *It Is Christ We Preach* (Boston: St. Paul Editions, 1982) 13.
7. John Hotchkin, in a homily, "Cardinal Bernardin: A True Person of Hope," *Origins* 26, no. 25 (Dec. 5, 1996) 409–11, at 410–11.
8. It is pertinent to note here that this homily was delivered within a Preaching the Just Word retreat/workshop at The Preaching Institute in Cincinnati.

Homily 29

1. See the tight summary by R. Mols, "Borromeo, Charles, St.," *New Catholic Encyclopedia* 2 (1967) 710–12.

2. This homily was delivered during a Preaching the Just Word retreat/workshop for priests of the Archdiocese of Toronto, Canada. It was the second of three five-day retreats, to accommodate all the priests of the archdiocese.
3. John Paul II, encyclical *On Social Concern* (1987) no. 28.
4. *Acta ecclesiae Mediolanensis* (Milan, 1599) 1177–78; translation from *The Liturgy of the Hours IV* (New York: Catholic Book Publishing Co., 1975) 1545.

Homily 30

1. Constitution on the Sacred Liturgy, no. 7.
2. For this translation and interpretation of verse 6, see Roland E. Murphy, O. Carm., "Canticle of Canticles," *The New Jerome Biblical Commentary*, ed. Raymond E. Brown, S.S., Joseph A. Fitzmyer, S.J., and Roland E. Murphy, O.Carm. (Englewood Cliffs, N.J.: Prentice-Hall, 1990) 29:24, p. 465.
3. I am aware that Paul has chosen the 15 verbs in this paragraph "in order to highlight virtues neglected by the Corinthians. The strong were not 'patient and kind' (8:1–13). The sexual ascetics tended to 'insist on their own way' (7:1–40). The community 'rejoiced at wrong' (5:1–8)" (Jerome Murphy-O'Connor, O.P., "The First Letter to the Corinthians," *The New Jerome Biblical Commentary* [n. 2 above] 49:62, p. 811).
4. Two popular TV shows at different ends of the moral spectrum.
5. Quoted from John Bookser Feister, "The Pope Visits St. Louis," *St. Anthony Messenger* 106, no. 11 (April 1999) 28–34, at 31.

Homily 31

1. Malcolm Muggeridge, *Something Beautiful for God: Mother Teresa of Calcutta* (London: Collins/Fontana, 1971/1972).
2. Remarks at an International Theological Conference at the University of Notre Dame, March 20–26, 1966; see *Vatican II: An Interfaith Appraisal*, ed. John H. Miller, C.S.C. (Notre Dame: University of Notre Dame, 1966) 374.
3. An intriguing possible interpretation; see Roland E. Murphy, O.Carm., "Canticle of Canticles," *The New Jerome Biblical Commentary*, ed. Raymond E. Brown, S.S., Joseph A. Fitzmyer, S.J., and Roland E. Murphy, O.Carm. (Englewood Cliffs, N.J.: Prentice-Hall, 1990) 29:24, p. 465.
4. Published in 1999 by the Children's Defense Fund, Washington, D.C.
5. Ibid. ix-x.
6. See ibid. xv.

Homily 32

1. For this translation of 8:6, see Roland E. Murphy, O.Carm., "Canticle of Canticles," *The New Jerome Biblical Commentary*, ed. Raymond E. Brown, S.S., Joseph A. Fitzmyer, S.J., and Roland E. Murphy, O.Carm. (Englewood Cliffs, N.J.: Prentice-Hall, 1990) 29:24, p. 465.
2. Murphy, ibid.
3. From the back cover of *The State of America's Children Yearbook 1999*, published in 1999 by the Children's Defense Fund, Washington, D.C.
4. See ibid. xv.

Homily 33

1. Second Vatican Council, Constitution on the Sacred Liturgy, no. 7.
2. I am not implying that these gifts were in the mind of the author(s) of this section of Genesis; more likely they are the result of continuing reflection on Genesis 1 down the centuries.
3. See *Washington Post*, March 30, 1991, 1 and 7.
4. See *Washington Post*, Aug. 19, 1999, 1 and 12.

Homily 34

1. This is a possible interpretation of the Hebrew; see Roland E. Murphy, O.Carm., "Canticle of Canticles," *The New Jerome Biblical Commentary*, ed. Raymond E. Brown, S.S., Joseph A. Fitzmyer, S.J., and Roland E. Murphy, O.Carm. (Englewood Cliffs, N.J.: Prentice-Hall, 1990) 29:24, p. 465.
2. So Jerome Murphy-O'Connor, O.P., "The First Letter to the Corinthians," ibid. 49:62, p. 811.
3. Statistics from the Children's Defense Fund, *The State of America's Children Yearbook 1999* (Washington, D.C.: Children's Defense Fund, 1999) xii and xv.
4. See ibid. xxvi.
5. For practical convenience, there is a World Share operation in Newark: 56 Freeman St., Newark, N.J. 07105 (973-344-2400).

Homily 35

1. So suggests Roland E. Murphy, O.Carm., "Canticle of Canticles," *The New Jerome Biblical Commentary*, ed. Raymond E. Brown, S.S., Joseph A. Fitzmyer, S.J., and Roland E. Murphy, O.Carm. (Englewood Cliffs, N.J.: Prentice-Hall, 1990) 29:24, p. 465.
2. See the text of the sermon in the *Alumni Bulletin of Bangor Theological Seminary* 43, no. 2 (April 1968) 12–14.

3. See Evelyn Whitehead and James D. Whitehead, "Christian Marriage," *U.S. Catholic* 47, no. 6 (June 1982) 9.
4. *New York Times*, Aug. 17, 2000, A30.
5. Aug. 18, 2000; reported at the State of Illinois website [http://www.state.il.us].
6. Figures taken from the National Center for Children in Poverty website [http://cpmcnet.columbia.edu/dept/nccp/cprb2txt.html].

Homily 36

1. This homily was preached at the liturgy celebrating the 35th anniversary of the ordination of Father Stephen Concannon, pastor of St. Charles Borromeo Church in Brunswick, Maine.
2. For problems on priesthood that the Epistle to the Hebrews raises with reference to other NT books, e.g., how illegitimate it is to generalize from Hebrews to the whole NT situation, see Raymond E. Brown, S.S., *Priest and Bishop: Biblical Reflections* (New York: Paulist, 1970) 13ff. A homily is not the place to discuss this; still, a homilist must tread carefully here. Still worth reading is the short article by M. E. McIver, "Priesthood of Christ," *New Catholic Encyclopedia* 11 (1967) 773–77.
3. From a Report (dated Sept. 15, 1971) of the Subcommittee [commissioned by the U.S. bishops] on the Systematic Theology of the Priesthood.
4. Dogmatic Constitution on the Church, no. 10.
5. I am aware that a 1997 Instruction from eight Vatican offices, "Some Questions regarding Collaboration of Nonordained Faithful in Priests' Sacred Ministry," quotes Pope John Paul II as saying, "Only with constant reference to the one source, the '*ministry* of Christ' (...) may the term ministry be applied to a certain extent and without ambiguity to the lay faithful.... [O]nly in virtue of sacred ordination does the word obtain that full, unequivocal meaning that tradition has attributed to it." The Vatican's English text can be found in *Origins* 27, no. 24 (Nov. 27, 1997) 397, 399–409.
6. So Avery Dulles, S.J., "The Church," Introduction to the English translation of the Dogmatic Constitution on the Church in *The Documents of Vatican II*, ed. Walter M. Abbott, S.J. (New York: Herder and Herder, 1966) 9–13, at 12–13. True, the Constitution does speak of "the distinction which the Lord made between sacred ministers and the rest of the People of God" (no. 32); see also canon 207 #1 of the Code of Canon Law. But note a shift in the thinking of insightful theologian Yves Congar: "The church is not built up merely by acts of the official ministers of the presbytery but by many kinds of services, more or less stable or occasional, more or less spontaneous or recognized, some even consecrated by sacramental ordination. These services exist...they exist even *if they are not called by their real name, ministries,* nor have their true place

and status in ecclesiology" (quoted from Congar's *Power and Poverty in the Church* [London, 1964] by Thomas F. O'Meara, O.P. "Ministry," *The New Dictionary of Theology*, ed. Joseph A. Komonchak et al. [Wilmington, Del.: Michael Glazier, 1987] 657–61, at 660–61; italics mine).

7. The quotation, from Father Robert Hovda, I have not yet traced precisely.

Homily 37

1. See the fine summary article by Edward Collins Vacek, S.J., "Work," *The New Dictionary of Theology*, ed. Joseph A. Komonchak, Mary Collins, and Dermot A. Lane (Wilmington, Del.: Michael Glazier, 1987) 1098–1105.
2. I am not implying that these two prerogatives were certainly in the mind of the author(s) of Genesis 1; a strong Catholic tradition has put the stress on knowledge and freedom (love). See the chapter on the image of God in my forthcoming *Long Have I Loved You: A Theologian Reflects on His Church* (Maryknoll, N.Y.: Orbis, 2000).
3. Vacek, "Work" (n. 1 above) 1102.
4. See Second Vatican Council, Pastoral Constitution on the Church in the Modern World, nos. 34, 67–68.
5. Vatican II, Decree on the Apostolate of the Laity, no. 5.
6. The number, "over 250 million," is taken from *The State of the World's Children 1997*, ed. Carol Bellamy (New York: Published for UNICEF by Oxford University Press, 1997) 4. But says the U.S. Department of Labor, "Statistics on child labor are in general fragmentary and suspect....Nevertheless, the International Labor Organization has estimated [as of July 15, 1994] the total number of child workers to be between 100–200 million" *(By the Sweat and Toil of Children: The Use of Child Labor in American Imports*: A Report to the Committee on Appropriations, United States Congress, [by the] Bureau of International Labor Affairs, U.S. Department of Labor [Washington, D.C.: U.S. Department of Labor, 1994]).
7. See *The State of the World's Children 1997* (n. 6 above) 4.
8. See the highly useful work of Frank D. Almade, *Just Wages for Church Employees* (New York: Peter Lang, 1993) e.g., chapter 5, "Criteria for a Just Wage for Church Employees" (115–49).
9. Marvin L. Hrier Mich, *Catholic Social Teaching and Movements* (Mystic, Conn.: Twenty-Third, 1998) 44.
10. John Sweeney, "Labor Unions and the Church," in the resource guide "Putting Labor into Labor Day Services" (Chicago: National Interfaith Committee for Worker Justice, n.d.). No pagination.
11. George G. Higgins, "Reflections of the Past Century on the Church and Labor Relations in the United States," ibid.
12. See Bob Herbert, "Nike's Pyramid Scheme," *New York Times*, June 10, 1996, A17.

Homily 38

1. Karl Rahner has put these words on the lips of Ignatius Loyola from his profound understanding of Ignatius; see his striking essay "Ignatius Loyola Speaks to a Modern Jesuit," the first section of his *Ignatius of Loyola*, with an Historical Introduction by Paul Imhof, S.J. (Freiburg. i. B.: Herder, 1978) 11–13.

2. *Spiritual Exercises*, no. 317; tr. Elisabeth Meier Tetlow, *The* Spiritual Exercises *of St. Ignatius Loyola* (2nd rev. ed.; New Orleans: Loyola Press, 1996) 118.

3. Francis Thompson, "The Hound of Heaven," in *Francis Thompson, Poems and Essays*, ed. Wilfred Meynell (Westminster, Md.: Newman, 1949) 107.

4. Ibid. 112.

5. See John Courtney Murray, S.J., "The Danger of the Vows," *Woodstock Letters* 96 (1967) 421–27. The text of this famous conference, given to the Woodstock College (Md.) Jesuit community, was reconstructed after his death (1967) from two of Fr. Murray's personal copies, one with his own handwritten emendations, together with a number of slightly varying mimeographed copies. Fr. Murray was reluctant to publish the conference without updating it in the spirit of Vatican II; he never found the opportunity.

6. Ibid. 426 and 427.

7. The New Revised Standard Version reads "live in love," not inaccurate, because the verb here (*peripateite*) is used figuratively of "the walk of life," a usage that is "decidedly Pauline" (William F. Arndt and F. Wilbur Gingrich, *A Greek-English Lexicon of the New Testament and Other Early Christian Literature* [4th ed.; Chicago: University of Chicago, 1952] 655).

Homily 40

1. John Bright, *Jeremiah* (Anchor Bible 21; Garden City, N.Y.: Doubleday, 1965) 287.

2. Guy P. Couturier, CSC, "Jeremiah," *The New Jerome Biblical Commentary* 18:89, p. 290.

3. See Ezek 11:19–20; 18:31; 36:26; also Isa 59:21.

4. Vatican II, Decree on Ecumenism, no. 6 (tr. *The Documents of Vatican II*, ed. Walter M. Abbott, S.J. [New York: Herder and Herder/Association Press, 1966] 350).

5. John W. O'Malley, S.J., "Reform, Historical Consciousness, and Vatican II's Aggiornamento," *Theological Studies* 32 (1971) 573–601, at 600.

6. See "Joint Declaration on Justification To Be Signed Oct. 31," *Origins* 29, no. 6 (June 24, 1999) 85, 87–92.

7. "Joint Declaration on the Doctrine of Justification," nos. 40–41, *Origins* 28, no. 8 (July 16, 1998) 120–27, at 124.

242 TO BE JUST IS TO LOVE

8. Ibid., no. 15, *Origins* 28 (1998) 122.
9. Ibid., no. 20, *Origins* 28 (1998) 122.
10. See "Joint Declaration To Be Signed" (n. 6 above), *Origins* 29 (1999) 87. See also the Note on certain Catholic questions, ibid. 89.
11. See Raymond E. Brown, S.J., *The Gospel according to John (I-XII)* (Garden City, N.Y.: Doubleday, 1966) 355.
12. "Joint Declaration" (n. 7 above), no. 29, *Origins* 28 (1998) 123.
13. Ibid., no. 30, *Origins* 28 (1998) 123.
14. Ibid., no. 29, *Origins* 28 (1998) 123.
15. *Weimar Ausgabe* 7, 36, 3f. (1520); see Gerhard Ebeling, *Luther: An Introduction to His Thought* (Philadelphia: Fortress, 1970) 212.

Comprehensive Index for Homily Books by Walter J. Burghardt, S.J.

compiled by
Fr. Brian Cavanaugh, T.O.R.

Reference Key: **TNG** (*Tell the Next Generation,* 1980)
LSJ (*Sir, We Would Like to See Jesus,* 1982)
PYW (*Still Proclaiming Your Wonders,* 1984)
GOC (*Grace on Crutches,* 1986)
ENH (*Lovely in Eyes Not His,* 1988)
TCL (*To Christ I Look,* 1989)
DBC (*Dare to Be Christ,* 1991)
CMC (*When Christ Meets Christ,* 1993)
SWB (*Speak the Word with Boldness,* 1994)
LFL (*Love Is a Flame of the Lord,* 1995)
JRD (*Let Justice Roll Down Like Waters,* 1998)
TTP (*Christ in Ten Thousand Places,* 1999)
TBJ (*To Be Just Is to Love,* 2001)

LITURGICAL SEASONS:

Advent Season:	TNG, pp. 25, 30
Advent: 1st Sun. (A)	LSJ, p. 17; DBC, p. 5
1st Sun. (B)	GOC, p. 19; CMC, p. 15
Vespers 1st Sun. (B)	JRD, p. 5
1st Sun. (C)	CMC, p. 20
2nd Sun. (A)	PYW, p. 19; ENH, p. 5; SWB, p. 3; TBJ, p. 5
2nd Sun. (B)	LSJ, p. 23; TCL, p. 21
2nd Sun. (C)	PYW, p. 25; TCL, p. 27
3rd Sun. (A)	LSJ, p. 29; ENH, p. 11
3rd Sun. (B)	LFL, p. 5
3rd Sun. (C)	LSJ, p. 33
4th Sun. (A)	SWB, p. 8
4th Sun. (C)	TTP, p. 7

Christmas:	TNG, p. 34
Solemnity of BVM,	
Mother of God:	TBJ, p. 12

Lenten Season: TNG, pp. 19, 44, 49
Ash Wednesday: GOC, p. 27
Sat. after Ash Wed.   DBC, p. 13
    1st Sun. (A)   ENH, p. 19
    1st Sun. (B)   PYW, p. 33; TCL, p. 35; TBJ, p. 17
    1st Sun. (C)   SWB, p. 14
    1st Mon. (Yr. 1)   JRD, p. 10
    2nd Sun. (A)   LSJ, p. 41; DBC, p. 16; SWB, p. 19; JRD, p. 15

    2nd Sun. (C)   DBC, p. 22
    2nd Mon. (Yr. 1)   TTP, p. 12
    3rd Sun. (A)   GOC, p. 31; ENH, p. 26; TTP, p. 17
    3rd Mon. (Yr. 2)   TTP, p. 22
    4th Sun. (A)   TTP, p. 28
    4th Sun. (B)   CMC, p. 33
    4th Sun. (C)   LSJ, p. 46; DBC, p. 29
    4th Mon. (Yr. 1)   CMC, p. 38; TTP, p. 34
    5th Sun. (A)   GOC, p. 37; ENH, p. 32; TBJ, p. 23
    5th Sun. (B)   GOC, p. 43; PYW, p. 39; TBJ, p. 30
    5th Sun. (C)   PYW, p. 45
Palm Sunday: TNG, p. 52
Palm Sunday (A)   GOC, p. 49; DBC, p. 35
Palm Sunday (B)   GOC, p. 54; PYW, p. 51; TCL, p. 41
Palm Sunday (C)   PYW, p. 55
Holy Week: TNG, p. 78
Holy Monday (Yr. 1)   TBJ, p. 36; TBJ, p. 41
Holy Thursday   TNG, p. 58; PYW, pp. 61, 67; JRD, p. 132
Good Friday: LSJ, p. 52; GOC, pp. 59, 65; TBJ, p. 47
    7 Last Words: LFL, pp. 17, 22, 26, 30, 34, 37, 41

Easter Season:
    Vigil (C)   ENH, p. 41
    2nd Sun. (A)   GOC, p. 73; DBC, p. 45
    2nd Sun. (B)   TCL, p. 49; TBJ, p. 55
    2nd Sun. (C)   PYW, p. 77; DBC, p. 51; TTP, p. 38
    2nd Mon. (C)   SWB, p. 25
    2nd Mon. (Yr. 1)   JRD, p. 20

FEASTS:

THEMES:

SCRIPTURE READINGS:

John 4:43–54	CMC, p. 38; TTP, p. 34
John 6:1–15	CMC, p. 51
John 6:41–51	LSJ, p. 186; SWB, p. 136; TBJ, p. 209
John 7:37–39	GOC, p. 191
John 8:1–11	PYW, p. 45
John 8:31–36	TBJ, p. 220
John 9:1–41	TTP, p. 28
John 10:1–10	LSJ, p. 65; GOC, p. 79
John 10:11–18	CMC, p. 164; TBJ, p. 67
John 10:27–30	ENH, p. 53; SWB, p. 186
John 11:1–45	GOC, p. 37; ENH, p. 32
John 11:17–27	TCL, p. 139; JRD, p. 235
John 11:20–27	LSJ, p. 192; TCL, p. 149; CMC, p. 170
John 11:1–45	TBJ, p. 23
John 12:1–11	TBJ, pp. 36, 41
John 12:20–33	GOC, p. 43; PYW, p. 39; TBJ, p. 30
John 12:24–26	ENH, p. 188
John 13:1–15	TNG, p. 58; PYW, pp. 61, 67; JRD, p. 132
John 13:3–5, 12–15	DBC, p. 129
John 13:31–35	SWB, p. 34; TTP, p. 43
John 14:1–12	GOC, p. 179; DBC, p. 196; JRD, p. 30
John 14:15–17, 26	PYW, pp. 183, 189; TTP, p. 211
John 14:15–21	SWB, p. 42
John 14:21–29	LSJ, p. 75; TTP, pp. 48, 93
John 15:1–8	LSJ, p. 70; GOC, p. 197; TCL, p. 55; SWB, p. 191
John 15:1–17	ENH, p. 168
John 15:9–12	GOC, p. 165; PYW, p. 206; TCL, p. 186; CMC, pp. 98, 115, 135; SWB, p. 157; LFL, p. 125; TTP, p. 198; TBJ, pp. 175, 186
John 15:9–17	GOC, p. 85; ENH, pp. 173, 177, 182, 194; TCL, pp. 55, 142, 174; DBC, p. 152; CMC, pp. 93, 121, 153; JRD, p. 180; TTP, pp. 53, 183, 193; TBJ, p. 72
John 15:12–17	GOC, p. 185; ENH, p. 163; CMC, p. 81; SWB, p. 40, 151; TTP, p. 204
John 15:26–16:4a	TTP, p. 57; TBJ, p. 79
John 16:12–15	PYW, p. 195; ENH, p. 143; DBC, p. 77; SWB, p. 82
John 16:16–20	TBJ, p. 75
John 16:29–33	JRD, p. 35
John 17:1–11	TBJ, p. 83

Romans 1:1–7	LFL, p. 89
Romans 1:16–25	JRD, p. 162
Romans 3:19–28	TBJ, p. 220
Romans 5:1–5	ENH, p. 143
Romans 5:1–2, 5–8	GOC, p. 31; ENH, p. 26; TTP, p. 17
Romans 5:15b–19	JRD, p. 68
Romans 8:8–11	TBJ, p. 23
Romans 8:12–17	CMC, p. 208; LFL, p. 98; TTP, p. 145
Romans 8:28–30	CMC, p. 141
Romans 8:31–35, 37–39	PYW, p. 206; GOC, p. 170; DBC, p. 152; CMC, p. 103
Romans 10:8–13	DBC, p. 173
Romans 10:13–17	SWB, p. 179
Romans 12:1–2, 9–18	TCL, p. 191; CMC, p. 127; SWB, pp. 131, 151, 157; LFL, p. 109; TBJ, p. 181
Romans 12:4–12	ENH, p. 168
Romans 12:9–21	CMC, p. 121; LFL, p. 149; TTP, p. 198
Romans 15:4–9	TBJ, p. 5
1 Cor. 1:4–9	LFL, p. 144
1 Cor. 1:10–13, 17	GOC, p. 93; JRD, p. 41
1 Cor. 2:6–10	DBC, p. 71; SWB, p. 65; JRD, p. 51
1 Cor. 2:9–13	PYW, p. 189
1 Cor. 3:9–11, 16–17	TTP, p. 154; TBJ, p. 214
1 Cor. 3:18–23	CMC, p. 64
1 Cor. 9:16–19, 22–23	LFL, p. 51
1 Cor. 10:31–11:1	TBJ, p. 99
1 Cor. 11:17–26, 33	LFL, p. 72
1 Cor. 11:23–26	TNG, p. 58; LSJ, p. 157; PYW, pp. 61, 67; DBC, p. 179; JRD, pp. 132, 136
1 Cor. 12:3–7, 12–13	GOC, p. 191; CMC, p. 109; JRD, p. 225; TBJ, p. 199
1 Cor. 12:4–13	SWB, p. 191
1 Cor. 12:12–27	ENH, p. 80; DBC, p. 65; TTP, p. 75
1 Cor. 12:12–14, 27–31a	JRD, p. 154
1 Cor. 12:27–13:13	PYW, p. 201; GOC, p. 175; ENH, pp. 177, 182; TCL, pp. 174, 180, 201; DBC, pp. 101, 106, 157; CMC, pp. 81, 93, 98, 115; SWB, p. 146; LFL, pp. 120, 125; TTP, p. 198
1 Cor. 12:31–13:8	TBJ, pp. 165, 170, 191
1 Cor. 13:1–13	LSJ, p. 189; DBC, p. 135; TTP, p. 204
1 Cor. 14:1, 6–12	TTP, p. 188